Bittersweet Lane

Bittersweet Lane

Creating Home(s) in the
American Affordable
Housing Crisis

Jamie Madden

BY ROW HOUSE

For all inquiries and usage requests,
please contact rights@rowhousepublishing.com or write to
Row House Publishing, PO Box 210, New Egypt, NJ 08533.

ISBN: 9798991642897 (Hardcover)
ISBN: 9781967182008 (eBook)

Printed in the United States
Distributed by Simon & Schuster

Library of Congress Cataloging-in-Publication data available upon request.

Edited by Nirmala Nataraj
Typeset by Iram Allam

First Edition
10 9 8 7 6 5 4 3 2 1

Contents

For Grandmy
For Mom
For Sean
For Sung
For Niamh

Introduction

I was four years old the first time we lost a home. It wasn't the last time. And we didn't all survive. I think maybe I've been trying to make up for it ever since. I've always told myself my work as an affordable housing developer is for the next kid. I work so the next kid has a home. But what I really want is to just fix it. What I really want to know is how we create enough homes for everyone.

And why we haven't.

Our housing crisis is not an unsolvable, abstract problem. There are physical realities at play, literal bricks and mortar. Our country does not have enough homes for the people and places that need them.[1]

So how do we create those homes we're missing? At the most basic level, creating new homes requires a place to build, permissions to build, and the resources to direct labor and materials. The price of accomplishing all that—the total development cost (TDC), in our jargon—is the real floor for how cheaply a new home can be produced. There is no magic technology that can reduce the cost of creating a home to zero. Your 3D printed nano drone swarms will still be made from materials, still require energy, and still require designing. Homes cost something, and there will always be people who cannot afford that something. That's the inherent market failure in housing: at any given time, a large portion of us cannot express our *need* for a home as economic *demand* for a home. The market does not even see us.

Everyone sleeps somewhere. That is an unavoidable physical reality. We are *all* better off when those somewheres are decent homes. It is in everyone's interest regarding public health, climate, and the economy that everyone has a home. The pandemic demonstrated how people living in overcrowded or unsanitary spaces—whether in houses, vehicles, or tents—share viruses at deathly rates.[2] Long commutes and inefficient buildings dump carbon into our atmosphere. Extreme weather leaves bodies in our streets each time a deep freeze, flood, heat, or fire encounters people sleeping outside.

My three-year-old daughter sleeps in her own room. I am exceedingly proud of that luxury. Each morning, we walk the eight blocks between our home and her preschool. On the way, she sees people sleeping on asphalt parking lots, in doorways, and in tents. She sees multimillion-dollar penthouses above it all. She sees a public housing tower and squat old buildings rehabbed into affordable housing. We say hi to the neighborhood crows, "Hi, Badb!" We say hi to Oliver, the cat stretching by its first-floor window. We pass expensive condos where my daughter's friends rent. We walk along together with another toddler friend of hers coming from their small, cheap apartment a few blocks away. We greet every neighbor we recognize, no matter whether they're housed, unhoused, or hustling. They are all our neighbors. I tell her this. Elmo tells her this. Our government behaves otherwise.

Our system assumes homelessness. The market is unable to serve a large chunk of our nation. Yet our government has never once budgeted enough to make up for the market's inherent inability to serve us. Because our government doesn't serve us either, we suffer homelessness at some point in our lives.

From the Puritans to the present, our governments prioritized their obsession with separating the worthy from the unworthy over simply providing help to all.

Well-meaning professionals do what good we can within the system we have, but a system premised on defining who is deserving will always include a group who is not. Sometimes the government defined my family as deserving, and sometimes not. At times I was deserving of one thing but not another, visits to a pediatrician perhaps but not to a dentist, this brand of bread but not that one. Being deemed undeserving of housing, however, may bring a sentence of homelessness.

Fortunately, Massachusetts did, eventually, decide we were deserving of some help with housing when I was a child. My childhood years living in the Bittersweet Lane Apartments weren't bad, and they certainly beat the alternative. They were real, and they were nice, but they weren't really nice. I've got my scars, but my childhood story is hardly exceptional. Plenty of people lived like us or worse.

Our housing shortage is a centuries-old, multibillion-dollar problem. Yet I stay optimistic because I must. I nourish that optimism, knowing it is possible to fix this. There are well-understood physical realities at play. What does it take to create homes? A place, permissions, and the resources to direct labor and materials. It is within our control as a nation to allow new homes to be created, wherever they are needed. It is within our control as a nation to build affordable housing and to correct for housing's inherent market failure. Every person in the US can have a home.

Maybe we as a nation must first finally, truly agree that every person in the United States *should* have a home. To date, we have not. But if we do, and if we decide to align our laws and our budgets with our humanity, we can solve our nation's housing crisis.

The money is there. The US currently spends four times more on housing benefits for the wealthy than the poor; the Home Mortgage Interest Deduction is a larger program than Housing Choice Vouchers, and its benefits accrue almost entirely to the richest fifth of Americans.[3] Even during the Democratic Biden–Harris administration, we spent twice as much money on Trump's Space Force as we did on public housing.[4] In just 2024, we spent over $22 billion on military aid to Israel; that money could have paid for more than 1.83 million housing vouchers and effectively ended child homelessness.[5] We spent nearly $70 billion on interstate highways in 2024, heedless of emissions, demand, or safety.[6] I could continue, but the point is that over a decade or so, for fewer dollars per year than we spend on research for orbital weapons systems,[7] we could build enough of the right types of homes, in the right places, to meet our tremendous need for housing today and for our children tomorrow. The price tag is within reach.

Housing for all would make Americans safer than any weapons system could. That's what my daughter's bedroom is: safety, security. But many of our neighbors don't have a room of their own. That's given our whole neighborhood a reputation for being unsafe.

This book is about how we create homes, once we've decided to. It's a book about how we lose homes, because we haven't. This book is about what affordable housing is, how we build it, and the things we've tried in the past. It draws on my career creating affordable housing. It draws on my education and on academic literature. But first and foremost, this is a book about affordable housing from a human perspective. I share my childhood struggles, my ancestors' survival, my family's present, and my sincere hopes for my daughter's generation.

Part 1 The Bitter is about us. How did my family fare in affordable housing? How did we end up there in the first place? I share our experiences in the hope that you understand the stakes. Housing is more than units, percentages, and dollars.

Part 2 The Sweet teaches how the US has created affordable housing, now and in the past. In this book, *affordable housing* is defined as "a home with a legal restriction that ensures it is available below-market price." This broad definition includes homes for rent, sale, or other tenure; development that is public, private, or both; architecture from detached homes to multifamily to institutional; housing built through new construction, renovation, rehabilitation, or adaptive reuse. The restriction on price is our core defining factor. This definition allows us to look at the full range of our nation's attempts to house people. But even using such a broad definition, affordable housing barely makes up 5% of the housing stock in the US,[8] so we will also discuss unrestricted, market-rate housing. Creating homes follows the same basic physical realities, regardless of type.

Part 3 The Laneway explores how we got here and where we might go. It challenges us to confront the unavoidably necessary steps towards addressing our housing crisis. We actually do know how to address it, after all.

Let's fix this shit.

PART 1

The Bitter

会吃苦吗？

ONE

We Didn't Grow Up in the Projects

We didn't grow up in the projects. Sean says we did anyway. It's easier to say. I doubt my brother even knows how to say the Bittersweet Lane Apartments were a Massachusetts Chapter 40B, SHARP, and 221(d)(3) financed, private, affordable housing development with our rent subsidized by a Chapter 707 voucher, and I doubt anyone would understand him if he did.

The Bittersweet Lane Apartments rose only three stories tall above surface parking and cracked suburban side streets. Its neighborhood was full of similar 1980s vintage three- and four-story buildings. Some were senior housing, some were condominiums; ours was for poor people. Projects or not, we grew up inside a shabby building occupied by people without better options, from single moms to refugees. *Sak pasé, zanmi mwen?*

When Sean says "the projects," it paints a picture in the American mind, but not always accurately, and not necessarily ours. Technically speaking, "the projects" means public housing, which is housing owned, managed, developed, and subsidized by the government through a local Public Housing Authority (PHA). From the 1930s to the 1970s, public housing was how our government built affordable housing.

In the beginning, PHAs usually built public housing projects on the sites of demolished neighborhoods. To unlock federal funds, combining slum clearance with public housing appealed to separate Congressional camps like putting peanut butter in chocolate. In a typical justification, the Boston Housing Authority claimed its slum clearances were a "service to slumdwellers that freed them from dangerous and indecent living conditions."[9] Yet few of the displaced slumdwellers had the money, connections, or citizen status to gain a place in the new public housing that eventually rose from the rubble of their former homes.

James Madden was one of those slumdwellers. No, not me, another one. The first of my ancestors born in America even. My immigrant Madden ancestors settled in tenements in Boston's South End, alongside fellow poor Irish refugees of *An Gorta Mór*.* Some would have spoken Irish, a language that was against the law at home and of little use in America. They found work as laborers. The South Bay docks were close enough to smell, not so bad at high tide but near intolerable at low. The Madden family moved several times over the decades but never farther than a few blocks. James, born just after his parents reached Boston, lived in the neighborhood long enough to see his first two grandchildren born there. Boston did not give the Irish a kind welcome, but our ancestors found freedom

---

* The Great Hunger, which will be referred to by its Irish name, *An Gorta Mór*, throughout. Let the poor potato off the hook for this tragedy of inhuman proportions.

from penal laws and from starvation to raise generations that would not know those horrors. They created homes.

James married an Irish American woman from the neighborhood, Mary-Ann Gormley. He had a tumultuous, violent life. But years before James was arrested for beating Mary, before Mary died and James fell from a third-floor window the first time, before James was found stabbed on Federal Street and refused to snitch, and before James fell out a third-floor window for the last time,[10] James and Mary raised three daughters and a son they named James.

This second James Madden also grew up to marry an Irish American woman from the neighborhood, Annie Hannafin. James Madden became friends with the neighborhood's more popular Irish American James, the one who would grow up to be the legendary Boston politician James Michael Curley. James Madden passed the civil service exam and became a postal carrier. His name showed up in the newspaper for Curley-related events. He and Annie decided enough with the Jameses and named their son Albert.[11]

Their neighborhood, around Washington Street and Harrison Avenue or so on the Boston neck, had been a growing middle-class Yankee area before we Irish arrived. It's a chore to find a non-British surname among the neighborhood's residents as late as 1821.[12] At the top of Washington Street, grocers and jewelers lived above their shops, often in buildings they owned. But lower down, closer to the docks where the Maddens would settle, tenements housed laborers and tradesmen. The area's landlords mostly came from well-known Yankee families. Several shared surnames with British landlords in Ireland.[13] There were Gibson landlords both here and in the Maddens' small home parish in County Cork.[14] By the first James's time in 1850, you'd be hard-pressed to find a non-Irish surname among the neighborhood's residents. The Yankees had left for the Back Bay, Brookline, and other such foreign lands.

While these once-refugees built families, the Cathedral of the Holy Cross rose above their rooftops. Builders used stone recovered from the Ursuline Convent for the brand-new cathedral's archway. The stones happened to be available as years earlier, a violent, white Protestant, anti-immigrant, anti-Catholic mob had burned the convent to the ground.[15] The forgotten site of the convent now hosts homes and a highway near my favorite Salvadoreño restaurants in East Somerville. But in the South End, these once-convent, once-rubble stones transformed into the jewel of Boston's Catholic archdiocese. Funded, designed, and built primarily by Boston's Irish, the cathedral signified arrival, community, and resilience in the face of a hostile, Puritan colony.[16]

Maybe that's why the City began to demolish the neighborhood in the 1880s—first along Washington Street, then Harrison Avenue, then the rest of the so-called slum, until the neighborhood was reduced to rubble-strewn lots and left untouched for decades. Whether for street widening or in response to disease, the City insisted they demolished the neighborhood for residents' *own* good, of course, and with no recompense, of course.

Like displaced South Enders ever after, James and Annie moved their family south to Roxbury. Albert grew up there, became a Boston police officer, and married an Irish American girl from his neighborhood, Anna Healy. Anna's parents had also moved to St. Patrick's Parish to escape slum clearances. Albert worked as a driver for the Maddens' former neighbor, Boston Mayor James Michael Curley.[17] I like to think he was in earshot when Curley said the "establishment politicians and business interests" left their once-neighborhood looking like an "ugly shell-hole in a bomb-wrecked European city."[18]

Albert moved farther south to Dorchester, St. Brendan's Parish. My grandfather Joe grew up there, and he too became a police officer. He too would grow up to marry an Irish American and name his son—can you guess?—James. And that James also grew up to marry an Irish American woman from his neighborhood, and he gave me his name. Legally, I am James Madden, Jr. I'm Jamie to family and friends, two names to navigate two worlds. Six generations of Maddens in Boston, and I became the first educated professional. My Madden relatives remain working class or poor. I doubt slum clearance was for our own good at all, *at all*.

Mayor Curley requested new federal funds from President Truman under the Housing Act of 1949 for the Boston Housing Authority to build the Cathedral projects on the site of our demolished neighborhood. Five hundred and eight new apartments rose from the rubble. Previously, Boston Housing Authority developments were not segregated, but the new federal dollars required racial segregation.[19] Cathedral initially provided homes for the South End's quickly growing Black community. African Americans leaving the legally established violence and oppression of the South arrived in Boston's South End to work in the nearby Back Bay rail yards. The old South Bay docks no longer existed, but the new rail yards were barely a screeching metal earshot away. Today, Cathedral's orthogonal brick towers still stand where the first of my name grew up. You can picture them; they look like "the projects." That block still provides homes for hard up newcomers—if they can get off today's years-long public housing waitlist.

"You know, I started in public housing, and here I am again. I lived at Orient Heights when Jed and I first got married. Now, I'm in senior housing." That's what Grandmy said when I told her my idea for this book, sending me dashing inside from my sunny balcony, phone on speaker so I could type up the quote and ask her more.

She continued, "Well, I'd gone on some dates with Protestant* boys. One had a car and drove me to the beach at Cape Ann. My parents were furious." They had reasons, having lived under English colonialism and the state terrorism of the Black and Tans.† Grandmy had also told me, "The scariest things I'd ever heard was when my father talked about the Black and Tans with a friend who was visiting from Sligo." I've never known Grandmy to scare at all. But back to my grandmother's dating life: "Anyway, the parish priest recommended Jed Fiske. My father thought he was a Protestant with that name, but the priest told us his mother and his grandmother were Irish Catholics. Anyway, when Jed and I first got married, he got a job at a funeral home up in Orient Heights. And I had to quit my job. In those days, once you were married, that was it. You didn't work. So we moved up to the Orient Heights projects where we had Jerry and your mother." Orient Heights was as far from her parents' Forest Hills home as one could reach on the MTA.

Then, as now, subsidized housing screened potential tenants for eligibility and for suitability. In those early decades, public housing authorities screened to ensure tenants were married, two-parent families, with no criminal histories, with no children born out of wedlock, and with a service record, proven stable employment, and enough income to afford the rent but not so much income as to be ineligible. It was a long list, but my grandmother's family fit the bill to live at the Orient Heights projects in 1958. If Grandmy were a single mother, they would not have. Then, as now, subsidized housing was a privilege, not a right.

---

* In both Ireland and Massachusetts, Protestant functioned as code for the settler-colonial dominant class. The divisions were not religious doctrinal arguments so much as a dividing line between colonizer and colonized.
† Infamously violent anti-Catholic, pro-English paramilitary group deployed in Ireland and Palestine

The Commonwealth of Massachusetts funded, and the Boston Housing Authority developed, the Orient Heights projects in 1952. The government intended to house veterans in 354 apartments there, near Boston's northernmost point, on land where the City had demolished tax-foreclosed properties. The Boston Housing Authority had claimed these projects would not be isolated, that they would be built in locations well connected to services and amenities. They were not.

MIT Professor Larry Vale wrote, "In 1957, a graduate student who mapped all retail facilities near Boston public housing projects found that the Orient Heights development—home to more than 1000 people—lacked even a single store within a quarter mile of its periphery, and that the distance was further accentuated by steep topography."[20] I asked Grandmy how she bought her groceries. "Ohh, that hill! If Jed couldn't leave work to give me a ride, I used to have to trudge up and down that hill with your uncle Jerry and your mother in tow, and carrying groceries. And they were toddlers at the time!" US public housing is often like this, disconnected from the other necessities of life.

"*She* started in public housing!? *I'm* the one who started in public housing. I was *born* there. She grew up in Forest Hills. And I'm back in affordable housing myself now too." That's what my mother said when I told her what *her* mother had said about my idea for this book.

By the mid-1960s, our government fundamentally changed how public housing worked and whom it was for. The federal government shifted its housing spending sharply towards FHA-subsidized mortgages, the Home Mortgage Interest Deduction, and other programs aimed at creating middle-class, whites-only suburbs.[21] These kinds of households, who in the 1930s–50s might have moved into public housing, instead became suburban homeowners on the back of that government largesse. Meanwhile, changes in public housing tenant screening rules and rent structure turned projects into places for poor people with the fewest choices. Then, our government stopped building new public housing altogether.

While public housing gave my grandmother a start in the 1950s–60s, my mother faced grim options in the 1980s. "Searching took lots of legwork. I was on the phone constantly. You'd hear that Waltham or some place was opening their list, and you'd pick up and go. I dragged you two along everywhere to fill out applications. You were little, and Sean was a baby. We spent hours and hours in stuffy waiting rooms filled with a lot of hard-off people. I'd try to make it a fun trip in town, go to the Children's Museum or something. It was all about getting your name on a list, trying to find the right person who had pull. I got a lot of broken promises; people would say 'I can get you to the top [of the list],' but they couldn't or didn't. It all felt very humiliating. I always worked and paid my own way from when I was a little kid, so it was really hard to ask for help. And, of course, it wasn't just housing. I needed food stamps and childcare and WIC and so on. Many of the office workers were unfriendly and unhelpful, but once in a while you'd find someone nice, like the woman who told me about the 707 program after many others didn't. She had just told me there was a five-year waiting list for Section 8, and I'd burst into tears right there and then. She paused and asked, 'Have you heard of 707?' 'No, what's that?'"[22]

We were lucky to be in Massachusetts, where the Commonwealth created the Chapter 707 program to provide additional housing vouchers when Congress wouldn't. We were lucky to come across a bureaucrat who wanted to be helpful, more than a gatekeeper. Parenting is hard enough, and I can't imagine how I would keep the rage off my face if my daughter's safety relied on such luck.

So we ended up in the Bittersweet Lane Apartments with support from the Chapter 707 Massachusetts Rental Voucher Program. We became part of the lucky 5% of US households to receive housing subsidies for the poor.[23] We had a fingerhold and could begin to claw our way up, not to luxury, sure, but to possibility at least.

We didn't grow up in the projects, but it turns out our family story is inseparable from public housing and slum clearance. I didn't grow up in the projects, but then no more than 15% of households in low-income, affordable housing do these days. The rest of us grew up in suburban developments, in pastel-colored townhomes, in rehabbed mill buildings, in anonymous detached houses, in shiny new towers, in crumbling mid-century modern mid-rises, in rented rooms, in family shelters, or worse.

TWO

Precipitating Events

In 1967, Grandmy had a third child while living at Orient Heights, but five months later, with baby Joe in tow, she moved across town again. They rented the upstairs of a Dorchester two-family house from Grandmy's friend. "It was a neighborhood," my mother told me, recalling fond memories of walks to school, to the library, and to the playground.

Unfortunately, Grandmy's friend had to sell the house after her husband died, and my grandmother needed to find another place to live. Worse, she needed to afford it on her nurse's wages. She'd earned her LPN while the youngest of her four children was two years old. Alcoholism had begun taking away her husband, and Grandmy was determined to provide.

They landed on the worse-off side of Washington Street. At the same time my mother Kathleen started high school, Judge Garrity started his busing plan. My mother told me, "It didn't seem real. I was just in survival mode, one of only three white kids. I didn't see any integration, just fighting. It was more the parents than the kids fighting, especially at first. But I was on guard all the time. I had long red hair, and the other kids would ask to touch it. It felt intimidating. My friend Lorraine at school was Black. We used to sneak up to the vacant third floor to smoke. But anyway, she used to protect me. She'd tell me when something was going to happen and to just run home. And then we all figured out we could use riots as an excuse to get out of school whenever we wanted. Our family wasn't political; we just went along with things. The anti-busing parents were worse than the kids. They were scary."

Kathleen's family tore apart at the seams around the same time her city did. Her father had been in and out of the first Dorchester house, but he didn't move with them to the second. "That was the beginning of the end of seeing him," my mother told me. At the time of my grandparents' divorce, fewer than 10% of US marriages ended in divorce, let alone Irish Catholic ones.[24] Jed did continue drinking in the neighborhood, however.

In 2010, my brother and I took our mother back to that neighborhood for its Irish Festival while Sean was home on leave from Iraq. We watched her point across Gallivan Boulevard: "That's where my father drank himself to death. He used to put me up on the bar, and the bartenders gave me cokes."

"The Eire Pub? Well, at least it was somewhere historic," I said.

"What, no, the American Legion Hall, behind the Eire Pub," she replied incredulously.

Mom, Sean, and I had a round of pints and whiskey in the Legion Hall. Sean didn't want to leave because the state's indoor smoking ban went unenforced there, but Mom and I wanted a clean breath. We three headed to the Eire Pub, where we watched a sitting US senator take a photo op pouring a pint of Guinness for his reelection campaign. He left more foam in that glass than the Atlantic leaves after a storm. He lost his reelection.

When I asked about leaving Dorchester, my mother told me, "Randolph just happened one day. I didn't want to move; I was tired of moving." In the summer of 1975, after a year of busing and with newfound resources from combining their households, Grandmy and her new husband, Tom Lally, moved the family to Randolph. They rented a modest post-war house on McDevitt Road. When not skipping school to take the 240 bus back to Dorchester, my mother and her brother Jerry hung out with another Irish American family on their new block, the Maddens.

My mother had a hard time adjusting to her new suburban school. "Randolph High was too white. I made a few friends over the summer, and I sat with them at lunch. I remember my first week at that new school in the cafeteria—the girls at my table were complaining that there were too many Black kids now. I was like 'Where?' and they pointed to two tables way at the other side of the cafeteria. Two tables! Randolph felt like the middle of nowhere to me then."

They lived on McDevitt for just a year, my mother's first sophomore year of high school. Then, a year later, Grandmy and Papa purchased their first home, on Lewis Drive in Randolph, with a mortgage subsidized by federal tax deductions like all buyers at the time. My mother recalls with flat enthusiasm, "It was fine. I had a bigger bedroom to share with Amy."

My mother lived five years in that house on Lewis Drive. Not having really had a freshman year in Dorchester, she repeated her sophomore year in Randolph before going on to finish high school and even attend community college. "I got sent to the principal one day during my senior year of high school; he was sick of me and sent me to the guidance counselor, who was on his way to take a student to Mass Bay. He dragged me along. He knew I was working at a preschool at the time, so he introduced me to the early learning program and helped me fill out the application right then and there. It all fell into place. Of course, there was no talk of college growing up."

At twenty-one, my mother began her career in early childhood education while living at home on Lewis Drive. In her desperation to leave her mother's house, she married her brother Jerry's friend Tommy's older brother, Jim Madden. He was tall and a carpenter, and he'd never lost his 1970s mustache. Jim and Kathleen moved to an apartment in a high-rise on the edge of the City of Brockton, the first time either of them had lived outside of their mothers' homes. "It was nice to get away," she told me. "It was a nice apartment, good location. We got along good the first couple years. I got pregnant just four months after marriage, so everything was all about the baby, really." (That's me! It's all about me, really).

My earliest memories kick in a couple years later. We came home through a red carpeted lobby at the bottom of that small Brockton tower. I'd wave to the building manager and once told him he smelled. I remember sitting up in a little bed filled with stuffed animals, yearning for something missing. I was too young to remember much else, and I don't know whether those were good times or bad times—celebratory times for a young married couple or the absolute exhaustion of two mismatched people caring for a fussy baby. My mother never really forgave me for being a colicky newborn, which, honestly, fair enough.

After a couple years in the small Brockton apartment, my parents rented a less small house in Randolph, closer to the day care where my mother worked, in the town where four of my six grandparents lived. We got a dog, a big gray Great Dane named Prince. The family next door had a child my age, and we used to explore our backyards together. They seemed enormous then, full of the mysterious ways of grass and trees, dirt and concrete, dogs and chain-link fences.

After I turned three, I had a big request for my mother. "Mom," I called. I found her in the kitchen doing dishes, staring out the window. "Ma." She must not have heard me. "Mom, mom, mom, mom, mom . . . MOM!"

"What! Jamie."

Her words didn't come out sounding like a question, but I asked mine anyway. "Can I have a little brother? I'd take good care of him. I'd help."

"We'll see," she told me, pushing down first-trimester nausea. Satisfied, I walked into the living room and climbed onto the pillowy tan-and-beige plaid couch with frills on the bottom that hid everything I put underneath it. Prince shuffled over to the couch and put his giant head in my little lap for pets. *Sesame Street* was on the TV, a floor model with a big dial that read 2 3 4 5 6 7 8 9 10 11 12 U. When Uncle Joe visited, the ColecoVision would come out for some *Frogger* or *Space Invaders*.

My parents were putting together the American dream: detached house, child, work. Jimmy Madden ran a growing carpentry business, framing up detached homes in the rapid sprawl of the 1980s. Then, he hurt his elbow. Then, he stopped working. Then, the painkillers were never enough. Decades later, my mother told me, "Jim started to change when you were fifteen months old. I didn't know he was taking pills and stuff; I was still pretty naive then. He had it all and just blew it."

The US Health and Human Services 1985 drug survey showed barely 1% of Americans actively used opiates at the time.[25] The survey in 2021 showed that number had at least tripled. Among people aged twelve or older in 2021, 3.3% (or 9.2 million people) misused opioids in the past year.[26] Decades before the twenty-first century opioid crisis, my father was part of a quiet trend.

My mother began to show as a hot and humid Boston summer settled in. She cut her hair short, suffering in the August heat with four weeks of pregnancy still to go. Her short bright red hair complemented her petite frame, but my father harassed her about it. "Why did you get that dyke haircut!?" He never let it go. I mean, fifteen years later, Jim's parish priest told me my mother was an "evil lesbian," as if that were a bad thing in the first place.

Mom delivered my baby brother, Sean, just a week before her own end-of-summer birthday. I was in love and heady with responsibility. They let me give baby Sean his bottle on that couch. I looked between his face and the face in my own framed baby photo on the side table. Sean had a full head of messy, dark hair, compared to me with my bald, golden baby fuzz. He was chunky and strong, the opposite of the tiny, premature, colicky baby in my photo. My mother, carrying Sean away, asked me to toss her Sean's brush for that head full of brown baby hair. I lobbed the brush. It hit baby Sean in the head.

When I was four years old, I tried to take the TV remote from my father, as toddlers do. He lost his temper and knocked me off the couch. My little head bounced off the coffee table and came up bleeding profusely, as head wounds do. My mother drove me to the doctor's office in Dedham, and I got my first stitches and first scar, just over my right eyebrow. I have an old photo of baby Sean and me sitting at Grandmy's table. A clean white bandage the size of my ear covers my stitches. I'm looking at someone to the photographer's right, smiling with my blue eyes and my lips both, one finger in front of them as if I'm shushing someone. I look happy. Baby Sean is holding a glass bottle of formula parallel to the table, pointing to the photographer's left. But from his high seat, Sean is looking directly into the lens, eyes a darker blue than mine, fixed in that thousand-yard stare Sean has always had. Prince stands taller than Sean's high chair. He'd rest his head on the tray and let Sean stuff Cheerios in his nose.

I could feel it coming in the air that one night. I'd been in the living room watching TV to ignore the thickening tension. Stillness was just the anticipation of an explosion. Waiting felt dangerous. More and more, my parents began to leave us in the living room watching TV while they argued in the kitchen. "Shut up. I don't want to hear one more fucking word out of you. You keep your god-damned trap shut," my father yelled at my mother, honestly expecting against all experience that she would in fact keep her mouth shut.

They got so loud I couldn't hear *Sesame Street*. I closed my eyes and I thought, *Be quiet, be quiet.* I hoped the fight was over when I opened my eyes. It was not. I yelled, "Shut up! I'm watching TV in here!" in imitation of Jim himself. I've always remembered that moment, but I couldn't tell you what happened before or after. My childhood memories are shards and fragments.

The last day stands out most in my mind. Dad carried a few boxes out to his truck. Mom took a photo of him from the living room window. His face in the photo is furious. Even his mustache frowned. Then Mom gathered me and Sean up to go to Grand-my's. I hopped down the four steps from our door to our car while my mother carried Sean. She loaded us into the back seat. The idea was to take us out and let Dad pack and leave on his own. But he wouldn't let us leave. He stormed towards the car, screaming at my mother. She opened the car door, and he grabbed her arm as she tried to sit down.

"Where are my lottery tickets!?" he screamed. He tore her out of the car and reached back in to grab her purse from the passenger seat. "They're in here, aren't they?" His arm hit the horn. We were screaming. My mother sobbed and gave up the purse. She managed to get into the car and drive us off towards Grandmy's home. The tears rolled down my face, and I cooled my hot red cheek against the car window.

Then, my father disappeared for months. When I woke up without a dad for the first time, I felt free, and I felt lonely, and I felt scared. And I began to worry almost immediately, not being used to being the next oldest person there. And I put responsibility on my skinny five-year-old shoulders and looked out for my mother and brother. Dad didn't contribute, and it would be decades before I could.[27]

As far back as I can remember, I worried a lot. Not just little five-year-old worries, big adults taking-the-world-on-their-shoulders worries. My mother saw my anxiety, and she did her best to help me through, telling me to relax and not worry. But I could see her own questions worrying her green eyes. *How long can we afford the rent? Where would we go? Will the courts side with Jim? Can I really handle a five-year-old and one-year-old on my own?*

She told me, "The only thing *you* have to worry about is what's in your lunchbox." And what was in my lunchbox, underneath the juice box and above the peanut butter and jelly sandwich cut into four triangles, was a folded-up napkin with a smiley face and a little note from my mother: *I love you. Have a fun day.* =) It meant so much to me to have this tiny bit of my mother's touch at preschool, distracting me from my four-year-old worries. Then, some other kid reached across the lunch table, picked up my napkin, and blew his nose into it. I could see his snot over the smiley face.

In social science, misfortunes like divorce, unemployment, injury, disease, etc., are called *precipitating events*. These are the moments that set everything else in motion. Not the whole cause, nor the full story, but the crack in the structure that marks the beginning of collapse. The rent on the detached home on Reed Street was more than my mother could handle alone on a preschool teacher's wages. So, like Jim, we had to move out too. Rents and incomes. It's just math to see how we would end up without a home.

And we were not alone in our situation. My generation are the children of an all-time high divorce rate.[28] But we were still the minority, the handful of kids in each classroom moving among households, needing support, and being looked down upon for that need. There was still tremendous stigma associated with single mothers like my own, whose gender-gap wages were supposed to support an entire household.

In the late 1980s, homelessness as we now know it was a new phenomenon. It was the consequence of the system's change away from creating affordable housing and towards exclusive zoning, inequality, deindustrialization, deinstitutionalization, and defunding social supports.[29] The emerging system turned the bad luck of daily life into the proximate cause of homelessness.

At the same time we were losing our home, on the other side of town in Cambridge, economists Richard B. Freeman and Brian Hall published "Permanent Homelessness in America?" They warned: "Rapidly rising land values, rents, and housing market problems for the poor in Massachusetts raises the possibility that future economic progress, including full employment of the type enjoyed in Massachusetts, may exacerbate rather than alleviate the housing problems of the poor. One can easily devise a scenario in which economic growth raises demand for land, inducing landlords to develop higher-quality properties, pricing out of the market those whose incomes do not rise with the rate of growth."[30]

To translate: an exclusive focus on job creation makes our sort of housing crisis worse, not better.

History has proven Freeman and Hall's prediction correct. I first encountered that quote on page 48 of Colburn and Aldern's

Homelessness is a Housing Problem. I circled the paragraph, and in the margin, I wrote, "They knew! They always knew!"

A permanent class of the homeless and housing insecure. That was my permanent worry. Ever since it happened to us when I was four years old.

Oh, and Prince didn't get to move out with us. A driver hit him in front of the house. We had to put him to sleep.

THREE

Grandmy's

P apa invited me home," my mother told me. The three of us moved into one bedroom back at Grandmy and Papa's house just four years after my mother had made her first escape from that house.

The US Department of Education commissioned a study that showed 76% of the 2.3 million students experiencing homelessness live in doubled-up situations.[31] The Department of Housing and Urban Development's homelessness report doesn't count people living doubled up.

My mother, Sean, and I shared one bedroom upstairs. The other upstairs bedroom belonged to my teenage aunt, Amy. She'd put her Bon Jovi T-shirt on me, sing Aerosmith's chorus as "Jamie's got a gun," and bring me chocolate crayons from her job at the mall. My grandparents' room was downstairs, next to the one full bathroom we all shared. When not working, Grandmy liked to sit in the sunlight in her rocking chair with the *Boston Globe* or a *Reader's Digest* and a cup of tea. Papa liked to rest in the dim light of their finished basement, eating potato sticks with the dog and watching sports.

Grandmy and Mom took turns dropping me off at kindergarten and dropping Sean at daycare so that my mother could work. I was the only kindergartener in my class who could read, but I couldn't tie my shoes. The teacher didn't believe I could truly read. She asked me to stay behind when everyone else went to play. She pointed at a little seat next to her desk. "Sit here. Read this." She trained skeptical eyes on me, trying to catch me pretending. Eventually, she believed me and encouraged my love of books. But she'd already left a chip on my shoulder.

As divorce proceedings began, our father decided he cared about seeing his children after all and demanded visitation rights. We stayed with him in his bedroom at Nana's house every other weekend, every Wednesday evening, and one week in the summer. His small room fit a TV stand that sat inches from the foot of his bed, a night-stand with yellow, lined pads of 8.5"x14" legal paper piled beside a lamp on top, a dresser, and a bookshelf that he'd made—poorly—which was filled with encyclopedias and more of his notepads. Every now and then for years, I watched him write up his own imagined, untrained legal arguments in those notepads. He was certain that made them legal. They were written on legal paper, weren't they?

Grandmy's crowded home was peaceful compared to hectic visitations with Jim at Nana's. He could turn any happy situation bad. Holidays and birthdays were the worst days, battlegrounds in the custody wars. Jim did try though, especially in those early years. He'd always take us somewhere on our Saturdays together, sometimes to the beach, sometimes to join him for under-the-table landscaping work. It felt good to get out of his mother's house where he sat chain-smoking all day.

Nana's house stood alone on a corner lot only a mile or two from Grandmy's house. Nana and Grandpa Herb spent most of their days in their glass-walled parlor watching game shows and Mother Angelica on television. My youngest Madden uncle, Tommy, had the back bedroom and fixed cars out of the garage. Sean and I slept in cheap sleeping bags on the floor of my father's little bedroom until he eventually bought cheap cots to put those sleeping bags on. During the day, we folded up the metal-frame cots and leaned them up against the random boxes and cases of Pepsi cans that lined the wall.

Long autumn afternoons smelled like motor oil and Marlboros. They sounded like Oldies 103.3 FM playing Van Morrison. Uncle Tommy kept on the radio while he worked on cars in the driveway. He usually worked outside and left the garage a wreck of empty Mobil motor oil bottles, empty boxes of Marlboro cigarettes, and empty cases of Budweiser beer. Who could afford to let the $0.05 each can was worth go to waste?

I spent long afternoons sitting on the concrete ledge above the driveway at Nana's, maybe reading, maybe watching Tommy work, but definitely avoiding my father and counting the hours until Sean and I could go back home to Mom. If I took my book and read inside for too long, my eyes stung from the cloud of cigarette smoke in my father's cramped room. Motor oil vapors smelled comparatively fresh.

Tommy worked from Nana's driveway because that was his home, the best he could afford. He worked from home because he'd lost his license for drunk driving, and it was miles walking to any of the auto garages that might hire him. So he fixed cars for cash at home and drank to his heart's content. In the evening, he'd tune the TV to *Star Trek: The Next Generation* or pop a VHS of the original *Star Trek* into his VCR. I loved getting to watch nerdy sci-fi shows with my uncle. My father didn't like it. Which is ironic, really.

One day in kindergarten, our friendly principal came to my classroom. "Jamie, you are getting released early today." I was confused, and I held her hand on the walk to her office. I was excited to go. I decided it was a nice surprise. Then, I sat in the office. I watched the clock tick. And tock. Tick. A red second hand stuttered around the circle, and I stared at the minute hand to see if I could catch it moving. Hundreds of hours of my childhood were spent just sitting, waiting for officious adults, waiting for them to decide our fates or to simply move some paperwork one way or another. I decided this was just another time like that. But my frustration grew as the minutes turned into what felt like hours. Eventually, Grandmy came and picked me up.

I learned later what had happened. My father had come to the kindergarten with a girlfriend pretending to be my mother because he himself was not on the approved pickup list. He wanted to take us back. We belonged to him, like property. It was a near thing, but the good staff at my school got suspicious and held me in the principal's office until it was all sorted and Grandmy could come rescue me. A federal government report that same year estimated noncustodial parents abducted 350,000 American children annually, something of a high-water mark for the rate of family abductions in the United States, which still remain four or five times more common than non family abductions.[32] Strangers aren't the dangers.

That ruse failed, thankfully. But it was one of many my mother dealt with continually, as if it weren't hard enough for a twenty-eight-year-old sharing a room with her two sons, back in her mother's house, and back arguing with her mother. Back then, searching for a place she could afford to live in was a job in itself.

"I started looking to get on Section 8. Remember, there's no computers. I had to travel and fill out applications in all these towns and cities, taking the Red Line to the Boston Housing Authority. One day, I was passing the Old Harbor projects on the Red Line and just burst into tears. I looked at some really bad places before Bittersweet Lane."

FOUR

Bittersweet Childhood

An uncommonly helpful bureaucrat told my mother about the 707 state housing assistance program and even helped her apply. My mother recalled, "I got awarded 707 certificates in two different towns—Wilmington and Randolph. I used the 707 voucher on one of the affordable apartments at Bittersweet Lane. I paid a third of my income, so rent would go up. I believe in paying more if you make more money. It wasn't really a problem, but things were always tight. You find tricks."

We moved into the Bittersweet Lane Apartments just before I started the first grade. The unremarkable gray thirty-five-apartment building sat in the back of a neighborhood of dozens of similar three- and four-story buildings, hidden away from the people who lived in detached houses in Randolph and adjoining suburbs. Still, it was exciting to have a place for just the three of us.

The two-bedroom, one-and-a-half-bath home at the Bittersweet Lane Apartments became my mother's first place of her own. She said, "I liked the apartment; I had a half bathroom of my own. I was very happy at Bittersweet Lane, except for the occasional ATF raid, of course."

Sean, Mom, and I like to joke about the day we left our apartment, pushed the button for the elevators, and then jumped back as a group of ATF (Alcohol, Tobacco, and Firearms) agents spilled out of the elevator with guns drawn. We huddled in the corner until they went down the hall, and my mother hurriedly ushered us into the elevator and out. I never did find out what it was all about.

When I interviewed my mother about her search for affordable housing, she left the academic silo implicit in my question. It was never just housing. "I hated using food stamps. Back then, they came in this humiliating large tear-off book. They were never enough for the food we needed, so I used to buy more food stamps from Jenae* for fifty cents on a dollar, cash. I would shop late at night because I was embarrassed when people saw me shopping with them. Jenae also used to pay me money to drive her to 'visit uncle' or run whatever errand in Mattapan. It took me a few trips to catch on to what she was really doing, and I told her I can't be doing that. I had you two in the car!

"But what used to torment me was childcare. It was really easy to go over-income and lose childcare, even when I was working there. I'd be on the phone crying to South Shore Day Care. They always seemed to find a way to make it work out. Without them, I'd have been screwed." People don't experience hard times narrowly. It's never just one thing.

After we moved into the Bittersweet Lane Apartments—certainly a more stable arrangement in the eyes of the Commonwealth of Massachusetts—my father did what he always did when my mother found some smidgen of progress. He threw a tantrum. He directed some of his anger towards our building full of Black families, and we kids were subject to all the racist tirades.

---

* Name changed for privacy.

Boiled potatoes left a starchy humidity in Nana's kitchen. I sat at the table trying to figure out what to do with the cold, boiled-to-death green beans I'd be punished for not eating. My father's family started cracking jokes: "Did you hear about the Polish Navy's new submarine? It had a screen door." "Why are there no Puerto Ricans on Star Trek? They don't have jobs in the future either." "Why don't Black people take Aspirin? They refuse to pick cotton." Racist jokes about Black people inevitably turned the conversation towards the Los Angeles riots and then to welfare. "Can you believe all these lazy welfare queens? Just having more babies and living off of us." We may as well have had Rush Limbaugh himself at the table, but I thought, *Welfare queens? That's us. That's Mom, Sean, and me. It's even the people here at this dinner table who collect one benefit or another.* I couldn't say it aloud without everyone turning their anger towards me, so I said something like, "Almost everyone in my building works. I don't think people choose to be poor."

My father retorted, "Oh, is that the liberal nonsense you get from your friend Bill Clinton?" I'd been unaware that the president who had ended welfare as we knew it was my own personal friend. I liked when he played saxophone anyway.

"No, he's been listening to his mother's lazy excuses. She needs to get a job and stop trying to be a career student welfare queen," said Nana. Then, looking towards me, she said, "And he's too smart for his own good, that one."

"Bit of hard work will learn him," said my father.

I stared at the clock. Eight p.m. could not come soon enough. After another weekend of being captive to my father's impotent anger, he'd drive us home in his beat-up old station wagon. He would drop us in front of the lobby because he was not allowed inside. He never left the car.

Sean and I walked to the vestibule, rang the electric buzzer, and strolled through the plain, undecorated lobby to the elevator. Today's elevator trash special was pizza crust. Sean rushed to hit the button for the second floor before I could. The doors stutter-stopped and threatened not to close, but up we went. Doors opened. Turn left. Our apartment was the first one on the left.

It wasn't a bad place. We had a kitchen with a little three-seat table, a dishwasher, a living room that we furnished with things out of storage from the Reed Street days, like the floor model television with channels 2 through U on a dial. (I was the remote control.) Sean and I shared a small bedroom, just big enough for our bunk bed, two dressers, and a toy box. My mother was thrilled to have a master bedroom with a half bath, even if she shared a wall with the elevator shaft. The noise woke her up in the early morning when our neighbors started off to work or, worse, when they came home from a night shift or whatever else brings you home at 3:00 a.m. Our living room had sliding doors for what should have been a balcony but instead was an opening with large red horizontal bars. We couldn't step outside, and the apartment didn't get much airflow. So I never really had any idea how to dress for the weather, which in Massachusetts could be anything you might imagine. When we did open windows, the sudden influx of stale cigarette smoke from the apartment downstairs got us coughing and rushing to close them again.

One small street called Highland Glen separated my neighborhood of three- and four-story apartment buildings from a neighborhood full of single-family detached homes and duplexes. As a child, I thought the people on the other side of Highland Glen were well-off, but they were just stable middle- and working-class families.

Occasionally, my father would have a friend or acquaintance drive us home for him. Some of them were shocked that my neighborhood even existed back there. I could sense their nervousness grow, driving down Highland Glen, seeing Black families cooking dinner on a smoking grill. Our neighborhood shocked these white families, even though they also lived in Randolph, even though they'd also been here the whole time. And, of course, they all complained about my mother and where we were living, so I got it. I got what they found shocking.

I went to Martin E. Young Elementary just a mile or so down the road for first grade. It was the elementary school that covered South Randolph at the time, a decent one, somewhat diverse but still majority middle-class and white. The Town didn't allow my neighborhood to stay at that school for second grade.

Randolph had diversified as the town grew with new subdivisions and apartment complexes through the 1980s and early '90s. The Town needed to accommodate a larger student population and converted a mothballed junior high school into an elementary school, the JFK. I was just a fourth grader when I saw a district map in an office at JFK and noticed that the other four elementary schools in Randolph served the neighborhood around them, but the JFK served nearly every dense multifamily apartment complex in town, regardless of location.

Even as a seven-year-old, I could see what was going on. It wasn't hard to notice it while walking along the street that separated multifamily buildings from detached homes on big lots and separated the JFK Elementary kids from the Young Elementary kids. The old townie clique, of which my father was a part, didn't want to integrate. They didn't want their children going to school with all these families who had moved from Dorchester or immigrated from Haiti. So they tried to contain us in one school.

I was always bored in school. My mind wandered in search of stimulation. My eyes settled on the classroom globe, which still featured the USSR. That didn't surprise me since our reading primers speculated whether people might land on the moon one day in the future. I flipped to the beginning of my textbook to read the student names written down in the 1960s and '70s. I always checked to see whether one of my uncles or aunts or parents had held that very same book. Sometimes they had.

I found that teachers treated us more as adversaries the less our class looked like them. At the end of our weekly art class in third grade, for example, the art teacher raged after some art supplies hadn't been returned. It was not the first time she had accused us eight-year-olds of being thieves. She refused to let us leave the room. She interrogated us one by one, letting only the favorites she deemed not guilty return to our classroom. I grew increasingly anxious as the room thinned out. The red second hand on the wall clock raced. Fluorescent lighting glared off its surface, obscuring the six. I could swear I saw the hour hand moving. Then the art teacher got around to me, the last left. "You have a guilty look on your face. Give them back. I know you took them." She badgered me for I don't know how long, maybe until I started crying.*

I've a few stories, but for many of my Black classmates, these sorts of false accusations and damaging assumptions were a part of daily life. They happened to me only occasionally. One day in fifth grade, while walking through the hallways to recess, my classmate turned around in line to sucker punch me in the face and call me honky.† His aunt lived at Bittersweet Lane with us. He and I played

---

* In the process of writing, I learned from classmates the identity of the art supply thief, who was never suspected.
† For the record, the correct slur for me is *paddy* or *mick*.

basketball in the parking lot. I have no clue what happened to him that day or what I might have done or said to set him off, but I can say with absolute certainty that adults' condemnations—like the art teacher's—hurt me far more for far longer than that punch.

South Shore Day Care helped raise us. I went to their after-school programs through elementary school, and Sean began there with preschool. My mother occasionally worked at their preschool too. At six, I met two friends there who would become like brothers. All three of us had single mothers; all three of us were some shade of poor; all three of us lived in multifamily buildings, me in affordable housing in Randolph, Gary in the affordable housing complex in Braintree where Grandmy's youngest brother drank his tragedy away to death, and Wayne in a small condo by the railroad tracks in Braintree. Gary, Wayne, and I would play street hockey behind the former parochial school where the after-school program was located or build massive block or Lego projects inside on rainy days.

Best, though, was that South Shore Day Care ran a day camp at Hale Reservation, southwest of Boston. Summers were the only time I ever rode a yellow school bus. It was always stuck in Route 128 rush hour traffic, but afterwards I could enjoy a day of meals outside, sports, art, hiking, swimming, boating, and especially music. Several of our camp counselors were musicians. I learned to swim there. I learned to paddle there. I made friends. We existed in a place where most everyone came from a family that did not fit America's ideal, nuclear, two-parent, suburban family. Some people didn't make it to adulthood; others are far from where we started. One friend is now a tenured professor. Another retired from the Army as a master sergeant after nearly two decades and four combat deployments. A third works retail and lives with his mother.

South Shore Day Care gave me a stable and compassionate place to be after my father's suicide attempt. I was not the only child there with a parent locked in an institution. During the handful of times we visited him at the mental hospital, I remember sitting down to do arts and crafts. We made a leather wallet with an *M* for Madden.

Jim met his second wife at the mental hospital. They married within a few months, and he moved into her four-bedroom on a cul-de-sac in Wilmington, Massachusetts. Jim liked living so close to New Hampshire, where he could buy cigarettes tax-free. It was probably the largest house I had yet been inside. Sean and I slept in twin beds in a room left to us but not ours. Jim wouldn't tell my mother where the house was.

So I paid attention to the drive during our next visit. I marked down directions as we drove. I lied when my father asked me what I was doing. It is the first lie I remember intentionally telling.

That house never became home. Shockingly, this marriage that began in a mental institution did not go the distance. They divorced a few months later, and it was back to the little bedroom in Nana's house.

Jim continued driving to New Hampshire to buy packs of Marlboro Reds, even though it was fifty miles from Nana's house, even though it took up half of the every other Saturday he got with us. I steamed on the sticky vinyl seats of his old, beat-up station wagon while he chain-smoked in the driver's seat. On long drives like that, I got in the habit of doing arithmetic in my head to pass time. What's the sum of the numbers on the license plate of that car? What's its product? How many dollars per gallon of gasoline times gallons per mile times the number of miles minus the savings on excise taxes divided by how many hours?

Jim spent money on cigarettes, scratch cards, and twelve-packs of Pepsi. Meanwhile, back at home, we were stressed about being able to afford basics like housing, food, and medical care. My feelings of resentment, disappointment, and abandonment grew with every hardship we faced, every pack he smoked, and every lecture he gave me or Sean about laziness or hard work. His hypocrisy and selfishness wounded me. I expected perfection—or at least best efforts. Isn't that what was required of me?

I expected perfection because imperfections lead to deprivation and disaster. Poor people in the US constantly face life-altering dangers over small sums of money. Being one hundred dollars short on the rent or getting a fifty-dollar parking ticket can easily grow into eviction or additional fines and could ultimately leave you homeless or unable to get to work, which is a distinction with only a few weeks of difference. According to the US Interagency Council on Homelessness, "More than half of Americans live paycheck to paycheck and one crisis away from homelessness."[33]

I thought perfection would get me out of that mess. Treating every dollar like a matter of life and death would protect me from those small-sum disasters. Being perfect at school and afterwards as a soldier or worker was the path to the middle class, to putting a net under the tightrope of daily life. But as any good writer will tell you, failure is a necessity. Failure is how we learn and grow. I never felt like I could risk it; failure is not allowed for the poor.

Perfectionism is anxiety. Hypervigilance and outsmarting people were my survival skills. But as a child, I wasn't wrong about perfection's necessity. Raj Chetty's groundbreaking research quantified just how unlikely poor Americans in my generation were to ever escape financial distress and how even less likely people affected by systemic racism were to achieve "economic mobility."[34] Americans who start from a disadvantaged class are unlikely to escape a lifestyle dominated by the daily anxieties of living on the edge in the

US, struggling for basic needs. I'm there in Chetty's massive dataset somewhere, pulling the data ever so slightly against the odds.

In the 1990s, I was a child listening to nonstop vitriol against poor people as Republicans and Democrats alike worked to transform our country's safety net. The cultural zeitgeist was full of welfare queens driving superpredators in their Cadillacs to go wilding. It all felt like so much propaganda to me, so at odds with the realities I witnessed. Welfare reform's goals focused on creating a system to punish imagined laziness and support only the deserving poor, with a faith that our bureaucracies are adequate to decide who truly "deserves" help. But me, I believed I would prove my worth myself and escape through effort and perfectionism so I wouldn't end up like that. So I wouldn't end up like my father.

My mother's younger brother, Joe, got married in a quick private ceremony in Texas. Marriage must have been the best way to prepare for a combat deployment, I supposed. We wrote letters to him, looked up where Kuwait and Iraq are in my grandparents' atlas, and learned that FOB means Forward Operating Base. Papa walked us to the corner store where he bought his Lucky Strikes and scratch tickets. For two dollars, we could send our letters to Uncle Joe across the planet over phone lines. Fax machines were the height of communication technology when the US invaded Iraq the first time. Try not to think too hard about that. Anyway, it was a very big deal. Desert Storm was the first war in which families and deployed soldiers could communicate like this, almost in real time.

After returning, Joe and his new wife, Jeannie, planned a proper wedding in Killeen, Texas. While Sean and I stayed at our father's, my mother left New England for the first time in her thirty-one years of life. Out of curiosity, she stepped into a Texas pawn shop. She walked out with a stenograph machine.

When my mother had found herself responsible for two boys on her own, her preschool teacher's wages no longer cut it. And then, the Commonwealth began to require a bachelor's degree though the work no longer made ends meet anyway. That was the end of my mother working at something she both loved and was good at. So she took a job doing bill processing for Travelers Insurance, a job that the company soon moved to Florida. We were not going to move to Florida. So my mother came home from Texas with a stenograph.

She enrolled in the court reporting program at Massachusetts Bay Community College. Court reporting was an associate's degree, but it also required speed tests in which my mother had to accurately transcribe a mock deposition with people speaking at 225 words per minute. (I type quickly, and I am only typing this at about fifty words per minute.) For the next six years—my elementary school years, our Bittersweet Lane years—my mother balanced going to school, working, raising two boys, and practicing nonstop to pass her tests to begin work as a court reporter. To make practice fun, she'd watch *Animaniacs* with us and transcribe their fast-paced songs, the very model of a cartoon individual. She never had much downtime. I did my child best to help.

I'm not sure whether the smell or the fluorescent lights was the more agonizing bit of our laundry room. The windowless room existed in the timeless banality only perpetual fluorescent lighting can achieve. The smell was more subtle. At first, the gauzy chemical fragrance of detergents and softeners covered the stale, moldy air. But after the first half hour or so, my nose was not fooled by either and thirsted for fresh air. Still another fifteen minutes until I had to move the clothes to the dryer, and then another hour of babysitting laundry. The last time I left the clothes unattended in the washer, a neighbor moved them to the table, where they marinated in that laundry room smell. That was still better than the time I left them in the dryer. Our clothes were gone, disappeared, by the time I remembered to go back downstairs for them. So 106 minutes in this timeless, stale room was the least bad option. My mind wandered back to the scene from that morning.

I'd burst into tears in Mrs. Dziergowski's fourth-grade classroom. Fear and pure emotion shot through my body. I had no idea why. It was a normal day. There hadn't been any recent tragedies. I'd enjoyed a weekend away at my mother's uncle's pondside cabin in Orange, Massachusetts. I tried to swallow the tears. Boys don't cry. I did my best to hide the first sobs behind a book at my little desk. But I couldn't help it; the sobs spilled out. Mrs. Dziergowski noticed, and then each of the sixty or so eyes in the classroom were on me. Shame rose up my throat to join my crying breakdown. I liked my fourth-grade teacher, and she was kind. Still, I didn't like being noticed. She helped me get out of my desk and took me to the hallway.

"Shhh, shh. It's OK. Do you want to tell me what's bothering you?"

"I . . . I don't know."

"Are you OK at home? Are you hurt?"

Still sobbing, I replied, "I'm OK, I think. I . . . I'm sick."

"OK, go to the nurse, and let's see about sending you home early."

There wasn't always a school nurse present, and there wasn't one that morning. They let me out anyhow, and I got home somehow. And I felt shame and embarrassment and sorrow because I wasn't physically sick and I had no idea why I'd burst into tears. But at least I made good use of the half day by getting some laundry done.

I thought about what to do after the laundry. *Homework's done. I'll play trumpet when I get upstairs.* It was my first instrument. Public school, fourth grade, a student trumpet my mother couldn't afford, but there was a payment plan. I was thrilled to have an instrument of my own, and I took to it quickly, practicing every single day.

Then, I found out my neighbors could hear me through our apartment walls. Our building did not have good acoustic separation—a topic I had to learn much about decades later as a developer. I didn't know what was or wasn't in the walls or ceiling assemblies back then, but I did know that everyone could hear whoever was above, next to, and, sometimes, below their own apartment. I still shudder at memories of upstairs neighbors screaming, getting hit, crying, and vacuuming at 2:00 or 3:00 or 4:00 a.m.

But anyway, someone complained, or maybe just made a comment, about hearing me play my trumpet. Our next-door neighbor, Jenae, told me she liked to hear me play. Still, I never played at home without a mute again, and I played less often. I was terrified of people hearing me make mistakes, of disturbing people with the noise of playing poorly.

My mother played guitar as a teenager. She had two imitation Les Paul electric guitars and an acoustic guitar with a crack in the neck and three-quarters of an inch of action above the twelfth fret. They were impossible, but I loved trying them anyway. Mom would take them out every now and then to play for Sean and me, but less often as court reporting work on the stenograph machine tired her hands. She played the songs she could remember learning as a teenager in the 1970s.

My mother sold her two imitation Les Paul guitars. She used the money to take me to Guitar Center and buy me a guitar for Christmas. I chose a Mexican-made Fender Stratocaster. Mom had Les Paul-style guitars as a teenager because she wanted to imitate Jimmy Page and Eric Clapton. Rock bands in the '90s played Stratocasters, and I loved Jimi Hendrix besides. Unlike the trumpet, I could play my guitar into headphones or turn my little practice amp down—safe to play, deep in the dream chamber, disturbing no one.

Jim promised to take us to the comic book shop right after the dump. The Falmouth dump had a swap area. What I would give now for one of those old stereo receivers with a tape deck or a VHS player, *sigh*. We weren't there for that anyway. We were there for the copper wire.

The dump made junked wire available to strip, and it paid for fully stripped copper by weight. Jim had some wire he collected and stripped at home. We loaded it into the station wagon. But the swap had three times as much piled up and waiting for us or someone like us. Jim taught us how to use the wire stripper, sizing it for the copper so we removed only the plastic insulation. And we sat there in the shade on a hot Cape Cod summer Saturday stripping wire, Sean, me, and our father. It felt like hours, but I was a kid, so who knows? Tighten, strip, tighten, strip, tighten, strip, roll it up from hand to elbow, stack it with the rest. Clean up all the shredded plastic bits. Tighten, strip, tighten, strip . . .

I thought to myself as I stripped wire that maybe someday I'd be an electrician. Then I decided I'd rather have a new comic book to read. And with cash for copper in hand, I got one. The rare kept promise from my father.

Sean and I watched the town names scroll underneath *Rocky and Bullwinkle* as snow fell outside. *Plymouth . . . Plympton . . . Quincy . . .* "Come on, come on." *Randolph.* "Snow day!"

I ate my strawberry Pop-Tart quickly and rushed to put on my snow pants, my boots, and my jacket. Sean wasn't ready to go, so I went alone to knock on the doors of the neighbors who would pay me fifteen dollars to shovel out their parking spaces. No school, and it was snowing money. It was a good day.

I took my shovel and brush outside and hung a right towards the surface parking lot on that side of our building. The snow was still white and pretty, untouched by cars, grime, or second winter's slush. It was powdery enough that I just used my arms to brush the snow off the first car's roof. Even better, I could brush the snow off the windows too—no scraping at ice today. After the car was clean, I shoveled the snow out from behind it, around it, and under it and tossed it onto the snow-covered landscaping strip.

Sean came out just before the snowplow arrived. I was shoveling the last spot, and the plow just pushed through the parking lot, adding an icy eighteen-inch snowbank behind all the cars. "Sean, help me out with this."

"I don't have a shovel."

"Kick it," I said. "Like this." And I drove the heel of my Timberland boot into the middle of the snowbank, knocking down a chunk of ice the size of a basketball. I picked it up and shot it at the big snow pile left by the plow.

Sean didn't need to be told twice. He demolished the snowbanks with kicks and tackles, and I shoveled away the rubble. Work done, Sean ran to the big snow pile. "I'm the king of the castle!" he yelled from the summit.

I threw a couple snowballs at him and charged up, boots driving through the soft snow, and grabbed Sean's legs to pull him down into the snow with me. That's one thing we had over the families in detached houses on the other side of Highland Glen. We had a giant snow pile in our parking lot.

The lights flashed on at 6:00 a.m. My father lit up a cigarette and bent down to his stereo. He turned on the most blaring, annoying music he could find. "Get up! Shower! Get dressed! Can't be late to Mass."

We pulled into St. Mary's parking lot half an hour before the 8:00 a.m. Mass. Jim insisted on the 8:00 a.m. Mass because it was the quickest one—no singing—so he could get in, get out, get some Dunkin' Donuts to bring home, and then get on with his day. We emerged from the smoke-filled, wood-paneled 1984 Chevrolet Caprice Classic station wagon. Sean and I pulled at our clothes this way and that, trying to find a way to move comfortably in the cheap, tight clothes we'd outgrown. Sean's little teal-blue shorts that once reached his knees were nearly vulgar now, reaching bare inches past his crotch. My jeans left nothing to the imagination, and they made walking difficult. Jim took forever to get through the parking lot anyway, stopping to chat with every townie on the way in.

Finally stepping into the church, I paused to dip my index and middle fingers in holy water and remember the Father on my forehead, the Son on my heart, and the Holy Spirit by making a cross of my chest. The cool water felt refreshing on my skin.

Tall, conspicuous Jim Madden strode up to the nave, nodding or waving to people already in pews on either side before finally choosing a pew near the altar. Just as I finally got to sit and rest for the first time since being roused from sleep, we all stood to watch the small parade of priests, deacons, and altar boys. The boy in front got to carry the cross up to the altar. His was a coveted position.

"In the name of the Father, and of the Son, and of the Holy Spirit."

"Amen," I muttered. I resolved myself to the routine, the responses automatic but the kneeling, sitting, and standing still annoying. The ritual of it all eased my mind a bit, but I found it hard to say *lord* and *king* so many times. I knew too much Irish history at a young age.

We all stood for the Gospel reading and the many introductory rites on the way to it. I listened more closely and read along in my missalette. It was harder to read along during the first two readings because I read too quickly. Most of the volunteer deacons didn't read as well as the priests.

"Jesus said to him, 'If you wish to be perfect . . .'" That caught my attention. "'Go, sell what you have and give to the poor, and you will have treasure in heaven. Then come, follow me.' When the young man heard this statement, he went away sad, for he had many possessions. Then Jesus said to his disciples, 'Amen, I say to you, it will be hard for one who is rich to enter the kingdom of heaven.'" I liked where this was going. "'Again I say to you, it is easier for a camel to pass through the eye of a needle than for one who is rich to enter the kingdom of God.'"

Church was one of the few places I encountered adults of a higher-class status than ours. I looked around at the middle-class families with two parents and at the old ladies as fragrant from perfume as their jewelry was gaudy. "Gaudy" was a vocabulary word at school that month. The 8:00 a.m. Mass was always whiter for some reason, but I looked around and counted a couple Haitian families at least. Inequality always riled me. I thought about how I wasn't allowed to continue at Young Elementary. I thought about last summer when no one would help us when my little brother fell off his bike and was bleeding badly. We'd ridden our bikes over the path through the road barrier to the wealthier side of Shorewood Drive. I wrapped a sock around the wound and walked him the long way back.

"'But many who are first will be last, and the last will be first.'" This faith in justice manifest, in the next life if not this one, appealed to me. It matched my desires for equity and salved some of the pain, like the pain in my crotch at that moment from jeans that hadn't even fit last fall. Our priest's homily did not go out of its way to justify wealth or to temper the passage's plain meaning. "Riches and greed, these are obstacles in the way of our path following Jesus. It is impossible, humanly speaking, for one who has many possessions to enter the kingdom of God, as Matthew reminds us. Only the poor can enter the kingdom." He did, however, reach out to us parishioners with a path to heaven regardless of where westarted. "The Twelve Apostles gave up everything to follow Jesus, and we can follow their lead to also have as our reward eternal life in Jesus."

I was getting hungry and impatient for the Eucharist. But first, the one piece of music at the 8:00 a.m. Mass. The priest intoned, "Christ has died, Christ is risen, Christ will come again." Now, everybody sing! The somber early morning chant of the insufficiently caffeinated Boston Catholics droned from the pews, "Christ has died, Christ is risen, Christ will come again."

Finally, finally, I sidled down the pews and into the line, walked up to the altar, received the Eucharist, and put the first food of the day on my tongue. I let it sit there. Someone had told me not to chew because it's Christ's body. The wafer slowly broke up, and I savored the nourishment. It never tasted like cardboard to me.

The alarms went off again. The hallway's blaring horns played tenor to our smoke detector's anxious soprano. "Mom, do we have to go outside?" I groaned.

Mom stood up resignedly. "Yeah, we should go."

"But that's the third time this week! It's just someone burning their dinner," I reasoned.

Sean said, "But *The Simpsons* are on!"

I stood up resignedly as well and sighed. "We can't hear it anyway, Sean. Let's go."

Mom touched the doorknob, just cold metal. I covered my ears after she opened it. The fire alarms in the hallway were unbearably loud. The hallway wasn't any smokier than usual, but we couldn't take our normal right turn with the heavy steel fire door slammed shut. Sean and I ran the length of the hallway to our staircase. A few neighbors trickled down the stairs with us, and we all gathered outside the building to await the fire department. We could hear the sirens before we heard the trucks. We always heard the sirens, the station sitting not far from our apartment blocks. We heard sirens get closer, then farther, then gone. We heard more sirens approach and turn the other way. We listened until they finally showed up to turn off what amounted to a poorly functioning, exceptionally disruptive oven timer.

The silver lining was staying up well past my bedtime and staring at the one constellation I could recognize, Orion, standing over the neighboring building. Mom got us off to bed, but she would not sleep well that night.

The air was clear, and the water was clean, but the bottom of the glacial kettle pond remained unfathomable. Sean jumped in, perhaps to find out, but five-year-old Sean could not swim. My mother dove in after him. There he was, just on the edge of the underwater drop-off. She kicked hard and reached her hand out to him, but he just sank deeper. She kicked harder and harder and reached longer and longer, but each time her fingertips brushed his little five-year-old hand, he slipped deeper and deeper.

My mother woke up from the nightmare in a panic, though thankfully dry. She calmed herself and walked into our room to see us sleeping peacefully.

Later on, we woke up excited. Mom was planning to take us to her uncle's camp house by the pond. Massachusetts only has so many nice weather days; it's a sin to waste any. But then, over a quick Pop-Tart breakfast, Mom told us, "We are not going to the pond today."

"Can we go to Houghton's Pond in the Blue Hills then? It's close," I suggested, hoping to be helpful.

Mom quickly responded, "No, no ponds today. Let's, um, go on a hike to . . . Cat Rock?" And so we did, and on the drive up 128, Mom told us about her nightmare.

"So that's why no pond," I said, just to state the obvious. And we had a pleasant walk through the reservation that also hosted our day camp, now empty on a Saturday. Sean and I showed Mom the trails and found Cat Rock, and we climbed all the way to the top.

It was a magnificent wilderness feat for five- and nine-year-old city kids. Cat Rock loomed a towering 360 inches or so above the ground below. Anyway, it seemed plenty tall when Sean fell over the edge.

Mom's body slammed to the ground, head and shoulders over the edge of the rock. She could just about reach Sean where he had foot- and handholds. Then Sean fell again. Sean, with his signature brand of luck, landed butt-first on the only two square feet of dirt between jagged granite rocks. Mom and I jumped to our feet and ran down. Sean was scraped up but cried just for a minute. "I want to go back up," he said once he'd gathered himself.

"No. We're going home," said Mom with the tone we didn't question. "I knew it. I knew it. It was one of those dreams. Maybe we should've gone to the pond after all! Just my luck," Mom babbled as the parental adrenaline rush faded. We talked about it on the trail. We talked about it in the car. We talked about it walking to our building. We talked about it in the elevator.

Then, the elevator dropped. Free, free falling.

Mom shouted, "Bend your knees, boys . . ." Time froze for us as the elevator fell. "Annnnd, jump!" Emergency brakes grabbed the car a foot or two below the first-floor lobby. We landed. Jumping was fun.

The doors did not open. An eternity passed as we pressed the emergency buttons and pulled at the doors until they finally gave way. We climbed out of the elevator and turned towards the hallway. "Let's take the stairs," Mom said. "Tomorrow, you can stay home and play Nintendo."

"Mom, why did you tell us to bend our knees and jump in the elevator?"

"Honestly, I didn't know what else to say."

The next time the elevator dropped, Sean and I bent our knees and jumped without being told. After the third time, we could time our jumps perfectly whenever the elevator fell. Survival is more fun as a game.

That's poor kid housing math: bend your knees, count to three, and hope the brakes catch. Currently, 23% of the Department of Housing and Urban Development's (HUD) public housing and 4% of homes assisted by project-based Section 8 failed their last physical safety inspections.[35] Behind stats like that are stories like these: A young wheelchair user in the Bronx couldn't go to school for days at a time because of an elevator outage.[36] Kansas City families felt forced to send their children away to live with relatives because their

Section 8 landlords refused to fix water leaks, black mold, sewer backups, and air conditioning in summer heat.[37] Charleston tenants suffered rats chewing through their electrical wiring at the same time their plumbing leaked.[38] Always a good idea that, to mix electricity and water. There are thousands of stories of harm to residents in HUD housing. Even buildings that pass HUD's REAC (Real Estate Assessment Center) inspections—which are more concerned about torts than tenants—aren't necessarily in decent condition. As *Pro-Publica* reported, "HUD Inspections Pass Dangerous Apartments Filled With Rats, Roaches and Toxic Mold."[39]

My father drove right up to the lobby doors at Bittersweet Lane. Just in time. I couldn't take what he was saying anymore. But arguing always made it worse. I hit my limit. I popped open the door before the car even got into park, and I moved inside with quick, long steps. Sean trailed behind, and I had to hold the door open for him.

Nana had spent that sunny afternoon with me—one-on-one. Grandpa Herb napped in his recliner. I sat on the couch and listened to Nana tell me about the end times. She told me about Revelation, and I read it. She told me what the TV told her Nostradamus told people Revelation meant. She told me it was going to happen to my generation, the coming of the anti-Christ, who would take control of the US government. She told me we'd have to choose between getting the mark of the beast, 666, tattooed on our foreheads or starving. She told me the choice between food rations and my eternal soul would make for no choice at all. She told me about hell. She told me about the torture, the beasts, the demonic fallen angels, and the hellfire.

And then I had to listen to another of Dad's rants about Mom and liberals and all? I needed out of that car.

The humid summer air stagnated inside our glass-walled lobby, a little greenhouse with buttons and names where, hopefully, you wouldn't have to stay long. I rang my mother on the buzzer and she let us in. The dark interior felt cool compared to the summer heat. As I waited for the elevator, I could smell the stagnant smoke from the apartment just to the right of the elevator. I hoped it wasn't coming in through the window upstairs. The elevator opened, and a garbage smell hit my face. The carpet had a new stain, with chicken bones and a balled-up paper towel sitting just next to it. Sean and I rode up to our floor and quickly turned the corner towards our apartment, happy to be home.

But that Sunday afternoon, our neighbor Jenae sat in the hallway, back against her door, head drooping and eyes half open.

"Jenae? Jenae, are you OK?"

"Huh? What? Oh, Jamie. Yeah, I'm . . . I'm locked out. Can you get your mother to open the door for me with her Blockbuster card?" Her son must have been with his father that weekend too.

I lay awake that night. Monday morning arrived too fast. I couldn't sleep the next night either. I repeated the Our Father and Hail Mary prayers over and over in my head until insomnia gave up and released me to sleep. I did that every night for months.

Monday night meant pasta with red sauce, bagged salad, and if we were lucky, Italian bread with butter. Wednesday is traditionally Prince Spaghetti night, but we had dinner with Dad at Nana's on Wednesdays.

"Jamie, put down the parmesan," said Mom.

"Yeah, Jamie, don't take it all," Sean piled on.

I put the green plastic shaker of Kraft grated parmesan powder back down after three shakes. Three shakes of parmesan. Three scoops of ice cream. Three slices of pizza. But only two donuts. There were rules, after all.

I finished my bowl and wiped up the sauce, then I stood up to get more pasta from the strainer sitting over the pan on the stovetop. The strainer was empty. When I sat down again, my mother picked up her bowl and gave me the rest of the food on her plate. She did that. When things were tight, she'd go without to give us more.

Sean and I were watching *The Simpsons* after dinner when the phone rang. And hung up. And rang. And hung up. And rang. And rang. After an hour of *The Simpsons*, I got up to turn the dial on the TV from Fox 64 Rhode Island to Fox 25 Boston to watch another hour of *The Simpsons*. I heard the answering machine click on.

My father's voice boomed from the machine, angry, rabid, threatening violence, ". . . I will come break down the door and drag you by your hair if I need to, you dyke. Someone's gotta smack some sense into you."

I tried to plan how I could defend us. We had no real weapons in the apartment. I pulled out the model rocketry equipment Uncle Jerry had given me, and I arranged it so I could launch one at someone. (I was ten; it seemed like a good idea at the time.) I waited, scared, staring at our door with my dry fuel rocket. I forgot about *The Simpsons*. I stayed ready for action until the phone stopped ringing and the ticking clock slowly proved Jim's threats hollow.

In the process of writing this book in 2022, I dropped by the Bittersweet Lane Apartments, now known as the Woodlawn Apartments. I hadn't visited since the '90s. I knew they had been purchased, refinanced, syndicated with Low-Income Housing Tax Credits

(LIHTC)*, rehabilitated, and renamed. Marketing photos online focused on green leafy trees, obscuring the building that may or may not have had a fresh coat of paint. Maybe the landscaping tricked me into thinking it might be better now.

The drive there felt natural, automatic. When I pulled up across the street from the building, my eyes creased in anger at its obvious disrepair and mismanagement. I walked around the building, taking photos. Dilapidated, split siding. Trash and toys scattered on the ground beside the building. Overgrown weeds. A garden of satellite dishes sprouting from the barred sliding windows. Chipping paint. With the decades away and the cognitive dissonance of an educated professional, I felt like this was just another site visit for work. The feeling of home was too big to handle, safer to keep at a mental distance.

Within a couple minutes, an SUV pulled up beside me in the parking lot. The driver's sister leaned out the window and, with equal courtesy and aggression, asked, "Excuse me. Who are you?"

I'd guessed, hoped really, that this might happen so I could talk to current residents. With tone and body language to communicate I was not the threat I embodied, I replied, "Hi, my name's Jamie. I'm working on a book about affordable housing, and it focuses on this place. I grew up here," I replied and then asked, "So, what's it like living here these days?"

The women visibly relaxed, and the woman, who told me her name was Monique, said, "It's nice. Except inside." I didn't think the outside looked nice either. Monique apologized for being aggressively suspicious of me at first. "I'm sorry, but my daughter is in there, you know?"

---

* Don't worry; this is defined at length in later chapters.

"No apologies at all! You're defending your home. My old home. That's the right thing to do, isn't it? You kidding me? You made my day!"

We began trading stories. They told me about the current rat infestation. I told them about our constant mouse infestations and the day my mother tossed a sticky trap and its mouse like a frisbee out our window. She'd panicked that my toddler brother would see it. But the punchline came the day I saw a neighborhood stray cat with the sticky trap stuck on its face, no mouse in sight.

It sounded like the roaches were the same now as they were then: mostly fine if you kept clean, awful when someone caused a roach migration with fumigation or a move-out. But the mold, that shocked me. "My sister has asthma and has to come use my bathroom because of all the black mold." I told them that's not legal and cursed myself for not keeping good tenant's rights contacts to connect them to.

They also complained that the landlord was raising rents, again.

FIVE

Which Way Out of Bittersweet Lane?

What does it take to survive? How do we rise from oppression to thrive?

TOUGHEN UP

Never underestimate violence. Don't dwell on it either. Just know that the neglected foundation of the hierarchy of needs is bodily autonomy.

As a child, I loved music, books, video games, and *The Simpsons*. People kept telling me I was smart—even when they meant it as an insult—and teachers kept giving me A's. Why wouldn't I sit around with my books and music, just thinking and learning? My father had forced me to play little league baseball for years, and it really wasn't for me. I looked like a tree standing in right field, dissociating. Let's just say I wasn't a very active kid.

I got into kung fu through my friend Wayne when we were both sedentary, fat, awkward preteens. Wayne was getting less so. And the stories about his sifu, Kevin Rice, were incredible. His classes were very hard on me at first. Then, they got harder. Sifu Kevin taught at the Wah Lum Kung Fu school in Chinatown, and he taught his own private classes, usually on a concrete platform by his house or one of the South Shore's parks. After a few months of my eight-year-old brother Sean stuck waiting and watching us every Monday and Thursday, he and Sifu Kevin convinced Mom to let him join too.

The basics were challenges in and of themselves. I worked hard to be able to kick high, to sit in a stance, to become flexible. I threw punch after punch, block after block. I progressed, but class was always that bit harder. Sifu had a gift for bringing students into the space between where we thought our limits were and where our true capacity was. During that moment when we were sweating and wondering whether we would quit, Sifu would have us yell out, "Suffering is the bread of life; through pain is born strength; that which does not kill us will only make us stronger."

We trained outdoors, year-round, in New England. We learned to ignore mosquitoes, and we dumped water on ourselves in the summer. We trained on ice or snow wearing layers and boots in the winter. We fought with four-ounce gloves, and we fought with wooden weapons and dull-bladed knives and swords. We fought in groups of all sizes. Learning to fight alone against a group saved me from a gutter years later. Fighting as a group against one didn't matter when the opponent was Sifu, but it taught us to confront fears and how to take a hit to allow your brother to follow up.

Sean and I had fun practicing kung fu together in the apartment, in the parking lot, on the beach, and in Nana's yard. When we got into brotherly squabbles, we understood and respected each other—even when Sean tried to choke me out with a Nintendo cord. Sean and I became brothers twice over, as blood and as kung fu family.

I was lucky to find belonging both inside and outside my family. Community carries us. With six grandparents and dozens of aunts, uncles, and cousins, not a month went by without a family gathering or four. It's just math. I cherished the holiday dinners. Well, holidays were split and traded, but I cherished the ones with my mother's side anyway. Better food, better conversation, less emotional abuse.

Besides dinner and dessert, I loved being there for the stories. I fought to be at the adults' dinner table so I could listen in on the conversation game. Everyone competed for the biggest laughs, and what was funniest was getting in and out of trouble with the authorities. Uncle Jerry's pre-sobriety stories were always good contenders, but Papa's old escapades had Jerry beat. He once drove away from the cops by driving onto the T tracks at Forest Hills. Grandmy laughed loudest. "I remember that! I thought, 'What kind of dingbat would do something like that?'" She was a teenager living in Forest Hills when that had happened, decades before she'd meet Tom Lally.

Jokes gave way to serious conversations sometimes. I always listened, rapt with attention, when the older generation talked about the Troubles, immigration, the peace process, and their labor unions. Papa won the conversation game again with a riveting tale about his uncles fleeing to America during the 1920s. It was all very confusing until I put together that they were talking about two very different political groups with the same big word, Republicans. At our table, the good Republicans were the Irish ones, the Fenians. They struggled for self-determination and the reunification of the island. The bad Republicans were the political party in the US. We're a Boston Irish family; at any given time, someone's union was on a strike or in a negotiation while Presidents Reagan and Bush and Governor Weld fought hard against workers' rights.

In mid-'90s Boston, the Troubles were all over the news as well. Headlines seemed to alternate between peace talks and bombings, up until the 1998 Good Friday Agreement created a lasting détente. I noticed 26+6=1 bumper stickers and graffiti. The math stumped me until Papa explained that it meant the twenty-six counties of the Irish Republic plus the six counties in the north of Ireland would equal one united Ireland. That made sense of the South Boston mural of a map of Ireland with a Union Jack covering the six northern counties, followed by a minus sign, a map of England, an equals sign, and the tricolor flag of the Irish Republic. Just across Broadway from the mural, the D Street projects loomed, angry and half empty, three even rows of windows covered by bloodred boards in the buildings awaiting demolition. I sent out thoughts of gratitude that I lived at Bittersweet Lane and not D Street.

Learning about the injustices my Irish ancestors faced raised my pride in the Irish. But if colonialism, forced labor, poverty, displacement, and language repression were wrong then and there, they must also be wrong here and now. My Haitian neighbors especially seemed to me to be suffering nineteenth-century-style impoverishment. Ireland paved a path towards anti-racism for me. Yes, these are the kind of thoughts I had in the fifth grade when my messy cursive spilled into the margins as I journaled excitedly about St. Paddy's Day and the Irish Republican Army's ceasefire that, in my eleven-year-old words, created "a light of hope for peace."

Besides, in our diverse, immigrant-heavy Randolph schoolyard, it was impossible to get by without knowing where your people were from. You're Haitian? Cool, I'm Irish. You're Polish? Did you hear that one about the Polish submarine? No? No, you wouldn't like that one, would you? You're from Hong Kong? I heard the best water park in the world is there; have you been on the waterslides? I'd never left New England myself, so I paid attention when my classmates talked about the larger world.

But at the time, I hated going to a school with textbooks my parents' generation had used, where authority came first, creativity and truth later. I got in trouble for arguing with a teacher who'd misread Newfoundland for Massachusetts on a textbook's climate map. I got in trouble again for asking, "Did you mean every year?" after she'd said, "The Earth orbits the sun every twenty-four hours."

I wasn't *entirely* a know-it-all brat. I was honestly baffled. When we learned about Jim Crow era segregation, I asked, "But what about Asian people? What did they do with them?" The teacher told me, "There weren't any."[40] I was a Randolph kid, and it was unimaginable to me that any racial group would be absent anywhere in America. I thought Randolph's diversity was the norm. "How?" I asked. I can't recall the teacher's answer, but I know I left still puzzled.

I had bigger things going on anyway. In my journal, I tried a thing I'd been told to try, and listed three things I was happy were happening:

1. Dad is moving to Nana's house in Falmouth.
2. Mom only has three tests left to graduate, and she got a job.
3. Soon I'll be old enough to legally be left alone for long periods of time.

Alone in the room Sean and I shared, a week or so later, I put more anger on the page. Dad was refusing us visits. No weekend visit. No Wednesday night dinners. Who even knew about the holidays? He was furious my mother wouldn't sign some documents he needed in order to get a housing subsidy. She didn't want anything to do with potential fraud, as he was living in his mother's home, not actually paying any rent. The hypocrisy infuriated me. This man ranted about "welfare queens," which was practically a nickname he had for my mother. This man ranted about how unfair the courts were to fathers when it came to custody and visitation. And here he was holding our relationship hostage to force cooperation in potential fraud for a housing subsidy, one that was not even worth all that much money.

Randolph Jr./Sr. High School was only a ten-minute walk from the Bittersweet Lane Apartments, with only one especially danger-ous street crossing. I was happy to start going to school in my own neighborhood, and that was good because I was about to spend six years there. The school temporarily served grades seven to twelve while the Town found a way to open a middle school.

I loved walking home from school far more than I loved walking to it. I'd take the closest stairs two at a time to leave the basement the housed the seventh-grade classrooms, maybe say a quick hello to the girls laughing and having fun out front, and then turn towards home. One afternoon, as I turned at the landing, rough arms pushed me back up against the brick wall. An older, bigger Black kid held me against the wall with his forearm pressing my neck. I'd dropped my chin to stop him from choking me, like I'd been taught. As I grabbed his arms, another kid quickly grabbed my wallet out of my pocket. Then, a third called out, "Yo, hold up, hold up. That's Jamie. I know him. Stop. He's a'ight. Let go. He's a'ight." It was Mo, from South Shore Day Camp.

I pushed forward as the boy who had my neck backed off. Mo got in between me and him. He grabbed my wallet back from the second kid and handed it back to me. "Sorry, man. Sorry. You're good. Go home." I took my wallet back. Mo clapped me on my back like we were all just having a good time. "You good?"

"Yeah, we good. We good." I pushed the door open and turned left to head back towards my neighborhood. I checked over my shoulder once and kept going. I didn't feel afraid or angry, not really. I felt a bit of pride. Mo counted me as one of his own. This was my school, my neighborhood, and at least one six-foot, two-hundred-pound teenager had my back, at least that much. That's a good feeling. That kind of feeling helps you stand straighter.

Leaving school, I crossed Highland Avenue to walk home down Highland Glen. Detached homes and duplexes with yards and driveways and garages lined the left side of the street. Children in those houses were the ones who still went to Young Elementary nearby. To my right were the couple dozen three- and four-story buildings comprising my neighborhood. The Town of Randolph allowed these incomparably towering behemoths to be built, but it still kept them hidden away from the main streets where most homeowners might drive by and see them. The first section on my walk was the Highland Ave Apartments, plain brick rectangles where the families were as poor as we were. But hey, their complex had a pool at least. We'd use it sometimes, alongside the family of Ukrainian refugees I knew through the kid in band class.

Then I passed the Woodview Apartments and wondered how nice it would be to have a little balcony off our apartment like they had. Next were the Castle Square Condominiums. They had balconies too, and the people there owned where they lived. That meant everyone did as they pleased. Spicy, smoky scents drifted down from a balcony where someone was grilling jerk. I considered cutting through that section's parking lot to get home, but I didn't like the way the cars whipped around it, and I'd had enough excitement already that afternoon. Instead, I walked to where the road dead-ended at the senior affordable housing complex. I turned right onto Bittersweet Lane.

I listened a bit. Beats fell from balconies, boomed from cars. My neighborhood had music. The legends of '90s hip-hop were in the air—2Pac, Biggie, Nas—but here, it was the Fugees above all.

THE BITTER

My Haitian neighbors and classmates took pride when *The Score* went multiplatinum, following nothing but disrespect, erasure, and bigotry towards Haitians. The Fugees' deft mix of styles and musical references even caught a punk like me. They were my Clash before I knew about the Clash.

Getting closer to our building, I kept an eye out for the maintenance man. He tried to get familiar with me in his unrelenting attempts to get closer to my mother. I didn't like it. No sign of him as I crossed the broken asphalt street to the Bittersweet Lane Apartments. My head jolted to the right when a stray cat yowled from the scrubby cedar swamp behind our building. The first brown leaves of the season scattered in the crisp early autumn wind. I turned onto a dirt path through dead grass and wood chips, a path cut by thousands of footfalls in lieu of an actual sidewalk. I walked towards our lobby over a driveway painted with FIRE LANE NO PARKING. I finally reached my door. The correct key was already in my fist, pointing itself towards its lock.

The lobby smelled of stale cigarette smoke again. I held my breath as I waited for the elevator, but when its doors opened, the stench only gave way to a faint garbage smell. Fast-food wrappers and an unidentifiable ooze lay on the carpeted elevator floor. Someone's trash must have busted open on the way out to the dumpster. Again.

The hallway was empty as the elevator doors opened on my floor. Didn't need to make any small talk with neighbors. Though I half wanted to tell my neighbor, Jahal, what happened with my almost mugging. My other half just wanted to be gone. I slid the key into the lock and stepped into the empty apartment. I had three or so hours before my mother and brother would be home. I turned the television on to MTV, or maybe I hit play on my boombox with The Smashing Pumpkins cassette waiting in it. I turned it up loud and lost myself in the elsewhere of the music.

GET OUT

I'd learned how to open locked doors watching my mother slide her Blockbuster Video card into door jambs. Credit cards were too stiff; the Blockbuster card had the perfect balance of thinness, flexibility, and strength to push the latch back into the door. Lockouts were good opportunities to get closer to our neighbors too. My brother and I were the only white kids in the building, and our ginger mother certainly stood out. Everyone knew the redhead who was always forgetting her keys and having to jimmy her own lock. So they figured she was good at it and would ask her help whenever they locked themselves out. "I learned to pick locks pretty well to help the latchkey kids who came home after school to figure out that they forgot their keys. That Blockbuster card opened a lot of doors," my mother told me.

So I could open a locked door without them, but I treated my keys like precious jewels. The keys gave me the freedom to explore by letting me know I could always come back home. I was twelve the first time I left Randolph on the T by myself. I would take the 240 bus to Ashmont or the 238 to Quincy Center and then hop turnstiles to take the Red Line in town up to Harvard Square to hang out with the punks in the Pit or browse records at Newbury Comics. Maybe take the Green Line to Hynes instead to walk Newbury Street and stock up on one-dollar books at Trident Booksellers. I'd walk down the street wearing my one pair of jeans that fit and some black band T-shirt, taking in the scents of wine, clam broth, and garlic. I wondered what it would be like to have a meal on one of those pricey patios, imagined myself on a date with a well-dressed woman on a crisp fall evening, stars above, historic streetlamps like wisps lighting a line towards the Boston Public Garden. No, too ambitious of a dream, I thought. Instead, I imagined myself reaching onto a patio, grabbing a rich person's meal, and running away with it.

Every time I went in town, the world opened up to me a bit more. I began to understand how far up and how far down societal divisions went, and I began to understand where I stood in them. And as much as I wanted to belong on one side, I wanted the other as well. I needed money. How could I start making money?

GET A JOB

I babysat occasionally for families in our building, but I needed more regular work. Papa hooked me up with my first job when I was thirteen—too young under Massachusetts law to work legally. His friend, "The Irishman" from Limerick, ran a pallet business in Brockton. I spent a Saturday lifting and sorting pallets. By the end of the day, my thirteen-year-old muscles had given out. The Irishman and his friend sat me down with a hammer and nails to continue repairing pallets when I could no longer lift them and place them at the top of the tall piles. His friend encouraged me, "You're doing a good job, kid. Good to learn a trade early. You're just thirteen? You'll be set, kid. Just keep swinging that hammer. It's a good trade."

At the end of the day, The Irishman gave me a hundred bucks, more than twice what a minimum wage job would pay for a full day's work. The pay excited me, but the excuse to spend a day away from my father was just as good. I went back to Nana's house that evening and spent the rest of the night lying flat out on the bottom bunk of our bed in Jim's room, listening to the original Dropkick Murphys album and feeling my sore muscles.

I turned fourteen at the end of 1997. Finally legally allowed to work in Massachusetts, I walked downtown to look for a job. Up and down sidewalks, cutting across bleak, empty asphalt parking lots, I awkwardly asked for applications at registers. I would sit in a booth or prop up by an entrance and fill out applications in my messy handwriting before handing them right back to whatever assistant manager happened to be around at Burger King, Shaw's Supermarket, Wendy's, Sudbury Farms, anywhere that had a sign posted. Not one called back.

My father reached out to his friend Norman, who owned two shops in town—The Video Store and Butts 'n' Bets—and got me a job. The Video Store was the place where my father took us on Friday afternoons to pick out a Nintendo game to rent for the weekend, a movie to watch, plus a carton of smokes and however many scratch tickets he could afford that weekend. Also, Norman had paid Jim under the table to tear down the wall between The Video Store and an adjacent storefront where Norman created an annex called the Keno Room.

Despite the store's name, I spent most of my shifts at The Video Store selling cigarettes and lottery tickets for $5.25 an hour. I loved learning the Massachusetts lottery machine and its unique keyboard, so I could work it faster than anyone. I was intrigued as the regulars asked me to read the barcode numbers on the back of scratch tickets and half shared their secret, special scratchie strategies with me, holding back enough to try to keep their competitive edge against the Commonwealth of Massachusetts. But the house never loses.

I had fun carding people with my puberty-cracked voice: "Um, can I see some ID, please?" as a six-foot-three man towered over me. "Are you even old enough to work here?" he asked. "Hey, this kid's asking for my ID!"

"Do you want those Newports or not?" I asked to put an end to it.

The store got crowded on the first and fifteenth when social security or disability or whatever other checks came. The regulars would buy their lottery tickets and their cigarettes (Butts 'n' Bets!), then hop across into the Keno Room to smoke and dream in four-minute intervals between games, between losing and winning just enough to get a few more tickets and dream some more. Hopes drifted out the wide interior doorway alongside rancid cigarette smoke, and they amounted to as much.

I didn't get a lot of hours at The Video Store, but it was enough to keep me going, and it was fun. The Commonwealth of Massachusetts finally noticed the Keno Room and shut it down as an illegal gambling establishment. Then, as things got worse with my father, I felt more and more awkward working for his friend. Did people only see Jim's good sides? Did they understand how a teenager would have issues with one of their regulars, especially one of the first-and-fifteenth people like Jim? I also imagine Norman lost a fair bit of money when he had to close the illegal Keno Room. In any case, that job came to an end while I was still fourteen and still unable to find a job on my own.

I walked downtown to look for a job again, cutting across all that Randolph asphalt again, this time in the bright early summer sun, heat radiating from the pavement. My headphones in, as always on these trips, playing Social Distortion. I was learning that connections, 关系 guanxi, hookups, are how you get a job. Unknown to me, striving middle-class teenagers built résumés at internships or camps. Privileged teenagers just played all summer. I pounded the pavement for minimum-wage work serving them all. The only goal in sight for me was $5.25 an hour and the minuscule slice of independence it bought.

My kung fu aunt, Caryn, hooked me up with my next job. At the time, she was teaching kung fu, attending photography classes at UMass Boston, and had gotten a summer gig managing an ice cream and sub shop at Hewitt's Cove Marina in the ritzy suburb of Hingham. All summer, I would walk up to North Street to catch the 238 bus to Quincy Center and lose myself in music or some epic novel. As we pulled into Quincy Center station, I'd make my way to a door so I could hop out first and sprint to the other end of the platform, hoping that a 220 bus to Hingham would be waiting and I wouldn't be late to work again. More often than not, I'd be left to post up, one foot on the concrete wall, reading Steinbeck's *East of Eden* or maybe eating a chocolate donut I'd grabbed from inside the station, eyes always over my shoulder, ready to run back out of the coffee shop if my bus arrived. Time, tide, and the T wait for no man.

And if that tide was a good one for fishing, when I finally got to the sandwich and ice cream shop, I'd have an impatient line of middle-aged white men eager to get their boats on the water. They were tired of their kids whining for ice cream, probably thought their wives should be watching the kids anyway so they could get some peace on the water after working all week for Chrissakes. I learned to scoop fast, to perfectly slice tomatoes, to make and wrap every sub on the menu, and to not talk back to the entitled Hingham men complaining about every little thing. By contrast, the workers from the adjacent shipyard were our best customers, always ready with a good tip and a better joke.

Sifu Kevin took care of my brother while my mother was at work that summer. Sometimes they would drop by the shop after visiting nearby Bare Cove Park. Sean and a friend took on the Titanic—a massive thirty-scoop, ten-topping ice cream sundae we served in a plastic beach pail.

The worst day on that job was the annual Chowder Festival. We always had a batch of clam chowder kept warm in the shop, but for the festival, it was all hands on deck—all three of us. Caryn led the chowder making all morning. The place stank of clam chowder. She sent me into the back to clear out a refrigerator to make space for the batches as she prepped. As I pulled out items, cleaned, and rearranged, I found—at the back of the fridge, way over to one side, behind everything else—an ancient, unpreserved batch of chowder. Surely it had been made by the Pilgrims and had some historic value, but it was rancid. I held my breath and pulled the heavy steel kettle out of the fridge and turned it over above the trash barrel. The pungent ecosystem it held fell out in heavy glops. Deed done, I only made it a few steps before my stomach emptied in heavy glops as well. Caryn saw it as an opportunity for a photography project and made me pose by it before I cleaned up.

I saved up enough that summer to not have to work during my freshman year of high school.

Then my mother finally finished school, and she landed a position with a court reporting firm in Downtown Boston. She bought professional-looking blouses and pants. She commuted to South Station. She made friends with her coworkers and joined happy hours at Fajita's 'n' Rita's. She even got a new car, a little Dodge Neon. Randolph had some public transit but not to rely on. My mother had driven a string of falling-apart, cheap, used cars. Breakdowns happened. A lot. We spent a lot of time at the mechanic's or at my Uncle Jerry's while they fixed my mother's cars. Being reliant on cars when you are poor is high risk. Missed appointments, missed work hours, any little thing could metastasize into a crisis because we did not have the resources to make mistakes.

法关系 (MAKE CONNECTIONS)

And every time my mother moved up in the world, my father upped his harassment. Of her, of us. At the time, he lived year-round at his mother's second home in Falmouth, on Cape Cod. Sean and I suffered forty-five minutes of cigarette smoke and verbal abuse in the winter, or ninety minutes of cigarette smoke, sweating, red brake lights, and verbal abuse in the summer. "I brought you into this world; I can take you back out."

He was jealous that we were doing better. He was jealous that Sean and I looked up to Sifu Kevin and preferred kung fu to baseball. He was especially jealous when my mother started dating Kevin.

My relationship with my father deteriorated alongside our building. Never particularly nice, the Bittersweet Lane Apartments began to look like trash. Instead of caring for the aging building, the maintenance guy busied himself stalking my mother. He would always, always be there when we arrived or left and would always corner my mother into some forced conversation. We dreaded having to call maintenance if anything broke.

To avoid default on its SHARP[41] mortgage, the building depended on collecting ambitious rents. But Bittersweet Lane was not a place where people who could afford choices ever chose to live. To make up the difference in rental income, ownership filled the entire building with households using Section 8 or other vouchers. They filled unrestricted apartments that might otherwise remain vacant or rent for even less than what a voucher would pay. In this way, a building program envisioned as mixed-income became home exclusively to poor people. That's not necessarily a bad thing, but it puts the lie to affordable housing policy. Of course, even an "affordable" rent is only good if it's affordable to your household. I remember some hard up refugee families crowding maybe ten people into a two-bedroom at Bittersweet Lane so they could begin making ends meet. They took pains to hide it from management, but neighbors knew. I remember the scent and steam of kitchens always cooking.

With her new job, my mother's income got high enough to pay the full rent of $900/month ($1,876 in 2025 dollars). She began looking for a better place to live than the Bittersweet Lane Apartments. Papa came through for us again.

Whenever Papa drove someone to the detox at Gosnold, which was often, he stopped on the way back at the Tin Man Diner. He got to know Barbara, the owner, and when Barbara confided that her daughter was suffering from addiction, Papa helped get her into rehab. She survived her addiction. To return the favor, Barbara offered a house she owned in Randolph to my mom at a discounted rent. The house was on Chestnut Street, just through a patch of woods to Grandmy's house, if not over a river.

My uncles and friends helped us move out of Bittersweet Lane. My friend Justin tried to ride my mother's TV stand out of the elevator and through the lobby. The pressed wood stand splintered and collapsed under him. We never did replace it. When the old floor model television with the dial that went from 2 to U gave up the ghost a few months later, we took the smaller TV from Mom's bedroom and plopped it on top. My friends told me it was artistic— a TV TV stand.

Sean, Mom, and I each got our own bedroom in our new, very old house on Chestnut Street. The basement had a washer and dryer, a big step up for us, even if the basement ceiling was barely five-foot tall and a rich habitat for spiders. We had a kitchen, a living room, and even a dining room. There was a yard (that I mowed), and we got a dog for Sean (that I took care of). We were moving on up.

The only thing I missed about Bittersweet Lane was being able to walk to everything. There were only a handful of destinations near our new home on Chestnut Street. I could walk to Grandmy's or to the corner store where they called Papa "Lucky" because he always bought Lucky Strikes and a winning scratch ticket. But with a twenty-minute walk, I could reach Friendly's Ice Cream and Restaurant, Dairy Barn ice cream, and the 240 bus to freedom, or, um, Ashmont Station.

And I had a new feeling, I found myself wanting to stay home when I could. The first time I had a room for just myself, I made too much of it. But I enjoyed it all because God hates it when I let gifts go to waste. And I wandered through my mind in my little room with the radio on.

I lay there and pondered what had happened, what could have, and what didn't. Between family and Massachusetts-funded affordable housing, I never spent a night of my childhood in a shelter, or car, or tent. I never spent a childhood night alone. Housing stability gave us access to lawful employment and education, and those were the fingerholds to claw our way out. We ate bitter for years and years in the hopes of finding sweetness.

SIX

Kicked in the Head

With the help of family and 关系, we'd found stable housing. Most poor people find housing that way, which does not speak well of the affordable housing system. Only about one in four extremely low-income families who need assistance receive it in our nation.[42] Worse, the systems meant to help Americans often create harm, and it's always hard for us to tell whether they'll help us or harm us until it is too late. It was too much to navigate for a teenager, but I found my way.

I took the stairs down from Boylston Street two at a time to a basement at Emerson College. It was my first underground show. Caryn's boyfriend played drums in a ska-punk band called Hag, and they were on the bill with Kicked in the Head, The Sellouts, and Metro Stylee. I lost myself to the music and the crowd. Pure flow-state joy. Dancing around the pit, I caught an elbow in the nose, and people fell into me, and we all fell to the floor. The crowd lifted us back to our feet instantly. Blood streamed from my nose. I felt free.

John, Justin, and I could be found any weekend at the rented halls and basements of Massachusetts's DIY punk, ska, and hardcore scenes. I could let loose, and people would be there to pick me up when I fell. Honesty and emotion were not looked down upon. I felt belonging, even with the strange people I met from wealthy white suburbs. We learned about each other's struggles, despite our different situations. We'd all leave with a feeling that we always belonged, that we were together and stronger for it.

One Sunday night, I lay down on my bed in my new room. My. Bed. My *room*. I felt rich. I couldn't wait to have friends over to hang out in *my room*.

I gazed up at the beige ceiling, felt the cool breeze flit across my feet from the window, and I let my back settle into the comforter and mattress beneath me. I inhaled deeply into my belly, fragrant incense smoke mixed with New England autumn air. I exhaled. My mind went free. *This must be what relaxed feels like. It's nice. Or am I being lazy? Homework's done. I practiced bass and trumpet today. I didn't work out at all, but I don't feel like it. What is it I'm not doing? What am I missing? It'd be a sin to waste my talents. Maybe I'm just bored? I wonder how I'd feel if the lazy smoke came from pot instead of incense. But I don't have the money. I can't do drugs anyway because I need to be perfect to make it to college and get financial aid. It's a mercy the Boston DIY music scene is so straight edge.*

I pulled myself out of my thoughts and turned my head to the right, to the warm blue glow of the 1980s-era stereo receiver I got as a hand-me-down from a relative. Sunday at 8:00 p.m., I reached out my right arm to turn the cold silver volume dial for the local music show coming up on WERS, the last channel on the left. The DJ welcomed Kicked in the Head, live in studio.

I swung my feet over the right side of my bed, grabbed my cassette Walkman off my small guitar amp, plugged a short quarter-inch cable into the tape player through an eighth-inch to quarter-inch adapter, plugged it all into the receiver's auxiliary output with a satisfying click, and pressed record on the Walkman. I spun the volume dial again.

I didn't always know how to feel, but the music knew for me. The frustration and anger I couldn't find surfaced when I yelled the lyrics. More tension left my body as the tempo churned it up into joy. I jumped on my bed, banging my head, dancing, and singing along through their set before I decided to call it a night.

John Connors told me, years later, "Oh God, you were so proud of that bedroom. You always wanted to hang out there, even though it was only like eight feet by ten feet, but you had your guitar and bass and turntable with like a one-foot gap from your bed." I covered the walls in flyers for punk rock shows. There was always music, always. From my amp, from my stereo, from WERS until late into the night, the warm blue glow emanating from the radio dial.

I began hiding out in the basement during visitation weekends at Nana's house. I sat on a wooden stool in front of my little practice amp and played my black-and-white Stratocaster guitar for hours. Off to the left, I could see the collection of bottles behind the bar. I decided to take a break for more Kahlúa. May as well put some gin in a water bottle to bring home too.

I got back to playing. Dad wouldn't let me go out for New Year's Eve. Sean was up there still arguing with him about it, I think. I could barely hear the banging and yelling in my father's room upstairs over my banging and yelling "X.Y.U." downstairs.

Sean ran down the rickety stairs, crying. The heat and anger in me went cold. He didn't cry easily; an older sibling knows. No doubt he'd just been told "Quit crying or I'll give you something to cry about" too. Jim thought it a clever turn of phrase.

"Fuck this. I'm going to run away. You coming? Let's go," Sean said. I don't know what happened between Sean and our father, but it was bad enough that I flipped immediately into big brother mode.

"Woah, woah, Ma's out of town, and we don't have keys. I don't know if he'd let us go, and he'd follow us if we just left. Maybe I can convince him that Wayne invited us over for New Year's and get him to drop us there. Kevin's there."

I left Sean in the basement to cool down, and I went upstairs to ask our father to drive us to Braintree. He started yelling about Sean and how disrespectful he was and how Sean owed him an apology and all.

"Well, Wayne asked if I could come over for New Year's Eve. Maybe I could take Sean with me? Can you drive us?" He looked me up and down with those jackal eyes, searching out the lie. He agreed to drive us anyway, ranting and screaming at us the whole time about how horrible we were, how aggrieved he was.

I walked up the concrete steps and rang the buzzer. I hoped someone would pick up. I hoped my father would just drive away and not see either way. No one knew we were coming. There was no way we could have called without Jim catching on. Luckily, Janet, Wayne, and Kevin were all home having a quiet New Year's Eve. Sean practically ran into Kevin's protective embrace. We recounted what happened that night and debated what to do the next day. I couldn't sleep. I listened to Alice in Chains' "Don't Follow" on repeat.

Jim came back to pick us up the next morning. We climbed into the rusty station wagon that reeked of cigarette smoke. Jim drove us silently back to our mother's place on Chestnut Street. We opened the car doors quietly. None of us had risked breaking the angry silence, until Jim yelled at us from his open window, "Don't expect to see me. Don't call me again until you are ready to give me the respect I deserve as your father." The words reverberated in my head. They haven't stopped.

But in the moment, I had a more immediate concern. We didn't have keys. I stopped to survey the old house. Sean started checking the windows. "I think I can break this one to get in."

"No, Sean. We aren't breaking in." Sean followed me through the yard. We stomped through the woods to Grandmy's house, trampling through drifts of leaves and old snow.

"Hii! What're you doing here?" said Grandmy, as she opened the door.

It occurred to me that the date must be January 1. "Hi Grandmy. Um. Happy Birthday?"

Back in school, after the holiday, I stared at the clock and quietly packed my things as the third period teacher droned on. It was lunch ticket day, and my fourth period French teacher had been giving automatic detention for being late. I saw the seconds ticking down to the end of third period. I was out of my seat as the bell rang.

I hustled out of the classroom, weaved through hallway crowds in a dash from one end of Randolph High to the other. A grumpy administrator handed out our federally funded free and reduced lunch tickets only once every two weeks. By the time I made it to her office, there was already a line out the door. The line did not move. A classmate hustled by and said, "What are you doing!? You're going to be late again."

The bell rang. The hall emptied out. Teachers started fourth period in their classrooms. Our slow procession of poor kids advanced in fits and starts. I thought up five different ways this could all be done more efficiently and more fairly while my anxiety grew. I finally made it in, and the interrogation began. "Name? Address? Paperwork? Oh, let me check. I'm doing you a favor even letting you in. I don't know as I like that. I should've closed the door and stopped giving these away the second the bell rang. Why can't you kids be on time?" I bit my angry, Irish tongue and kept quiet because I was hungry, and I needed those damn lunch tickets to eat. I thought about Mom's many stories about her big mouth earning her detention in that very building. I bit my tongue harder.

I hustled back across the building to my French class. The door was locked. I knocked. Mr. Putnam came to the door, opened it, told me *en français* to see him after school, and closed the door on me. A Haitian classmate who was behind me in the lunch ticket line saw that happen to me. He decided to just turn and walk away.

My body dropped back against the lockers, and I sat in the hallway staring at the ceiling. It occurred to me that I could get up and leave. But I didn't have the pad of dismissal slips I'd swiped, and I did have band later, so I didn't want to skip the rest of the school day. Not knowing what else to do, I pulled out a book and waited there in the hallway for fourth period to end.

After the bell rang for lunch and the class shuffled out, I walked into Mr. Putnam's room to ask him what the homework for tomorrow would be. I might miss classes, but I didn't fall behind. I was going to be the top student in my class. I was going to get scholarships and get out. I was determined.

"If you cared, you'd have been here on time," scolded Mr. Putnam. "I let you all get away with too much, and you need to learn respect."

"*Ce n'est pas ma faute!* I had to wait for lunch tickets."

"What kind of excuse is that? What are you even talking about?"

"They give out the free lunch tickets—which we need to eat— once every two weeks. It's right before your class. That's why we're always late."

"Well, you need to be responsible and figure that out. It's not their job to get you to class on time. It's yours. See me for detention later."

I bit my tongue hard enough to taste blood, but I succeeded at not cursing him out. I hustled off to lunch, with twelve minutes left to get food, find a place to sit, and eat.

Why did it seem like French classes were where these things always happened? I thought back to the time freshman year when Madame Laurent tried to force Tyera Toussaint to remove the scarf that wrapped her half-done hair.* There was not much time before our 7:15 a.m. first bell. She was not about to unwrap it. Madame Laurent prided herself on being a disciplinarian and had taught at the school since the years when it was predominantly white. She raised her voice and stepped towards Tyera. When her student refused again, Madame Laurent reached up to pull the scarf off herself. Tyera pushed her backwards, but Madame Laurent was a large woman and able to grab Tyera's head and bang it against the desk before dragging the teen girl screaming into the hallway for security guards to collect. *Sak pase?* Oh right, *that's* why French classes were where this sort of thing always happened.

Speaking of racism, the Randolph schools tracked me into the top-level classes, always. Tracking started when we moved from elementary school to junior high school in seventh grade and was every bit as racialized as researchers would later publish.[43] Tracking widens the achievement gap for Black children and for poor children. Despite using race-neutral language, tracking further segregated schools by race.[44]

By high school, things shifted for us only slightly. Some undeniably talented students rose up in spite of racism, and some middle-class students dropped levels despite having received the benefit of the

* Names changed for privacy.

doubt. By the end, we enjoyed an odd sort of mix. Two Jewish girls and I were the only white students in BC Calculus, where everyone else was Asian, mostly Chinese. One of those same Jewish girls and I were the only two white students in AP French, where everyone else was Haitian. The two of us also got the best grades in that class, even though the rest of the class were native speakers. Or, perhaps we got the best grades *because* the rest of the class were native speakers. The teachers were determined to stomp out their Kreyòl in favor of Parisian French, or at least Québécois. Back in the 1970s and '80s, French classes took field trips to Montreal or Le Quebec, only a six-hour drive from Boston. My generation didn't get that. We got state-mandated assessments, ID cards, and security guards. At least school shootings weren't yet common.

The high school security guards became a real problem for me after I broke with my father that freshman year winter break. My father spread stories about me around town. Most security guards were white townies. The best of them, Joe Prevetti, was a retired cop who used to bust my mom and uncle drinking in the woods with their friends in the '70s, but then call their parents and get them home safe. Word was, Joe was a tough guy when he was young, found some success at boxing, became a cop, and then took up the school security gig for fun during retirement. He made a point of learning the names of kids who found themselves in trouble, bent rules to help them, and encouraged boys into boxing to channel our anger and energy. He didn't pay attention to me one way or the other.

Judy, another security guard, was my father's friend. (I suspected girlfriend.) She followed me whenever she saw me in school. I could usually duck into the classroom of a friendly teacher, but the times she caught me alone, she'd use the opportunity to berate me for being a bad son, for defending my mother, for upsetting my father, for whatever. She made certain I knew she had disciplinary power over me and could choose to use it. I began to contemplate the exercise of power in low-stakes situations.

Another friend of his was the school librarian. I used to go to the school library if I had time between classes or after-school activities. I always loved perusing books, but this library was also the only place I could access the internet or a printer. After I broke with my father, the librarian kicked me out every time she saw me print something, whether it was an English paper or guitar tabs. I continued to go to the library when I needed to anyway. Sometimes she wasn't there, and I could stay.

I finally lost it when she tried to kick me out one day senior year. "Why do you keep doing this? Do you realize I'm on the State Board of Education?" I said.

"So what?"

"So, my meeting packet this month includes a vote for grant funding for school libraries, and Randolph is on the list. I vote on your funding."

"I'm an adult. I'm in charge here. You do what I say, or you leave."

"Well, all right."

"All right nothing. You need to learn respect."

"Let me see the head librarian."

"Get the hell out. Now!"

I left. I thought more about power and wondered how petty I could be. It didn't take more than a minute's thinking to know that I'd rather use what power I had to get more resources to my school than to try to withhold any.

Randolph was going through a transition. The amazing diversity of families who began moving there in the 1980s and '90s now had children in the schools. The white New England town of the

1940s that became the working-class Jewish and Irish town of the 1970s had just become the most racially, ethnically, and linguistically diverse place in Massachusetts—a title it holds to this day. But the town was still run in every way by the mostly white, mostly high-school-educated townies. As my classmates and I grew up, we watched school funding dry up and youth recreation funding completely evaporate. We watched the freedoms and respect our older relatives had received transform into security and discipline. None of it was lost on us as teenagers. We saw the racism and the classism for what they were. We knew who security was for, and it was not us.

My brother Sean recalls, "I picked up the phone, and a recording said, 'This is a collect call from . . . Kevin Rice . . . at MCI-Concord,' and I was like, 'Kevin! Kevin? Are you there?' as it said 'Do you accept the charges?' I yelled, 'Maaaaa, I think it's Kevin.' I was ten years old, what did I know back then?"

Mom accepted the charges, got the story, and then got the word out. Kevin also got in touch with his kung fu sister Caryn, and she took over teaching us while Kevin was incarcerated. The story as I've heard it is this:

Coffee and cigarette in hand, Kevin was crossing Comm Ave from Dunkin' Donuts to teach his Boston University kung fu class. Police lay in wait to arrest him on his way. The cops ran out, guns drawn, and surrounded him. Kevin, dressed in his typical loose-fitting black workout clothes, stopped, relaxed his six-foot-two frame, stood calmly, and gave the cops that stare of his. Calm, focused, ready for violence. Kevin's eyes could remind you of a predator you instinctively fear—whether or not you outnumber it, whether or not you are holding weapons, you fear it. Someone must move first, after all.

"Put the coffee down and kneel in the street! Now!" Kevin complied, slowly. An officer walked up to him with cuffs. "Don't kick me or anything, Mr. Kung Fu."

Years before, Kevin had moved back to Weymouth from New Hampshire when his mother grew ill. New Hampshire's gun laws were far laxer than Massachusetts's, so Kevin sold his guns before he moved. Cash, no paperwork involved. A man who bought a handgun off him used the gun to pistol-whip his girlfriend in Massachusetts. The prosecutor gave him a break from the domestic violence charge in the hopes of getting a big-time gun dealer conviction. Instead, she got a penniless martial arts instructor. But, hey, a conviction is a conviction, am I right?

She didn't get one. A conviction. Kevin spent a year in jail anyway.

Kevin was a dad to us. As our biological father dove deeper into anger and resentment, Sean and I received encouragement, lessons, discipline, and unconditional love from Kevin. First, we lost our biological father to his hatred and mental illness. Then, the system took our chosen dad.

I woke up in math class to a question and a clearly frustrated middle-aged man waiting for an answer. The gleam in his eyes showed he was excited to have caught me asleep. My cheek stuck to my forearm slightly as I lifted my head.

My teacher repeated himself, "Mr. Madden, can you tell us the simplification of $(a-b)(a+b)$? Since you seem to know this lesson enough to not listen."

"A squared minus B squared," I replied groggily.

He grunted at my correct answer. "You'll need to apply yourself if you want to go to college."

"Why would I want to go to college?" I said with teenage defiance. Fuck it, I wanted to do music anyway, and no one graduates from Berklee, you know what I mean? They make music.

The teacher moved on, and I rearranged my books to rest my head on. I woke up again when the bell rang.

I put my sneakers and headphones on and walked out of the house to try to quiet my mind. Saw a raven against the cool gray day as I walked along. I loved the ominous feeling in the air and moody colors in the sky. Walking aimlessly, I took a right at the end of Chestnut Street. I started to wonder where I was going. I took another right on High Street, but I still couldn't tell you why.

One more right onto Canton Street, and I saw a beat-up red station wagon driving towards me. When I saw that car last month waiting at my bus stop, I dashed into an alley to escape and caught the bus at the next stop. This time, I decided to try my hand at forgiveness.

My father pulled his station wagon over. I took my headphones off and just stood there, waiting for whatever would come. He started talking like nothing had ever happened.

"Do you want a ride?" he offered.

"No, I'm enjoying the walk. It's nice out." I wasn't ready to let down my guard, but I wanted to give him a chance to reach out.

He started one of his monologues, complaining about town politics, laboriously recounting tedious conversations he'd had. Then he said, ". . . granted my children come from a family where both parents were involved . . ."

I waited until he finished making a short story long and asked, "About that both parents being involved thing, you should call Sean . . . call us."

"Well, why haven't you called me!?" he angrily snapped.

My anger surfaced in response. "Who's supposed to be the father here? I have a job, do you? You talk about respect, but respect is earned. Earn it." I turned and walked away. It was the first time I stood up for myself to blood.

I pulled my headphones back on so I wouldn't have to hear anything else from him and cranked the volume just in time to hear Less Than Jake sing about holding your ground and not giving up in what you believe.

I could not afford to give up on me. I had big plans to make it. I couldn't give up on me, so I gave up on him.

"Hey, James, are you going to try out for drama too?" Justin asked me at the start of our freshman spring.

"What? No, I can't sing," I replied.

"There's no singing. It's a play," corrected John. "You should come. It's a play about 'disadvantaged youth.'"

I went with my friends to the drama club audition. It was for some play called *A Stand-Up Tragedy*. It felt like a knock-off of *Stand and Deliver* or *Dangerous Minds*—probably more affordable for our school to put on. The play was "relevant." It had poverty, dysfunctional families, suicide, violence, teen pregnancy, and interminable high school classes. My friends and I all got parts. I ended up with a lead part, a troubled student named Henry who was on the edge—the edge of unplanned parenthood, the edge of committing manslaughter, and the edge of expulsion.

With no money for costumes, the school gave us T-shirts of different colors meant to signify . . . something? onstage. I do not like a spotlight. I do not like being the center of attention. But I pushed the emotion of the year I'd had into that role, and it seemed to work.

After rehearsal one evening, the beautiful junior who was cast as my teacher in the play slipped me a note with her phone number. I was dumb enough to think she gave it to me so we could rehearse more.

That spring, I had the opportunity to leave New England for just the third time in my life. Our school band went to Washington, DC, for a festival. That junior, Candice, made it clear she wasn't interested in me for rehearsing. The two of us snuck away from the group at every chance to spend time together in the hotel. We were inseparable, attached to each other during the trip and wrapped around each other during the eight-hour bus ride home.

Even in our amazingly diverse town, a white boy–Black girl couple was unusual at the time. I didn't know how some of my family would react, but the first time we bumped into Papa walking around the neighborhood, he broke into that big, charming smile of his and welcomed Candice into the fold. Her parents were less accepting. Their daughter was dating a lower-class, younger, white, Irish Catholic guy from a broken family. Her immigrant parents had worked for, hoped for, and expected better for their children.

We navigated as best we could. Candice was angry about racism. I was angry about classism. We were both raised in postcolonial cultures. We shared all of that with each other, establishing a shared anger and a shared intersectional worldview before I knew that "intersectional" was a word. Each of us caught shit about our relationship. Black men harassed Candice about me. A pizza place refused to serve us. I knew just one song about it, and I loved hearing Art sing when I wondered whether we'd find a place where we could just fit in.

The only place Candice and I regularly ran into couples who looked like us was in Cambridge's Central Square, pre-gentrification. We felt comfortable there, and it didn't hurt that it was a center of Boston's music scene.

Candice and I fell for each other with teenage first-love abandon. She opened worlds for me, including the world of college. Two grades behind, I was by her side while she navigated the college admissions process with plenty of help from her older sister, Audie. They demystified the entire idea of college for me. Maybe higher education was the way out. I'd never earn make-it-out money anyway.

I wrote down, "God made mornings beautiful for the poor, wretched souls who are dragged from their beds before dawn." The 6:00 a.m. March air was cold and crisp but not freezing. As the sun rose, the scent of spring, of melting snow and budding flowers, of the return of the salty ocean air, rose to my nostrils.

In the still, quiet morning, I stopped and thought about Papa. He had survived emphysema; could he survive lung cancer? He quit smoking after that one. Now, when "Lucky Lally" went to the corner store, he bought his scratch tickets but left the Lucky Strike cigarettes behind. We all started spending more time with him. I hoped he would make it to Red Sox opening day. Every year, Mom let me stay home from school to watch the opening game on TV with Papa, while Grandmy made us Fenway Franks for lunch.

My Aunt Amy hoped Papa would make it to her wedding. She was a baby when her parents split and still little when her biological father died. Papa was the only father she knew. Papa did not make it to the wedding, but the wedding party took their limo to the hospital for photos with him between the wedding Mass at St. Bernadette's Church and the reception at Lombardo's.

Papa went from a cancer diagnosis to the grave in only six months. His death came quickly but not suddenly. We got to say goodbyes, but now we had to learn to live in a world without Tom Lally in it.

Papa was a rock. We were unmoored. Grandmy keened along to her Andrea Bocelli record in her rarely used living room. Time to say goodbye. But without the keening, her house was too quiet. No irreverent jokes shouted up the stairs, no Sox or Bruins game in the background, no potato sticks crunching, no Spike whining for potato sticks.

Papa was a Teamster, Local 25. He'd been a trucker and had worked for a railroad, but most of the time I knew him, he worked for the union itself. He ran a program that helped union members overcome substance abuse problems. I remember Papa taking phone calls during dinner or at odd hours, working late, and driving around the state.

Before the wake, I stayed behind in the funeral home parking lot. I cried enough grief out to get myself in order and went inside to stand with my family. I stood in the greeting line next to Papa's casket for hours. The line of people waiting to pay their final respects stretched through the funeral home and out the door. I shook the hands of scores upon scores of people. They told me, over and over, "Your grandfather saved my life," "He helped a lot of us guys out," "I wouldn't be here without him," and "He was a great man."

Papa gave me one last lesson: what a life can be worth.

Months blurred into each other following Papa's death. I finished my sophomore year of high school, recorded a CD with my band, and worked three jobs in the hopes of saving up for a car. At the time in Massachusetts, it was illegal for minors to work more than twenty hours a week. So I got three jobs and worked twenty hours a week at each of them. I scooped ice cream at Friendly's. I clerked at a music lesson studio and shop. Candice and I both took care of children at the Randolph Day Camp. I got involved in activism and education policy to push back on the Commonwealth's new high school exit exam. I went to kung fu class two nights and one morning each week. I got annoyed when I heard jokes about teenagers sleeping in. I could count on my fingers how many mornings off I'd ever even had to sleep in. And, we are not morning people in my family.

At the end of the summer, I took the train back from a few days on the north shore for the State Student Advisory Council conference. My mother picked me up at the Quincy Adams T on her way home from work. We started talking, and Mom shared news that would shake up my life again.

"We're in too deep. We can't afford rent. Even filing bankruptcy costs more than I can afford right now. My friend Marcia asked us to move in with her family. I need to do this. It's the only option. In six months, I'll end up having a heart attack like my brother just did. I'm losing weight. I can't handle it."

"I . . . I can't move to Lakeville."

"We'll see if you can move in with Grandmy. I know you can't move. You have too much here. I haven't talked to her yet. She'll love to have you. She's lonely now."

Thank God for family, I thought. I wouldn't mind living with Grandmy.

"Sean will be better off in Lakeville," Mom says. "He's already falling through the cracks in Randolph. I asked him and gave him a choice. I love that kid. He said he'd love to do it."

Back at the house, my head was spinning, trying to see the new shape my life would take. I wrote in a journal, "I don't know how I'll live without Mom and Sean around. And Seamus, we don't know what to do with the dog. If I leave Randolph, I'm screwed. I need to put myself through college. Here, I may be valedictorian; I have a job, friends, clubs; I just got elected as a state delegate to the Student Advisory Council from Randolph. I'd lose all of that and more. I can't go with them." I resolved to stay, to take care of myself if need be.

Mom filed for bankruptcy. Family helped her with the rent. The immediate threat passed. I stopped agonizing about losing my home, my first bedroom of my own. Mom kept worrying about the next thing, and the thing after that. The ground there on Chestnut Street never felt so solid again. Everything was temporary.

When school started, I dropped down to two jobs, and by December, I only worked at the music store. Candice left for Smith College in western Mass. I made the journey by bus a few times before I'd clocked enough minimum-wage hours to scrape together two thousand dollars for an eleven-year-old Mazda Protégé. Radio on, not feeling so alone, I sped up 128 in the dark to the Mass Pike, lost in contemplation. I'm in love with Massachusetts. I even thought I was an adult. How long could I keep it up?

In the past year, I'd lost my relationship with my biological father, seen my Sifu jailed, lost Papa, and nearly lost Uncle Jerry to a heart attack. I didn't put that thought together until six years later, awake with insomnia, staring at a ceiling lit by the glow of late-night Beijing. I'd barely spoken any English in months, and I'd just learned that my father's mother had died.

Despite the losses, I still had family. I had a chosen family in my kung fu class and a group of best friends united by music. I had a loving relationship with Candice. My relationships with my mother's family deepened in the wake of Jim abandoning us and Papa passing.

Tragedy and achievement, trauma and love, condolences and congratulations. At least life wasn't boring. And we had a home.

SEVEN

Evicted to Educated

Mom, Sean, and I gasped and cursed when we came home and saw it. There was a For Sale sign in our front yard. Mom went inside to calm herself before calling the landlady. Sean ran over, kicked the sign, and then stomped it into the ground. I mediated and comforted.

Back in my room—was it still my room?—I put a Dead Kennedys record on. You know which song I listened to. We'd just gotten past the bankruptcy and the threat of losing the house and needing to move to Lakeville. I hadn't even had time to feel like my feet were on solid ground again. Just as well I kept my sea legs, I suppose. The water is always trying to get into your boat, and we were sinking again.

Mom could only afford this house because the landlady gave her a cut-rate rent to return a favor to Papa. Papa passed, so the favor was finished as far as the landlady was concerned. Home was a favor, not a guarantee. It had been so nice having a little room to myself. Another step forward. Another two steps back. We had to be out. No legally filed eviction on record at least.

Still, it was hard for me to blame the landlady. A waitress's abusive ex-boyfriend had firebombed her diner. Then, a developer offered to buy the lot our (her?) house was on, alongside neighboring homes, to develop a cul-de-sac with twelve new homes. She could retire on the sale. Who wouldn't cash out in that situation?

I rushed from school to work to Burger King to kung fu class. I sat the food on my lap and drove my beat-up Mazda Protégé with Sean in the passenger seat and a collection of spears and staffs at his elbow, slipped between the passenger seats and the doors. Duffel bags of fighting gear, swords, and smaller weapons sat on the backseat. I parked in front of the house where Sifu Kevin rented a room. Sean and I rushed to our places just in time for Sifu to light the incense and *bai san* to start class. Sifu led warm-ups himself tonight. Sifu was an expert at seeing where his students' limits were and where his students *thought* their limits were. We all learned to trust that if Sifu said we could do something, we could do it, no matter how tired we were, how much it hurt, or how hot or cold the weather.

After class, we went inside to hang out in Kevin's room for healing and bonding. Sifu taught us how to care for our bruises, our strains and pains. Sifu's classes didn't just break us down; putting ourselves back together was a core part of it. A few times, he asked a relative of the kung fu family to teach us the first aid and trauma care she practiced in the Army. Sifu regularly brought experts in Chinese medicine, *qigong*, and countless other martial arts to augment our training. While we rubbed bruises out with *die da jiu*, we told jokes. We drank Irish whiskey and Miller High Life. And we listened to Kevin's stories.

"Kevin, how did you end up learning kung fu?"

"I started at a karate school when I was thirteen in the late '70s. Everyone fought back then. Guys wore Bowie knives on their sides at high school, leather vests on top. Anyway, karate was OK, but it was limited, is all. And then I left for the Army."

"The Army?"

"When I got arrested at eighteen, the judge gave me two options: jail or the Army. So I enlisted. They took me even though I had a psych profile and a criminal profile. Or maybe that's why they took me. I ended up in Nicaragua training paramilitary. Not just training. No, I won't talk about it. When we got back, they discharged me and anyone else with profiles."

"Wait—like in the Iran-Contra scandal!?"

"No, not Iran, Nicaragua."

"No, no, the Iran-Contra affair. When Reagan illegally sold weapons to Iran to illegally fund a right-wing insurrection in Nicaragua."

"Yeah, that."

One night, Ed brought his mother's homemade labouyi. Kevin had mentioned he loved labouyi but hadn't had any in years. Ed asked Kevin how he knew about this sweet Haitian dish.

"I was staying at the D Street projects when they tried integrating them again. This Haitian family moved into the building. Some guys were trying to mess with the father one day, and I let them know they shouldn't do that. His wife used to bring me labouyi now and then as thanks. I always had a hard time finding it after I left. Tell your mother thank you and let her know I'd been dying for it."

"Kevin, when did you leave Southie?"

"Oh, I left when I moved to New Hampshire for a while."

Kevin chuckled and said in a cartoonish, high-pitched voice, "This makes me very angry, very angry indeed."

We missed the joke and looked at him, waiting for an explanation.

"I love Marvin the Martian," he said with a glint in his eye and that tiny grin in one cheek, the only part of his smile he couldn't flatten and hide. Then he told us this story.

"They wanted me to come back and work for them in Southie. I was done with it. I was teaching kung fu in Chinatown, and you know, the Big Dig was going on. So, one morning, I borrowed a hard hat and safety vest and went and bought some Dunkin' Donuts. I walked right onto the construction site with coffee and donuts to share. You can always get in with coffee and donuts and looking like you belong. So, I got some explosives.

"I went to go meet with them. These guys that were trying to step up after Whitey left. They knew I was big and violent and scary. They thought I was crazy though. I always let them think that. Better to just listen, do the work you need to do, and get out.

"Anyway, I go into the room with them, and they pour some beers, and we're all sitting around the table. They start trying to tell me that I'm going to work for them, what I'm going to do, what will happen if I don't.

"I just look at them calmly for a second. Then I say in a Marvin the Martian voice, 'This makes me very angry, very angry indeed,' and put a Marvin the Martian Pez dispenser on the table. I said, 'Where's the kaboom?' and let my jacket fall open to show the explosives I'd taken from the construction site. 'My friend Marvin here is the detonator. I'll be leaving now, yeah?' I left, and they never reached out again."

Not a person in the room doubted Kevin's account. It sounded exactly like something he would do. His presence dominated any room with his charisma, his sharp dark humor, and his clear, calm capacity for violence. In precolonial Ireland, he might have been a fierce *fianna*, a warrior inspiring legends. In postindustrial Boston, he suffered crushing poverty. A starving artist. A man I called Dad.

I catch up to Jim, my biological father, with my nose just starting to bleed from his punch-and-run. I cinch my forearms around his neck, knee him with all my strength, and follow him to the ground. I'm on top, punching, and punching, and punching. My fists are connecting with his head, but there's no weight behind them. He laughs at me as I punch impotently, over and over, wondering why it isn't hurting him. I start kicking him in the head. Hard. But that doesn't do anything either.

I woke from the nightmare in a cold sweat, checked my clock: 4:30 a.m. The worst possible time for me to get any real sleep in before my 6:00 a.m. alarm. I could hear Sean talking in his sleep from the next bed too. That always creeped me out.

We'd moved in with Grandmy for my second time and Mom's third. This time, Mom got her own bedroom at least. Sean and I shared Aunt Amy's old room. Grandmy and Mom love each other, but they have a difficult time living together. Sean was just like our mother too. It was a stressful situation, and we all walked on egg-shells. I stayed busy and was rarely around.

Seamus was the first to go. Our beloved mutt wasn't a bad dog, but he did possess a certain spark. Grandmy gave our misbehaving dog away to Uncle Jerry, so at least Seamus got to go kayaking. We joked that Sean would be the next to go.

Grandmy's deck collapsed under the weight of the snow that winter. The carpenter who'd built it originally was my biological father, Jim, so we know it was quality work like. Grandmy's little Boston terrier, Spike, ran under the wreck, so she sent Sean in after him. Mom and I joked that Grandmy was just trying to get rid of Sean. We might've yelled, "Sean! It's collapsing! Hurry!" even though it wasn't. That sounds like something we'd do.

We weren't wrong, entirely. Sean and Mom were the next to go. Mom's boyfriend (coincidentally introduced by the same landlady who would later give us the boot) bought a house for them to share. I occasionally spent a night, especially if I had a meeting or a show in that part of Massachusetts. When I did, I had a forty-five-minute commute to high school, sucking down a Dunkin' Donuts coffee on the highway too early in the morning. Just like my teachers.

I absolutely refused to leave Randolph for Assonet. I had one year left at Randolph High School, and there was no place like it. It was (and is) the most diverse in the state, racially, ethnically, and linguistically. I represented Randolph on the Greater Boston Student Advisory Council, and in turn represented Greater Boston on the State Student Advisory Council, which had just elected me to lead it and to represent all the Commonwealth's students with a vote on the Board of Education, alongside eight Republican gubernatorial appointees. My band was in Randolph. My jobs were around Boston. The trip to Smith College to see Candice was shorter from Randolph, and she stayed in her parents' Randolph home on breaks. I had a shot at being valedictorian at Randolph High. I had a shot to accomplish enough to get revenge against the doubters and the denigrators, to get revenge against my father for abandoning us by showing I could do anything I set myself to. Mom always told me, "Success is the best revenge."

On the morning when I woke up in a room in Grandmy's house alone for the first time, I was cold because Grandmy had turned down the heat, so I put on a sweater. The clock stopped looking early, and I felt so anxious I practically ran from my bedroom out into the street. From the bus stop, I watched the world start to come alive. And I stood there, a pale apparition waiting for my bus, waiting for life to arrive. If the bus ever did.

It was just me and Grandmy now. We got along better, just the two of us. I knew the two tricks to living in my grandmother's home: pretend I didn't and leave no evidence that I did. I supported myself with minimum-wage jobs, tried not to use her groceries, tried to make my own food, and cleaned up after myself.

I made a mistake once by taking leftovers to work in one of her CorningWare dishes. When I got back home, I dropped the dish on the brick stairs while I juggled keys and bags trying to open the door. I cleaned up the shattered pieces and called my mother for advice.

"OK, well, she'll have you dead to rights on breaking the dish, but she doesn't need to know you took it out of the house. Tell her it fell and shattered in the kitchen while you were trying to put it back up in the cabinet."

That story must have been convincing because Grandmy found "pieces" of the shattered CorningWare on her kitchen counter for weeks. I had to hide my smile every time.

I was at home with my grandmother, even if it was walking a tightrope. Hell, wasn't that true of every home I'd had?

I read Grandmy's copy of the *Boston Globe* every day. Every day, I hoped to find my own name in the obituaries.

Does that date me? A teenager in his grandmother's breezeway, ink staining my fingertips, turning pages, newspaper rustling. Skip past the Nation/World section, put the special Spotlight section full of priests raping children on top of it. Look at the back of the Metro section, Obituaries. Find the *M*'s. Sometimes, there might even be a Madden and a flicker of exhilaration before seeing the first name wasn't James or Jim. Was my soundtrack 2Pac or Everclear?

I kept a stack of college admissions brochures next to the newspapers in the breezeway. I hadn't known many college-educated adults, and the ones I did know were only familiar with nearby community and state colleges. I can't remember any family talking about college with me as a child, except maybe mentioning West Point. I knew that Berklee College of Music students played on subway platforms. I spent a lot of time hanging out in Harvard Square, but the campus on the other side of that brick wall may as well have been another planet. I had my work cut out for me learning about this strange world.

Fortunately, I was not alone. I had Candice. I'd watched her go through the college admissions process two years earlier. Now, as I went through it, Candice gave me direction and taught me the questions to ask. I visited Candice at Smith College every chance I got, staying in her dorm, attending performances, visiting Smith's excellent art museum, sitting in on classes, and attending student anti-racist activist meetings. I fell in love with the cloistered academic atmosphere of the elite liberal arts college. I needed a break from the turmoil of my own world. I wanted somewhere I could learn for learning's sake.

At the time, I worked the desk at a small music lesson studio/store called My Music House. I used their computer and internet connection to research colleges during downtime. With my grades and test scores, I looked straight to the top tier.

Then, people told me I couldn't. One of the few college-educated adults I knew told me, "Well, yeah, numbers say that. But a good GPA from Randolph doesn't count. Those schools aren't going to take someone from Randolph High School."

"Phil Nguyen got into Harvard last year," I replied.

"Yeah, and what's the difference between him and you? You need to apply to safety schools." I did not welcome the racist subtext.

I had a chip on my shoulder from being poor and from Randolph. I pursued the top schools with an angry passion. I was angry at the people who said I couldn't. I was angry at my father for his abuse and abandonment. I was angry, and my mother always told me, "Success is the best revenge."

I took my mother to tour some of the schools I was considering, trying to show her what that success might look like for me. We walked around Amherst College, got coffee in the town center, and drove around UMass's gigantic campus. We drove to Hampshire College, where my mother flatly refused to get out of the car because, "It's a fucking barn. You aren't going here."

Our most memorable visit was Harvard. We took the Red Line in, as each of us had done hundreds, if not thousands, of times. Then, our familiarity vanished when we tried to navigate from the Harvard Square T stop to the campus admissions office, getting lost more than once in this elite otherworld that coexisted with our own city like dark matter, like the Irish Otherworld.

Before the tour, we sat in the back of a large room while the upper-class parents peppered admissions officers with questions. I began to wonder whether their kids did any of their own college applications work at all. My mother tensed up in the chair next to me. I had never realized how uncomfortable upper-class spaces made her. Come to think of it, I wasn't sure we'd ever sat together inside one. I looked around the room; save a couple well-dressed Chinese and Korean families, it was completely white. I joined my mother in her discomfort.

The admissions staff led us outside where students took over giving the tour. We waited while a group of visiting Black students filed out of a charter bus and joined our tour group. Mom and I relaxed a bit, hanging back from the intense, upper-class white parents and their ambitious children. We walked with the group of Black students and made small talk.

The white and Black groups were oil and water while we walked through campus. I had not yet encountered anything like that in my life. We all filed into Memorial Hall, listened to the guides talk about the building, and then were led back out through the very same doors we'd entered. The white families who always rushed to the front to question the tour guides would now be forced to walk through the group of Black students to catch up with the guide outside. Finally, I thought, there will be mixing. No. Oil and water. Within seconds, we were walking with a fully segregated tour group again. Mom and I had a conversation with our eyes. I could see her discomfort. "Should we ditch?" I asked.

"Uno's?" she replied. I nodded and we walked away quickly and quietly, not slowing until we crossed Mass Ave back into the city we knew. We ordered pizza, and my mom even ordered a drink for me while we complained about upper-class white people: their thin smiles, their rudeness, their judgment. I was more comfortable ranting about it all than my mother, but she knew the score as well or better than I. She told me the cafeteria story again and about taking the 240 bus back as often as she could—her experiences of first being upset by and then adjusting to Black–white segregation as a teenager moving from Dorchester to Randolph in the 1970s.

I asked for college application help from the guidance counselors at Randolph High, but they hadn't even heard of several of the schools I was considering. Plus, I found out that one of them was secretly feeding my files to my estranged father, and I stayed away from guidance counselors after that.

I worked hard on my applications through what still counts as one of the top three most sleep-deprived periods of my life. I got school-work done during the interstitial times on the T, waiting for the bus to work, during the odd slow time at work or school. I applied to Amherst (the closest I could get to Smith College), Swarthmore (which no one had heard of but always ranked in the top three and had the most diverse student body of its peers, an admittedly low bar), Brown (freedom, prestige, and proximity), Harvard (because fuck you), Oberlin (a liberal arts college with a music conservatory, but in Ohio), and UMass–Amherst (a good public university, near Smith, and the only school people thought I'd get into).

The first big packet arrived in the mail. I knew from Candice I wanted to get big packets, not light envelopes. It was Oberlin College. I got in! And they offered me a scholarship! An alumni couple spent an hour on the phone encouraging my questions and trying to recruit me. Then, Amherst came in. I got in there too! I thought that would be the end of my search—top school, near Smith, can't be beat. Swarthmore's acceptance package came too, and then UMass–Amherst. Four for four. One afternoon, I was taking a short nap upstairs between school and work, and Grandmy woke me up with her loud voice, calling up the stairs, "JAMIE, you have mail."

"Big packets or small envelopes?" I groggily replied.

"Big packets."

"OK, I'll look later," I yelled back down the stairs, smiled, and then turned over to finish my nap. I did what they told me I couldn't. I got into every one of those damn schools.

Then came figuring out how to pay for them, filling out the FAFSA myself, deciphering the complex financial aid letters the six colleges sent me, each with different combinations of loans, grants, work study, merit scholarships, and fees. Harvard stuck out from the rest. The parental and student contribution—i.e., cash money—that they demanded was nearly twice as much as the others. At the time, Harvard's policy was to include an estimate of noncustodial parents' income regardless of the reality. They assumed I could get thousands of dollars out of the guy I hadn't seen in years, the one who'd never shell out a few dollars so I could wear clothes that fit. Worse yet, Harvard's "Self-Help Offer" included work study in which I could choose to work serving food in a dining hall or cleaning dorm rooms my freshman year.

I thought about it throughout my evening shift at the café inside a chain bookstore. Every time I served a customer, I could see the stand-up display just behind them advertising Barbara Ehrenreich's *Nickel and Dimed*. Big blue letters exclaimed "Inside Minimum Wage America" above an image of the book's cover. I hadn't read it yet. I thought I had some sense of what was inside of minimum wage America. I eventually grabbed a copy and read it back-to-back with bell hooks's *Class Matters*. I saw my relatives, neighbors, and even myself in these books. They helped tell me how much it mattered and how much we were not alone.

After my shift, I took a photo with the sign, mop, and dirty yellow bucket, leaning on the mop to keep vertical, in my dark green apron, an honestly exhausted, disgruntled look on my face. I'd be damned if I was going to work a mop in college too, cleaning up after my classmates because I came from less money than they did. I'd worked as hard or harder to get in. Being alongside Candice for her Smith journey had primed me for how severe the socioeconomic and racial culture shock could be for me at an elite college. I was not going to put myself in that situation.

My families showed up for my high school graduation. They were loud—Uncle Jerry brought a boat horn—but they weren't the only ones. Many of my classmates were, like me, the first in their family to be going off to college. Some were the first in their families to finish high school in the US. We'd entered Randolph High School six years before as seventh graders, and from the 350 of us that entered, we were the 216 that stayed and survived.

When our very last day of school came, we rioted. At first, security and administration tried to move us back into classrooms. Then, they turned the auditorium into a holding pen. I don't know where the riot started, but it swept through our whole class. We ran through the halls together. We yelled and sang and banged lockers. Once the administration realized they could not contain us, they forced us all out of the building. We partied in the parking lot. A Jamaican kid jumped up on the hood of a car and started rapping and toasting through a megaphone. Head's high. Where did the megaphone come from? The party went on until people broke off to go to work or practice or home, but the celebration didn't stop.

On the morning of my graduation, I walked onto the stage to the sounds of the school band playing the same songs I'd played in the stands with them at prior graduations. The twelve of us sitting up onstage—the top ten GPAs plus class officers and speakers—beamed with pride. None of us was exempt from the struggle. We each overcame disadvantages to become a first of one kind or other.

I have a VHS tape of my high school graduation, and reader, I will tell you, I grimaced through the entire mortifying thing. The things I do for you, dear reader.

Teenage me is on-screen, lanky from too much exercise and too little eating, squinting at the gray light, wearing the jade Buddha beads Sifu made for me over cheap, blue graduation robes. The salutatorian, Sarah, and I both wore shit-eating grins on our pale, freckled faces.

Our principal started in with a heavy Boston accent. Back then,

I didn't think he had an accent. He rattled off the stats about our class: 58% going to a four-year college; 32% to a two-year program; 90% pursuing some form of higher education—that set an all-time record for Randolph High. He went on at length about September 11, which we were all still processing. That was an entrée for the principal to then talk about "The Greatest Generation" from a Boomer perspective and then to brag about his own Boomer generation's excellent qualities before saying, "Future generations may be lacking in these qualities. We will see . . . But, these ones are off to a good start." High praise indeed.

I was the last of the student speeches. The rest of my classmates and I had much stronger Boston accents than we do now, after years spent in the college and professional worlds. I launched into my speech, swaying side to side like a hockey player before the game, but I settled in with fierce determination. Nervousness disappeared as I poured my emotions through my words. I grew confident when I got some "yeah's" and "hmm-mmm's" from the crowd. My punchlines landed, and I was flying. Midway through, I broke the rhythm of the speech to stop and thank my mother. I said, "All of us here had to fight to make it. We had to work harder because of where we were born, the color of our skin, the languages we speak. My own struggle was being raised poor by a single mother." I paused and threw a fist up in my mother's direction and said, "Thank you, Mom." I turned back to my class and said, "We have fought. We have won! And we are just getting started!" It didn't sound quite so clichéd at eighteen.

The next night, I was waiting in line for soft serve ice cream at Dairy Barn* when a classmate came up to tell me, "Hey, man, I liked

---

* Some of you have the wrong idea right now, and I would wager you'd think "Kennedy's Fried Chicken" is also a typo.

your speech. I feel you, man. I've been through a lot, and my family sacrificed a lot for me, coming to America and stuff like that." That memory anchors me when the fog of time and distance blocks my view of where I'm from, when the ethereal fog makes me wonder if I was ever really there.

Not everyone was so complimentary. I opened the mailbox one afternoon to find an angry letter from a priest. Father Michael Harvey worked at St. Mary's Parish, where my biological father attended Mass. He was the parish's youth pastor, and as such, attended the graduation. He told me I may be smart but was not wise, that I owed it to my father and his family to go beg their forgiveness for what I'd said during my speech. What I'd said, mind you, was "Thank you, Mom."

I turned to my mother. "You *lied!*" She smiled. "You lied," I repeated as the Bronx's towers rose around us barely three hours into our drive. "You told me New York was a six-hour drive! I could've driven here in my car! All the shows I've missed . . ."

Before college, I had left New England only a few times. I arrived in distant, exotic Pennsylvania braced for culture shock. The last two years of frequent Smith College visits taught me a little bit about what to expect and the importance of finding my people. The people who get it, with whom I could be comfortable and honest. That can be a challenge when the issue is social class. Luckily, I'd made friends with Ana Chiu back in the spring, and she connected me to more friends from the TriCo pre-orientation for students of color, shared among Swarthmore, Bryn Mawr, and Haverford Colleges. I met a few older classmates from poor, racially diverse parts of Massachusetts, and I met amazing seniors who'd been through it themselves and looked out for me. I felt at home in the Black Cultural Center and the Intercultural Center more than anywhere else on campus. It was not until three years later that Hansi Lo-Wang pushed to organize Swarthmore's first Class Awareness Week, creating what I wished I'd had.

Anger fueled the motivation I'd used to make it that far, but Swarthmore was an absurd setting for anger. One day freshman spring, I was severely upset by some things back home and very angry about some things on campus. Maybe it was the day I threw my heavy physics textbook at the wall, completely frustrated and completely unprepared by RHS. I don't remember. I put on my headphones and cranked 2Pac. Now that hip-hop wasn't simply in the air around me as it was in Randolph, I had to reach out to it to connect. I stomped down the stairs in my boots with the hole in them and my scally cap on. Then, I stepped through the door. A bunny hopped around a grove of blooming magnolia trees outside my dorm. I fell to the petal-covered ground laughing at myself. How could I be hard around bunnies and flowers?

My mother was one thousand times more uncomfortable on Swarthmore's campus than I was. She got shy and anxious in upper-class spaces. She usually refused to walk campus or spend any time there, instead immediately turning around to drive six hours back home after having driven six hours there. By Connecticut, she'd be delirious. She grooved to Motown mix CDs to keep going. She made me sing backup. I refused. Once. She responded by swerving and yelling, "sing!" Worn Timbs on my feet in Mom's Montero jeep floating north on I-95, I belted out, "oo . . . oo . . . oo . . . oo . . . re-re-re-re-re-re-re-respect . . . just a little bit . . . just a little bit . . . just a little bit . . ." as if my life depended on it.

I had twenty-five dollars my freshman spring.

I was OK on the necessities. I covered tuition, food, and lodging with Swarthmore's grants, loans, work study, and excellent dining hall. I treated myself to a café breakfast on Thursdays before Chinese class—a double shot of espresso because it was only a dollar fifty. No food because it was too early and too expensive. I got creative acquiring the expensive books listed in my syllabi. Work study money came in and went right out, but I always had that twenty-five dollars. Lucky for me, I could get home on the Chinatown buses for cheap.

When my left toe poked through my only boots during a month of nonstop rain, I began putting my foot in a plastic bag before I put the boot on. My roommate was aghast. I figured he just didn't know the plastic bag trick because he'd never had to walk through deep snow in sneakers, having grown up in Lubbock, Texas, and all.

Before spring break, I carried my things through cold, pounding rain to the R3 train from Swarthmore to the ironically named Suburban Station in the center of Philadelphia. The rain turned to wintry mix—that hell-frozen-over sky slush—while I walked to the tiny basement shop that sold tickets for the Chinatown bus to New York. They played an old Shaw Brothers kung fu movie on the bus. The bright Hong Kong soundstage on-screen contrasted with the dark wintry mix outside.

Things were tense on the block of Chinatown buses in Manhattan. A crowd spilled off the sidewalk, waiting for late buses. Apparently, the storm was dumping snow on New England, and the Boston-bound buses weren't making it back. I bought tea and a char siu bao and waited until 10:00 p.m. to learn I wouldn't be taking a bus to Boston. I decided to splurge on an Amtrak ticket to Boston with points and most of that last twenty-five dollars. By the time I got to Penn Station—via Brooklyn because I was too tired to keep my directions straight—the last train to Boston had already left. The next train was scheduled for 4:30 a.m.

Cold, wet, and tired, I showed my ticket to get into the Amtrak waiting room. I watched a bootleg copy of *Dr. Strangelove* on my school laptop because I couldn't sleep on the chairs. Besides, any time someone looked a little too asleep, security roused them to check whether they had a ticket. I didn't know where New York expected people without homes to sleep, but it wasn't Penn Station.

I had no way to make it from Boston to my mother's place way down in Assonet, and she had to work that day anyway. So I took the train to Whitman to go to Sifu Kevin's. I hoped the conductor wouldn't check tickets, but he did, and I gave him my last five dollars. When I got to Whitman Station, I didn't know which direction to go. I walked over to a convenience store and asked for directions with no luck. I asked if they had maps. They did not. A nice, older woman with a small dog and a large SUV overheard me and generously offered a ride. I eagerly took her up on it because I was exhausted and because my left foot was already soaked, and I wasn't looking forward to a two-mile walk through eight inches of snow.

I got to Kevin's just as he was having his morning coffee. He took one look at me and said, "You look like shit. Did you know your toe is sticking out of your boot?"

"It's not so bad with a plastic bag."

Kevin gave me a look of amused pity, pulled out sixty dollars, and threw it at me. "Go buy some boots. Welcome home."

While I was home visiting, I helped Kevin apply for health insurance. Thanks to the Massachusetts Health Reform, Kevin, my mother, and tens of thousands of others received access to health care for the first time in years. I would later call home from college to check in and to encourage Kevin's way into the US health system.

After decades of abuse, his body had begun to turn against him. Doctors diagnosed him with the least bad kind of hepatitis, tried to find the right balance of psychiatric medicine, and told Kevin that the tingling in his fingers and toes was neuropathic pain, the result of advancing diabetes. Apparently, coffee, cigarettes, water, and booze do not a good diet make, but they sure were cheaper than insulin. Eating was a challenge for Kevin, a deadly piece of emotional shrapnel left in him from childhood abuse and poverty. Every doctor's visit brought more bad news, and he stopped telling me all of it on our phone calls. Very few of my classmates could identify. I was learning to code-switch, to hide everything away. But I could relax among the few of us Swarthmore students who knew what "one of those phone calls home" meant.

EIGHT

Leaving Home, Finding Home

New York City announces itself where Co-op City's orthogonal residential towers reach into the sky, five hours into a Chinatown bus trip from Boston. I was excited to get an invite to stay in Co-op with my college friend David Perez for a weekend.

Two and a half more hours of traffic after passing Co-op City on I-95, the bus inched towards the curb. I hustled past the jewelry shops and around the Friday night handbag shoppers down to the subway at Canal Street.

Three things did not yet exist in our world: smartphones, Harold, and Kumar. This is relevant.

David had given me directions: Take the 5 train to Pelham Parkway. Then take the Bx12 bus up Fordham Road and get off after you see a white castle.

I'd left Boston at 4:00 p.m., and it was past midnight when I handed over my transfer ticket to the bus driver. OK, almost there. As I looked out at the Botanical Garden, finding a castle seemed plausible enough. Still, I didn't see a castle there, and I didn't see one nestled into the Fordham University campus either. When the bus reached the 4 train stop, I knew I'd gone too far. I called David, "Hey, I think I took the bus too far. I didn't see a white castle. Hey, why is there a castle in the middle of the Bronx anyway?"

"BWAHAHAHHA! White Castle. White. Castle. Not a white-colored castle. The burger place!"

"The what? I don't think we have those."

David gave me directions back and met me at the bus stop. The six-foot-three bear of a man picked me up with his hug. The plan was to hang out there and then catch the last Metro-North train to New Roc where we could stay in David's grandparents' place while they were in Puerto Rico.

After a detour to Columbus Park for weed, at 1:00 a.m. we finally reached the apartment where David was hanging out with his high school friends, plus another of our college friends, a Polish American kid from Riverdale, who was also named Dave. We listened to Nas like the world was ours and told stories. We smoked blunts and drank whiskey and Hennessy. I hadn't eaten in almost fourteen hours and asked them where I could get food. "Any chance for Jamaican patties up here?"

"The only thing open this late right here is the White Castle."

They sent Riverdale Dave and me—the smallest and whitest guys there—to the Fordham Road White Castle at 2:30 a.m., where I yelled everyone's order through the thick glass.

You may be surprised to hear that we did not make the last Metro-North train out.

David found us a gypsy cab. We didn't have enough cash to make it to New Rochelle, but David negotiated a ride up to his mom's place in Co-op City. I talked to the friendly Haitian driver about Randolph; he said he had some people up there. The driver let us out on Co-op City Boulevard. David pointed out important places from his childhood as he navigated the quiet towers in the park. My eyes rose towards the sky. I'd never seen so many towers at once. I couldn't tell them apart, and I couldn't make any sense of why one was placed this way and one that way. I brought my eyes back down and pulled my jaw up. *Look cool. Look like you've been here before.*

Co-op City's towers rose above marshland on the traditional lands of the Lenape people. The marshes had been briefly developed into an amusement park called Freedomland USA. New York also used these marshes as a dump. But in 1966, the United Housing Foundation (UHF) built the largest single residential development in the world.

They envisioned Co-op as a city within a city, filling land between I-95 and the Hutchinson River in New York City's farthest northeast. Workers drove fifty thousand pilings through the marsh and landfill down to bedrock to create foundations for Cooperative City's thirty-five high-rises and seven townhome clusters, which include 15,372 homes. Co-op City boasts bountiful park space, the Harry S. Truman High School, two middle schools, three elementary schools, a firehouse, a cogeneration plant, and several houses of worship. But theirs was a mid-twentieth-century vision of a city within a city, so Co-op City also has eight parking garages, three suburban-style shopping centers, several surface parking lots, and a few highway on-ramps. There is no subway station or rail service, but the express bus to Manhattan could be a ticket to freedom.

Like Bittersweet Lane, Co-op wasn't technically the projects. UHF financed Co-op City with a mortgage loan from the New York State Housing Finance Agency. Using public resources to subsidize the *financing* of housing—rather than paying for the housing directly—was becoming the fashionable innovation to create affordable housing in the US. And moreover, this was a co-op, not subject to the management of a public housing authority.

In the US, cooperative housing represents a middle ground between owning and renting, more affordable and with less control than ownership but with more rights and stability than renting. Co-op residents do not buy their homes; they buy a share in the cooperative company that owns and manages the homes. It's as if you owned a significant amount of stock in the corporation you work for. Residents and their neighbors/shareholders use a democratic process to govern the community, which they fund through an ongoing co-op maintenance fee.

Co-op City's first residents—forty-four thousand strong—moved in between 1968 and 1973, mostly Jewish, Irish, Italian, and African American households from other parts of the Bronx. Construction defects and mismanagement plagued Co-op from early on, and Co-op City defaulted on its mortgage from the New York Housing Finance Agency in 1975. The state took control away from the cooperative board and demanded a 25% increase in maintenance fees. When the resident/owners refused, New York State threatened to foreclose on the property and evict the residents. The cooperators stayed united and held out for thirteen months before reaching a compromise and a return to cooperative management. By David's time, it was a pretty good place to grow up, everything considered. Maybe bittersweet too.

I took note of the wanted poster in the lobby of David's building. We reached his mother's apartment in Co-op City at four thirty in the morning. David turned the deadbolt as quietly as he could, pushed the door gently, and hit something. "Fuck. She put the chain on the door. Of course she did. I'm glad you're here with me. She *probably* won't yell at us with you here. If it was only me, she might just leave me in the hallway."

David knocked and rang the bell and woke up his mother. She welcomed me with open arms and made fun of David while she walked right back to her bed. David and I spent some time on his balcony looking out at the city. This was only my second night ever in New York.

I woke to the siren scents of coffee and bacon. Sandy handed me a cup of strong, angelic coffee from the beans she'd brought back from the island. She assured me she was only being nice because I was there and, OK, maybe a little because she missed David since he'd left for college. Within an hour of chatting in Sandy's kitchen, I felt like family. Except for the goddamned Yankees memorabilia on the fridge. And to my left. And behind me. Other than that, their home was always a happy place for me. It took thousands of people and millions of dollars to build Co-op. The Perez family made it home.

"Oh. I thought it got bombed in the war."

"What?"

"They say it was all better before the war."

Sitting in Chester High School, I could see how he came to that conclusion. Outside, derelict row houses lined the streets of this small city on the Delaware River. On the better blocks, grandmas sat on stoops and most homes were well lived in. On the worst blocks, most of the row houses were abandoned. Loose bricks hung from half-demolished and fire-damaged remnants of places children used to call home. Some had plywood ripped from the boarded-up doors or windows. By any social measure—educational attainment and achievement, income, wealth, racial segregation, violent crime, unemployment, public health, etc.—Chester struggled, badly.

A few of my older classmates—some of the same women of color from lower-class backgrounds who helped me through my initial culture shock at Swarthmore College—founded Dare 2 Soar to provide culturally competent mentoring and tutoring to the young people in Chester. Dare 2 Soar was my paid work study. It beat the hell out of what work study would have been at Harvard where I'd have been serving the privileged instead of the poor. Every other Saturday, however hungover, I looked forward to catching up with the young people who came to our campus from Chester. On weekdays, I tutored and mentored young people in Chester's public schools, churches, and a Delaware County family homeless shelter. My heart broke as I witnessed more hope among the children in the homeless shelter than in the Chester schools. The kids in the shelter came from all over the county, from every race. Many of my students in the Chester schools had little experience with life outside their small, devastated, postindustrial city.

I had asked the fourteen-year-old boy who just told me he thought Chester had been bombed in a war whether he'd ever left Chester. "Just once," he said, "to Atlantic City."

"Not even Philly? You've never taken the R3 train or the 109 bus in?"

"No."

"Why not?"

"Philly n****s don't like Chester n****s."

I knew what he meant and didn't press further. This boy had spent every day of his fourteen years in Chester. He was also functionally illiterate. We tried to combat the school-ingrained dislike of reading and writing by using lyrics. That afternoon, he and I made our way through 2Pac's inspiring "Rose that Grew from Concrete" and his honest and prophetic "Changes." While going through "Changes," he asked me, "How did Chester get like this?"

OK, I thought, let's see if I can explain this history both honestly and simply. "Well, Chester grew up on factory jobs and especially on building ships during World War II. People came up from sharecropping families in the South to work in the relative freedom of Pennsylvania. When World War II ended, the jobs went away. That hurt. And then, because the local elected officials couldn't control jobs for favors, they turned to taking money from stuff like your schools, the roads, and public housing. That hurt too. People took up drug dealing and other things when they didn't have better options to make a living, and that hurt. Then, the government tried almost every bad idea to 'revitalize' Chester. They built the prison, built the casino next to the prison, tore down random blocks to widen avenues, and gave the school system to the state, who handed your schools to a private, for-profit company that stole all your resources before quitting and leaving your school in this mess. All the while, many people who could leave Chester did, and things got harder for people who stayed."

"Oh. I thought it just got bombed in the war."

"What?"

"They say it was all better before the war."

This bright kid—who'd never been taught any history—made an insightful if tragically misinformed assumption about his hometown. On the van ride back to Swarthmore, I stared at the remains of row houses and at the derelict factories. I could see how he thought Chester had been bombed.

No child should have to grow up with all that, but they do. I went to Chester three days a week for three years, and the moral injury of it always got to me. I asked my mentor professor, Keith Reeves, how he balanced his two worlds. He'd grown up in Chester, attended Swarthmore alongside his twin brother against the odds, taught at Harvard, and now lived in a big house in Swarthmore on the road to Chester. He still visited Chester frequently to connect with family or to run classes for inmates. "Honestly," he replied, "I pour a glass of whiskey whenever I get home from Chester."

I got back to my dorm room, poured some whiskey for myself, and looked at the 2Pac lyrics on my own wall, on the poster I had made and printed in the campus library, the library named for the alumni family who had extracted their fortune from Chester.

When we took a senior year spring break trip to New Orleans, hurricane timber lined I-10. I snapped photos as we crossed the long bridge over Lake Pontchartrain, but once we entered the city proper, I put my camera away. I had no idea how bad New Orleans would look more than six months after the storm. It felt like descending into another world. Many of the stoplights along the way were still out. Wrecked houses bore spray-painted markings warning of toxic floodwater or dead bodies, though we couldn't decipher them at first.

We wound our way through the city towards Common Ground's community center at North Claiborne and Pauline. Friendly and upbeat long-term volunteers oriented, provisioned, and arranged work for more than five hundred students that weekend. We connected with our Swarthmore classmates who'd flown down and claimed cots in our barracks-style tent. I joined a group of volunteers signing up to pull security shifts. I signed up for the 12:00–2:00 a.m. watch.

After dinner, we headed to Frenchman Street with a car and trunk full of Swarthmore students and long-term Common Ground volunteers. The long-term volunteers reminded me of war veteran friends. I was the designated driver and made trips back and forth that night, dodging pothole craters through dark city streets. The power was still out.

At the morning meeting, organizers assigned us to a house not far away on Pauline Street and supplied us with Tyvex suits, respirators, gloves, boots, and tools. It was a double-barrel shotgun house—one-story, two apartments, no hallways, just two front rooms, a kitchen, a bathroom, and a back room. We were to gut the left side, while a group from Eastern Tennessee State University gutted the right side where the owners—Rose and her son—lived. They were amazingly hospitable. Rose shared stories about raising her son and daughter in that home. She told us about every family on the block, how they had survived the storm, where they were now, and whether they hoped to come back or would sell and move on. Before the storm, 80% of New Orleanians were born there, beating Boston for highest percentage in the US.

Returning residents faced harsh obstacles. There was still no running water, electricity, or garbage pickup. It was unclear whether the city would grant building permits for desperately needed renovations. It was ruinously expensive to clean out toxic storm debris, gut a house, perform mold abatement, and then rebuild. I suppose that's where our volunteer work came in, a small contribution to lowering the total cost of rehabilitating this home.

We spent the morning clearing flood debris from the house. We picked through toxic-floodwater-contaminated possessions and piled them up on the curb. Clothes, shoes, teaching manuals, indecipherable photographs, furniture, pots, pans, mirrors, a person's entire material life—all rotting, all to the curb. Then, we got to work with sledgehammers and crowbars, breaking down the plaster and ripping out the wooden slats that formed the walls, walls old enough to have well predated the use of drywall.

Common Ground volunteers brought lunch, and I needed the break. Sweat soaked through everything under my Tyvex. Then, President Bush's motorcade stopped just a few blocks away from us on North Claiborne for a sausage po' boy and a photo op. Traffic backed up for miles. We ran down there in our Tyvex suits and pleaded for help for NOLA until the motorcade drove off. The President's embedded reporters took no notice.

By the end of the workday, I was dead tired and sunburnt. It reminded me why I went to college in the first place. After dinner, my classmates and I went out to a bar in Bywater to catch a couple of the musicians we had seen the other night play again in a different band—the Palmetto Bug Stompers. Since I picked up a trumpet at the age of nine and began listening to Louis Armstrong, I'd dreamed of seeing jazz in New Orleans. I never imagined these circumstances.

The band was even better this time. I sipped on a small glass of whiskey and smoked a Black and Mild I'd picked up earlier that night. At one point, the band asked how many of us were from Common Ground. They thanked us and told us how wonderful it was that we were there and how much of an impact we would have. Between sets, we talked with the trumpet player and sax player as they shared a joint outside. The trumpet player said, "I know a little of what y'all are going through. I gutted my mother's house, my sister's house, and my aunt's house. That's hard work." What *we* were going through!? This man had lost nearly everything and gutted three relatives' homes. We'd barely put in an eight-hour day. His eyes watered a little as he shared stories about New Orleans during and after the storm. The musicians that night and two nights before played old jazz tunes with an energy I'd never heard.

We all woke up a little sore and tired Thursday morning, but ready to finish gutting Rose's house. The work seemed harder. Maybe it was just my already tired muscles, or maybe it was that we'd already finished with the easier tasks. By lunch, the wind that had been building all day turned into a severe storm/tornado watch. John and I returned to tent city to take down the tent while everyone else returned to decontamination at St. Mary's.

The storm passed before long, so we used the afternoon off to go see the Lower Ninth Ward, taking North Claiborne across the bridge over the Industrial Canal into the worst devastation. We rode in silence down the main drag until we realized we'd crossed Tupelo Street and left the Lower Ninth. We doubled back and wound through side streets, working our way towards the levee. Homes sat on their sides in the middle of the street. Rotting cars and trucks dotted the neighborhood, debris and garbage everywhere. Worse, the forty-block area closest to the levee was empty but for scattered rubble. The water rushing from the levee breach must have hit like a tidal wave.

We got out of the car about a block from the levee. John and Dave climbed stairs to nowhere, someone's former front stoop, and a cop pulled up. "This is still private property. Respect it and stay on the street." We complied. He drove away.

Places change us. Co-op, Chester, and NOLA certainly changed me. I used my time in college to learn more about them. I used my thesis for the public policy concentration to study Chester's seemingly contradictory housing problems—vacancy and unaffordability— how they could coexist, and what could be done about them. Moved by my trip to New Orleans, I used my thesis for my political science major to try to highlight the interplay among redevelopment, demographics, and politics in New Orleans.

The six-hour drive from Boston meant a smaller screaming section for me at college graduation than high school, but we still shocked the WASP families and amused the Black ones with loud shows of emotion. Grandmy, Uncle Jerry, Auntie Ellie, Mom, Sean, and my little cousin, Connor, made the trek down from Boston. Shockingly, so did Candice's parents, while she came up from law school in DC. My father and his side of the family were not there, of course. It had been years already. My Dare 2 Soar mentee Jaquille, his brother John, and their whole family came seven-strong from

Chester to campus for my graduation with a handmade congratulations sign.

I had people who loved me, who cheered loudly for me, who felt like home to me. I felt like I'd *earned* that love, proven myself worthy of these wonderful people. But I'd lost fathers and homes before. Experience taught me everything could be provisional. I was terrified that I would fail, that I'd prove myself unworthy. If I stopped earning it, I'd lose it all. Right?

PART 2

The Sweet

The child in each of us
Knows paradise.
Paradise is home.
Home as it was
Or home as it should have been.

—OCTAVIA E. BUTLER

NINE

The Institute

Finding my way around MIT's campus was at least as confusing as finding my way to graduate school period. I took the 85 bus down from the room I rented in Winter Hill. Riders on the 85 lined up in a neat little queue stretching down the block. I'd never seen such a thing on the MBTA before; it felt Canadian. The bus ride was easy enough at least; I'd been getting around on the T by myself since I was only twelve years old.

The walk through MIT's campus, on the other hand, left me stupefied. The buildings were numbered, but the numbers didn't follow each other in any order I could decipher. It was more like an Escher painting than the neat bus line. I walked up and down the Infinite Corridor, trying to find building 10 somewhere among buildings 7, 3, 13, 12, 4, 8, and 16. I did what I do when I'm a little lost and worried about being late. No, not ask someone for directions. Why would I ask for directions? I walked as quickly as I could, weaving between students who carried dangerously heavy backpacks while working problem sets in their minds.

Eventually, I discovered the building 10 elevator bank, but then I had to find room 485, which if you were to guess was on the fourth floor, you'd be wrong. When I finally found room 485 with not a minute to spare, I breathed a sigh of relief. Then, I walked in.

Room 10-485 was a large planning studio, double-height ceilings stretching deep into the building. One corner was filled with large iMacs and exhausted students drawing in CAD or Adobe. At least two were asleep on their keyboards, cans of espresso drinks and snacks scattered around them. Another corner was crowded with three-dimensional models of city blocks cut from foam, the acrid smell lingering. Whiteboards displayed planning ideas for studios focused on places from Lawrence, Massachusetts, to Shenzhen, China. Still another area had teams of students collaborating over large tables. None of these were the professors' offices.

Clock ticking, back sweating, I finally located stairs up to a mezzanine level with professors' offices, room numbers blissfully ordinal, and then I found a chair to sit in as Professor Lee finished up with another student. Someone had given me the good advice of meeting with whichever professor's work most appealed to me. Professor Tunney Lee taught a planning studio centered on a client in Shenzhen and ran a seminar on immigration and the development of Boston's neighborhoods.

"Come in, come in," said Tunney with a warm smile after opening his office door as the student leaving hurried past me. In this coldest of settings, Tunney radiated warmth. He had that natural charisma the most friendly, curious, good-hearted people wield without intention, *wu wei* 无为. "Make yourself comfortable. Good to meet you."

Tunney sat back in his office chair, skinny legs pointing forward, heels on the ground, a smile radiating from the lines in his forehead down through his eyes to his mouth.

I started, "Thanks for making the time, Professor Lee. I've been wicked excited to come meet you. Boston and China are two of my great loves, and I'm fascinated by your Immigration and Ethnic Neighborhoods class."

Tunney just smiled and said, "What part of Boston did you grow up in?"

"Randolph, actually."

"Ah! Your mother must be from Dorchester?"

This man had my number. "That's right. How did you know that?" I cannot think of anything else he could have said to so immediately gain my trust. I'd spent the last hour anxiously hurrying around a blank spot in my mental map of my city. I'd felt out of place, lower class, dim. But here I was, my background immediately honored.

We talked excitedly until a line of students had formed outside, waiting for their meetings with Professor Lee. I walked out knowing that it was our first conversation but would in no way be one of our last.

Tunney set me on a never-ending journey to try to make sense of Boston through its history, its neighborhoods, and its centuries of migrants. He told his students to "Learn one city truly well, and then you will know how to read the rest."

Few people loved, shaped, and learned from Boston as much as Tunney did. Over the years, I asked his peers about his accomplishments because he was never interested in rehashing old work. I cornered the legendary transportation planner Fred Salvucci once and listened, rapt, about the history they'd made. The two worked at the Boston Redevelopment Authority during the fight against the Inner Belt and Southwest Corridor highway projects. Fred told me how Tunney helped plan Resurrection City for MLK's Poor People's Campaign. Fred and others told me that Tunney could be credited with saving Boston's Chinatown from a program of slum clearance that would have replaced most of its remaining residential blocks with a hospital campus. Tunney couldn't stop urban renewal, but he redirected its substantial funding and political strength to construct blocks of mixed-use affordable housing that ensure a place for Chinatown's working class and elders into the future.[45]

Despite having a full course load already, I enthusiastically signed up for Tunney's seminar. The small group included master's, doctoral, and undergrad students, as well as Loeb Fellows, including the mayor of a sizable city in Brazil. We learned and shared with Tunney and a procession of Boston notables over the fourteen weeks.

Together we explored how, why, and where people move; how people shape places; and how places in turn shape people. Tunney charted the forever changing and interacting dynamics among people, place, exogenous macro factors, and planning. We were students of city planning, but Tunney made sure we understood: "Planning is not the driving force; it's the resulting one."

MIT's Department of Urban Studies and Planning (DUSP) required all master's students to take its "Gateway" course. We filled a lecture hall and listened to Xav Briggs teach us how to think about city planning. I looked around the room to take in my new classmates. Of the seventy or so, I knew four that I'd met while traveling in Asia over the summer, plus one Swarthmore classmate. It was a diverse group—students fresh from college and people with over a decade of experience in the field, people from all over the world, people from a variety of disciplines with many architects and landscape architects, some people who'd worked in finance, and others, such as myself, who carried on mission-driven work.

Quickly, I felt like many of my classmates were years ahead of me. Many arrived knowing what their questions were, what exactly they were there to research and learn. I felt irrationally intimidated by classmates' detailed ambitions around climate change adaptation, for creative real estate financing, for data analytics tools to reform public transportation. I didn't have my question yet. I wanted to make things better for the next kid like me by making places better for people and families, to create more opportunity, and to remove barriers. I wanted to figure out what could be done with Randolph, with Chester, with New Orleans, even with Beijing. Those were overly broad goals that required any number of fields of study.

I sat in class silently at first, still suffering some jet lag from my long trip to Asia and exhaustion from days of visiting Kevin in the hospital when I returned. He'd fallen into a diabetic coma while I was traveling in Thailand. He woke up before I returned, but he was still in such a state that I had to wipe shit off his back. I tried to unsee that. In class, I flipped between the anxiety of impostor syndrome (Do I belong here? Am I in over my head?) and my Bostonian self-righteousness (This is my town. I earned my way here, and you will listen to me).

I'd prided myself on never having to pull an all-nighter for academics at Swarthmore College, but I had four under my belt in just the first few weeks at MIT. I could be found at 4:00 a.m. on the steps at 77 Mass Avenue—my new stoop—smoking a Black and Mild with Sara Zewde. In addition to Xav's Gateway and Tunney's Ethnic Neighborhoods courses, I overloaded myself with the required Housing, Community, and Economic Development intro course, the required economics course, the Community Development Finance intro, and the Design Skills studio. Visual art of any kind was outside my skill set, but I knew how crucial understanding urban design and architecture would be. That studio course was often the reason for my 4:00 a.m. stoop time.

The most intense semester of my life left me exhausted but pondering the big question from Xav's course: what is city planning? I learned to view cities—any places really—as complex ecosystems. A city is a unit of governance, a collection of buildings and neighborhoods, a density of people, an economy, a polity, a culture, a transportation network, a sewer and water system, an ecology of diverse habitats, a school district, an energy grid, and so much more. To improve a place, one must know how to effect a specific change but must also understand how everything intersects and how one change affects the rest of the system. We had to go both broad and deep—become competent enough in design, finance, policy, community process, and economics to communicate, while also becoming expert enough in one to get a job in a complicated field like affordable housing, public transit, or climate adaptation. I had to learn to communicate in words, pictures, and numbers to accommodate the diversity of stakeholders crucial to the work. Not quite being everything to everyone, but being enough to collaborate well with everyone. We learned to consider both the forest and the trees.

Sure, I was spent from that semester, and the trip, and the family problems, but Tunney was leading a trip to China during the January break for his spring semester studio. I was excited to go to China for a third time, to cities I'd never visited, and with such an incredible expert. I now suspect I worked myself to exhaustion at MIT to avoid all the problems outside of it. I was glad I had left the state for undergrad. Being just a T ride away from it all might have broken me as an eighteen-year-old experiencing cultural dislocation for the first time.

Our studio class traveled to Shenzhen, Guangzhou, and Hong Kong. Tunney enjoyed having me—the pale Irish American kid—translate Mandarin Chinese for him, shocking the locals. He joked to me about his own times in Italy where he—the Chinese American man—translated for his Italian American friends, shocking the locals. Tunney's ever-present wonder heightened on the trip, eyes always scanning up, around, and down. At the end of a long day in Hong Kong, after visiting the Public Housing Authority and numerous new town developments, Tunney asked us if we wanted to go look at one more public housing development. At the time, about half of Hong Kong lived in public housing. Impressively, the public housing was nearly self-funding on revenue from commercial real estate development. Tunney had worn out our group of grad students only a third his age, but he wanted to keep going. I ended up being the only one who went. There was no way I was missing that walk.

My notes from Shenzhen included this gem of wisdom from Tunney: "You never achieve master plans because cities are not buildings. You can't control them. Change can be abrupt or gradual, inclusive or involuntary, dramatic or tiny; but there is no such thing as a stable neighborhood."

During our time in Shenzhen, we visited a variety of our housing developer client Vanke's projects. We also explored Shenzhen's "urban villages." Housing quality revealed stark class differences. We interviewed residents in Mandarin about what they needed from the neighborhood.

How do you get to work? "Bike or bus."

Where do your kids play? "There's no time to play. And school fees are expensive. And there's a lack of parks here."

What happens when you get sick, where do you go? A seamstress responded, "Don't get sick."

What do you wish the neighborhood had? Would you be open to more mixed-income community? "Yes, but not with the poor people."

Impoverished neighborhoods in Shenzhen resembled nothing I'd seen in the US. The so-called urban villages were dense clusters of ten-meter by ten-meter buildings, sometimes only an arm's length from each other. Urban land in China is owned by China and developed through ground leases between developers and the government. But in rural areas, China had given peasants ownership over ten-square-meter patches of land. Shenzhen grew so rapidly—from a fishing village border town of only twenty-two thousand in 1970 to a tech-driven economy and 17.6 million residents in 2020—that its rural farmers found their little plots quickly surrounded by dense city. Banding together as village corporations, they capitalized on every centimeter of their suddenly much higher land value by developing (or selling the right to develop) these ten-by-ten handshake buildings. The cheap, dense urban villages created space in Shenzhen for its lowest-income workers—migrants from distant rural areas without proper hukou registration who exist in a legal limbo not unlike undocumented immigrants in the US.

We spent three days drawing plans for a neighborhood on the fast-growing outskirts of Shenzhen, collaborating with Vanke's architects and Shenzhen planners. Translating between Chinese and American architects was easily the most exhausting workday of my life. I'm sure I could have lifted pallets without my arms giving out long after my brain had turned to static from communicating one group's visions in one language to another group in another language, listening to their critique, and then translating that back for the original group.

My brother, Sean, had joined the Army just before I started at MIT. He went to paratrooper school and joined the storied 82nd Airborne Division. Mom, Grandmy, and I traveled to Fort Leonard Wood deep in the heart of Missouri to watch Sean graduate from basic. Later, I'd make an annual trip to Fort Leonard Wood to visit my childhood friend, Gary, when he was stationed there. The first time Gary drove me in from Kansas City, I remarked, "Wow, it looks like every house has a swimming hole."

Gary laughed and said, "Those aren't for swimming. They're open septic pits." That was even newer to me than the urban villages had been.

Back in Cambridge, I started looking into enlisting myself. I could join the National Guard to help pay for MIT. I come from a family of enlisted men, but my degree meant I could be an officer. When my mind wandered during a lecture, I used my laptop to research the possibilities. I thought about the Army. The impulse strengthened after Sean's company received orders to deploy to Afghanistan in February.

Then, on January 18, a powerful earthquake devastated Haiti. Sean's company was the designated Global Response Force at the time, able to immediately deploy anywhere in the world. The Army sent Sean and the 82nd to Haiti to provide relief, and they sent the 10th Mountain Division to Afghanistan in their stead. I later met a 10th Mountain veteran of that deployment, and it sounded like an especially awful tour of duty. I was relieved that my little brother would avoid a deadly deployment to instead serve our Haitian neighbors. I worried about the relatives of my Haitian American friends. I grieved the latest in a centuries-long chain of horrific disasters to punish the first free nation in the modern western world.

I took one course at Harvard during graduate school, and I took it because Ed Marchant taught it. Whether rain, snow, or—actually, I'm not sure there was any other weather those months—I'd

walk down from my apartment in Winter Hill, Somerville, to the
Kennedy School of Government in Harvard Square to learn about
how affordable and mixed-income housing is developed. The walk
gave me plenty to think about. I'd stroll through my own gentrifying neighborhood, stopping to chat with the elderly woman from
Kansas City who was always on her Central Street stoop. I passed
the buildings that were no longer factories but not yet craft brewer-
ies, and then, I knew I crossed from Somerville to Cambridge when
the triple-deckers turned to mansions. The street turned one way
for just one block at the city border, just to keep the riffraff out.
There was a clear line between gentrifying and gentry, here where
the wealthy have kept estates for the last four centuries.

Ed Marchant was from Quincy and still spoke with a Boston,
South Shore accent. I never quite knew how to fit as one of very few
lower-class locals sitting in a classroom at Harvard or MIT, but Ed
made me feel at home.

The class was complicated because affordable housing development in this country is complicated. We've had a century of bright
people innovating ever more complex methods to squeeze shrinking
dollars ever harder. We use every tool in the box. We provide direct
subsidies for rents or operating costs, such as Section 8 vouchers or
public housing operating funds. We provide direct financing for real
estate through loans and equity investments. We provide inducements to financing like mortgage insurance, loan guarantees,
tax-exempt lending provisions, interest subsidies, Community Reinvestment Act (CRA) requirements, and other devices designed to
make direct financing easier or less expensive. We provide inducements to equity, usually in the form of tax credits like the Low-Income
Housing Tax Credit, historic tax credit, Brownfields tax credit, and
others. We reduce the costs of real estate development through efficient design and through donated land, materials, or labor. We

reduce routine operating costs with efficient utilities, insurance, taxes, and other sensible cost reductions.

One day in April, Ed brought in Willie Jones as a guest speaker. Willie was then a senior vice president at The Community Builders, where he had led several neighborhood redevelopments while ensuring the associated work helped grow typically excluded Black construction contractors.

Willie was* a force of nature. The son of sharecroppers in Virginia, he somehow worked his way to Brown University. There, he met his lifelong love and a powerhouse in her own right, Pam, who eventually moved him to her hometown of Boston. Willie was a legend in the field, and I hoped I would be lucky enough to maybe work with him someday. Willie never minced words, always cursed, and never let anyone forget the people and neighborhoods this work was supposedly for.

"See, you have got to control the corners. No, I'm serious. When we worked to redevelop the City West projects in Cincinnati, there were buildings and blocks where drug dealers had control, not the housing authority. Our redevelopment plan was going to disrupt their business. So they weren't happy about it. I was presenting at a public meeting when one of them got to the mic and said, 'This is ours. You aren't going to touch it. You aren't going to change anything. And if you do, we will find you. We know what hotel you stay at.' Then, he pointed to the gun on his hip. I acted all bad, cursed him out, and it impressed the rest of the residents that I was brave and confident that this redevelopment could happen. Then, I went straight to the airport without going back to my hotel room to get my clothes. In truth, I was shook."

---

* Our loss of Willie Jones in 2024 forced me to edit this verb from "is" to "was." https://www.whbryant.com/obituary/Willie-JonesJr.

Ed Marchant's class set my professional path. In addition to introducing some of the best practitioners in the country, it required participation in the Affordable Housing Development Competition. My team was lucky to be paired with Madison Park Development Corporation to plan for two vacant sites on Dudley Street, just outside Nubian (Dudley) Square. Today, dozens of households call those sites home.

I fell in love with the idea of project managing affordable housing development. Here was a way I could improve opportunities for the next kid like me, help build the city I love, and—not for nothing—have a job that I could probably explain to my family. Construction site stories go over much better than office stories.

Nevertheless, I worked as Tunney's teaching assistant for the Immigration and Ethnic Neighborhoods seminar the following fall. We redesigned the seminar together. Each week focused on one of Boston's communities, and Tunney would invite a friend from that community for each. I was thrilled to meet Tunney's people—friends, former students, collaborators—who had each shaped my city: Fred Salvucci, Antonio Di Mambro, Amy Schectman, Tony Pangaro, Kairos Shen, Janelle Chan, Byron Rushing, and many more. Tunney took us into the neighborhoods to walk about the places we talked about. And on those walks, I watched this man who knew this city as well as any person possibly could; I watched him looking up and around with wonder and curiosity, always learning.

Tunney gave me the opportunity to make my learning still more personal. With his guidance, I used my graduate thesis to explore what happened to my hometown through its family and community stories, in addition to the physical, political, and economic histories I researched. I'd never been able to properly explain my hometown.

Randolph was undoubtedly a suburb but with dramatically "urban" problems. Some part of every ghetto, city, and suburban place I'd been made me recall Randolph. Tunney gave me the framework to properly understand it.

Tunney also inadvertently introduced me to my wife Sung. We first chatted during Tunney's walking tour of East Boston, and we hit it off immediately. We stood together on the Blue Line and traded stories, and I can still picture the way she smiled up at me on the train. We sat together during lunch at a Salvadoran restaurant to continue the conversation. We had so much to say to each other and so little in common.

During the tour, Tunney showed us the steps to the former immigration station where he first set foot in America at the age of seven. And yet, Tunney was fourth-generation American . . .

Tunney's great-grandfather had worked on the railroad, digging tunnels through a particularly dangerous section of the Cascade Mountains. Once the job was done, he and his coworkers settled in Tacoma, establishing a vibrant Chinatown near the docks and tracks at the bottom of downtown. The federal government further isolated Tacoma's one-thousand-strong Chinese community with the Chinese Exclusion Act, which forbade nearly all new immigration from China.

Worse, sporadic racist violence reached a new pitch when whites in Wyoming massacred a large community of Chinese workers in Rock Springs. The violence crept closer to Tacoma when whites beat, kidnapped, and shot several Chinese working men in east King County, Washington.

Then, the City of Tacoma began passing laws aimed at making life more difficult for its Chinese community. On September 28, 1885, an "Anti-Chinese Congress" met in Seattle. Tacoma's Mayor Weisbach—an immigrant from Germany—proclaimed that all

Chinese people must leave Western Washington by November 1. Most of Tacoma's Chinese residents fled what was coming.

On November 2, a court acquitted those accused of the horrific massacre at Rock Springs, Wyoming. This meant open season for pogroms. On November 3, Tacoma's Mayor Weisbach led a mob of over five hundred whites to attack and expel any remaining Chinese people and to then burn down their homes and businesses. Desperate Chinese residents with faith in the rule of law sent emergency telegrams to the governor in Olympia, to the consulate in San Francisco, to contacts in Seattle. No help came. The mob violently forced the last members of Tacoma's Chinese community to march eight miles through unusually heavy rainfall to the Lakewood train station. They violently dragged a mother who'd refused to leave her home. At the station, the mob then forced their victims to buy their own train tickets. Those who could not afford tickets rode in the boxcars of a freight train or walked 140 miles along the rail grade. Two men died of exposure. Tacoma's whites then demolished Chinatown. Within four days of the expulsion, they'd erased all physical memory of Tacoma's Chinatown.[46]

A factory owner in western Massachusetts heard about the Tacoma Expulsion while his predominantly French Canadian workforce was on strike. He brought Tacoma survivors to western Massachusetts to replace his striking workers. It broke the strike, and when the whites agreed to come back to work, the Chinese workers were forced to move again. They ended up in Boston, where they formed the nucleus of Chinatown around Oxford Place.[47]

Tunney's great-grandfather had returned to China after Tacoma but rejoined this community in Massachusetts. Many made a living in laundries—one of the feminized trades to which Chinese men stuck after whites massacred Chinese miners and rail workers. The Exclusion Act did not allow Chinese women to immigrate, and race mixing was both illegal and violently suppressed. So the men in Tunney's family returned to Taishan to start families. Then, after a few years, they would take their sons back to the United States. Tunney's father was the last man to get married this way in his line. He attended the prestigious Boston Latin High School and apparently became a little too popular among the white women. His family quickly sent him back to China to marry and have children. He brought Tunney back to Boston when he was seven in 1938, one step ahead of the Japanese invasion, World War II, and the Communist Revolution. Neither the US nor the People's Republic of China would allow Tunney's mother and three sisters to emigrate. It would be decades before he saw any of them again.

Working with Tunney made it very clear to me that history is not past, not even passed. Absurdly, there's a direct line from the Tacoma Expulsion to my marriage. Billions of individual stories form our world. When people gather in our thousands and our millions with our stories and our ideas, we change places.

TEN

The Rent

MIT did not get any easier three semesters in. I wanted to learn everything, meet everyone. I wanted to prove I could live up to the highest expectations. I loaded up on design and finance classes with the hope of becoming an affordable housing developer. David Geltner's Real Estate Finance class ensured I would always feel behind. I choked down the nervousness in class as my mind raced to catch up. I didn't yet speak the language of finance, and I felt like I always caught up to concepts a week or two after I was supposed to have.

The best dumb question I ever asked came when a professor mentioned there was "no housing demand" in a neighborhood where I knew there to be a large homeless population. "Professor, I don't understand, there are thousands of people homeless or living in overcrowded homes in this market. How can there be no demand for housing?"

"Oh. No, there's no *economic* demand. The people who need housing there, which we'll call shelter demand, do not offer rents high enough to justify the costs of development." My mind lit up. That was a revelation to me.

This quick exchange revealed the core market failure in housing. Ours isn't a broken system failing to meet demand—this system was never intended to meet the needs of people who can't pay. I'd lived that experience, watched my own family navigate it, and felt the pressure of not being enough to meet capital's demands. Our system never fully addressed the hard reality that the market is utterly unable to serve households that cannot afford the costs of development and maintenance. I began to understand the concept of rent differently.*

I'd always understood "rent" as just one of those necessities of life, like taxes. That's how it looks from the perspective of those of us who pay: "rent" is the payment from the user of a property to its owner. Rent is more complicated from the perspective of those who collect it: "rent" is part of a cash flow that splits into paying for property operations, paying a return to any lenders/investors who may have funded development or acquisition of the property, and paying profit to the owner. Economists are even more specific. They use the word "rent" to describe those owner profits, the passive income that comes from owning, not working. Those rents are the extraction of our own labor, even to the point of leaving many of us out in the cold.

Housing development is a servant of two rents, and a third there is that matters the most. First, there's the *construction rent*, the rent level that allows developers to build new homes without needing subsidies. Then, there's the *operations rent*, the rent that covers maintenance, utilities, insurance, taxes—basically, the cost of keeping things running smoothly. But the only rent that matters to you, to

---

* These concepts function for the monthly costs of purchasing, owning, maintaining, and paying mortgage debt on an owned home as well as for money paid to a landlord. For simplicity's sake, this book will use "rent" throughout to represent both rental and homeownership payments.

me, or to anyone else living in this system is the one your household can actually afford.

Let's break this down, because understanding these three rents is key to understanding how housing is built and why our efforts to create homes have fallen so short.

CONSTRUCTION RENT

I define construction rent as the rent level that justifies the cost of creating additional homes, whether through new construction or rehabilitation.

The construction rent varies in place and time alongside changes in the economy, the market, and regulations, but a distinct and knowable construction rent exists in each place and time. Estimating it could help craft more effective policy, allow us to keep track of which households the market is able to serve, and allow us to trace where egregious rents drive large-scale wealth extraction.

In Seattle in 2018, the market was providing new apartments at $3.50/square foot—which roughly means a household must bring in $105,000 per year to afford a two-bedroom apartment at $2,300 per month. About half of the households in the Seattle metropolitan area could afford that rent. The development market couldn't even notice the other half. Their need for a place to live, their "shelter demand," does not translate into economic demand for new development. Instead, they must compete with other potential residents for whatever homes currently exist, a cruel game of musical chairs where the losers end up displaced or homeless.

To create homes for people who need them but cannot afford the construction rent, we must somehow close the gap between what it costs to develop and how much those people can afford.

It is possible for public policy to lower or raise the construction rent, thus leading the market to serve more or fewer people in need of homes. Local and state governments can change requirements for parking, land use, design, procurement, design review, labor, impact fees, environmental methods, construction materials, accessibility, and so forth in ways that reduce (or increase) costs.

Even so, our ability to lower the construction rent is limited. Experts must be paid to design a building, engineer a safe structure, lay a foundation, frame it, wire it, complete its plumbing, source and transport materials, and complete each of the hundreds of other complex tasks that go into creating new homes. The cost of doing so creates a lower bound on how cheaply private market developers can offer new homes.

The United States has tried a variety of ways to provide capital subsidies, including public housing capital grants, mortgage lending, subordinate debt programs, inducements to financing, and tax credit programs such as the Low-Income Housing Tax Credit (LIHTC).

It is impossible for the market to serve all Americans who need homes. The gap between what people can afford and what it costs to build is the inherent market failure in housing. The market cannot go it alone, and so we must publicly fund affordable housing.

Or, alternately, we can leave an entire slice of society locked into perpetual homelessness.

OPERATIONS RENT

Construction is just the first step. Those buildings must operate well. Water, sewer, taxes, insurance, maintenance, garbage removal, cleaning, landscaping, snow removal, management, services, mortgage payments, and so on require a solid operations budget. I define the operations rent as the rent level at which that budget is balanced.

Multifamily developers and owners generally know how much their buildings cost to operate per unit per year (my inner ten-year-old's favorite acronym "PUPY"). For example, in Seattle in 2025, an affordable housing apartment building would typically need $9,000 PUPY to operate without losing money. That means that the affordable housing provider can stably provide housing for households who can afford $750/month in rent. That rent is theoretically affordable to someone earning $30,000 per year ($15/hour working full time). To serve households that make less than that while properly maintaining the property and paying the bills, the affordable housing provider needs an operating subsidy.

Through our history, operating subsidies for renters in the United States have included public housing operations funding, Section 8 housing assistance, and some state and local rental assistance programs (such as Massachusetts Chapter 707, aka MRVP, which kept my family housed at Bittersweet Lane). These subsidies set a rent level the government is willing to pay, and then they provide the landlord the difference between that level and the rent the tenant pays (typically 30% of the tenant's income). For Section 8, that rent level is set each year by the Department of Housing and Urban Development (HUD) and called the Fair Market Rent.

For a time in the 1960s and 1970s, generous operating subsidy through Section 8 contracts drove a wave of affordable housing construction. When the operating subsidy provided was generous enough to equal or exceed the construction rent, developers could literally take a long-term Section 8 contract to the bank and use it to underwrite a mortgage loan to pay for development. That era is all but gone. HUD no longer allows Section 8 to create additional homes.

If the property is not bringing in enough revenue to operate in the black, it will quickly become a bad place to live—part of the story of the Bittersweet Lane Apartments where I grew up. Needed capital improvements like replacing a roof or boiler system will be deferred. Routine maintenance like painting walls or replacing light bulbs will be ignored. Broken things will go unrepaired. Needed services and staffing will go unprovided. The history of public housing in the US is littered with properties that deteriorated into terrible places to live after the federal government defunded housing.

RENT MATTERS

The construction rent and operations rent are conceptual tools to help us understand why current programs and policies are not solving our housing crisis.

However, these construction rent and operations rent concepts are not actually how professionals currently think about rents. Professionals in the affordable housing world talk about rents as a percentage of area median income (AMI) or perhaps by program name, like "Section 8" or "202." Here is a typical rental program summary adapted from an application to a public agency for funding:

Our team is committed to equitable development without displacement at FakeName Gardens. We propose to set rents for 55 out of 70 units at levels that are affordable to households that earn 55% of AMI or less, allowing us to make rents affordable to the average resident in census tract 1234.56. As requested by the community, 20% of the 70 apartments will be set aside for artists and their families and restricted to households earning up to 70% of AMI. The FakeName Gardens project intends to utilize HUD HOME ARP support on 8 units; these are restricted below 30% AMI but must be rented to a member of a Qualified Population as defined by HUD.

Clear, concise, and comprehensible, no? The reason for this focus on percentages of AMI is simply our government's consensus to use AMI to define program eligibility. That is, AMI is how those government agencies define which people are worthy of help and how much the government will help them.

Means-testing by AMI is admittedly an improvement over the worlds of health care and early education, where eligibility is attached to the federal poverty level (FPL) and professionals refer to limits like "250% of FPL." AMI means that affordable housing eligibility is at least tailored to each metro area rather than an entire, incredibly diverse country. But as an individual person, could you name your own AMI level? Do you know what percentage FPL you are?

Conceptual mechanisms for delineating who gets what and who doesn't are fundamental to public policy in a context of scarcity. But when we cannot think beyond the game as it exists, we do no favors to overwhelmed people navigating this byzantine morass to apply for help during hard times. We need to get real.

ELEVEN

Jackson Square: A Walk Through Affordable Housing History

Tunney asked me, "Where would you bring visiting academics to see affordable housing? We're hosting a group from China." Tunney and I bounced ideas back and forth, both of us a little giddy to talk about Boston neighborhoods, history, and development.

Tunney taught his students to understand urban change through the histories of peoples' migrations, society's planning responses to those moves, and the stories of places—a cycle and epistemology he called People, Planning, and Place. From this perspective, planning itself is an oxymoron because it is fundamentally reactionary, responding to and constrained by the dynamics of people and place.

This method occasionally conflicts with the supposedly scientific city planning methods that came to dominate Western Europe and America in the twentieth century. Those methods often failed the scientific process by omitting huge swaths of relevant data. They often mistook economically privileged white Protestant men's perspectives as neutrality. They believed that people's histories and stories—especially from oral or lower-class sources—were of no use or importance. Traffic counts, level of service, GDP, job counts, units, profits: those matter because we can count them.

Modern city planning intends to be more participatory, but can we truly collaborate with communities if we do not understand their origins? Our built and natural landscapes are physical records of our histories. The stories we tell about them track and assign value to who, where, and when we have been. The Irish have a word for these stories in the landscape, the *dindshenchas*. There is no word in English for this indigenous form of knowledge, this lore of place names.

Nothing in our world is free of history. Those of us who seek to shape cities or policies should always look back as part of our looking forward.

That day, Tunney and I settled on bringing our visitors to Boston's Jackson Square, where nearly the entire history of US affordable housing could be seen within a few blocks of the T stop. Allow me to take you on that walk through affordable housing history.

PUBLIC HOUSING - BROMLEY-HEATH

The brakes squeal as the Orange Line train shudders to a stop at Jackson Square. Cold wind rushes into the station from the door at the top of the stairs. Walk out into the brisk December day and turn right. You see the aged, rectilinear red brick buildings that conjure "the projects" in the American mind.

From that corner, the community now known as the Mildred C. Hailey Apartments reaches a quarter mile northwest. The eponymous Ms. Hailey led the Bromley-Heath Tenant Management Corporation, which in 1973 had taken over management of the Bromley-Heath public housing development from the Boston Housing Authority (BHA). It was the first public housing development in the nation to be directly managed by its residents, but it returned management responsibility to the BHA after Mildred's passing in 2012.[48]

The BHA constructed Bromley-Heath as three separate developments beginning with Heath Street in 1941, followed by Bromley Park in 1954, and Bickford Street in June 1961. That puts Heath Street within the earliest vintage of public housing in the US and Bickford Street among the latest.

American public housing construction occurred during an era when Americans were less pessimistic about our government's ability to solve problems. Yet even then, we did not fully agree on which problems public housing was meant to solve. The US had experience developing institutions for the public benefit, such as schools, parks, libraries, and hospitals. And it had experience developing places meant to punish, like prisons, asylums, and poorhouses. According to Professor Larry Vale, American public housing has always fallen in between the two, never clear whether it's humanitarian or penal.[49]

As I shared in the first chapter, early public housing was aimed at working- and middle-class veterans. In the 1960s, the US changed its mind about who public housing was for. Public housing became the housing of last resort for the people with the least money, falling on the hardest times. In a telling reversal, housing authorities that once had a policy of forbidding unmarried mothers ended up with a policy forbidding men from living with mothers.[50] In *The Pruitt-Igoe Myth* documentary, former resident Jacquelyn Williams described how her family moved into Pruitt-Igoe from the tenement housing she'd been born into, "The welfare department came to our home. They talked with my mother about moving into the housing project, but the stipulation was that my father could not be with us. They would put us into the housing project only if he left the state. My mother and father discussed it, and they decided that it was best for the twelve children for the father to leave the home, and that's how we ended up in the projects." Or, as another former resident, Sylvester Brown, put it, "Who are these people and how do they have the power to make my mother lie?"[51]

Today, 958,000 public housing units are spread across all fifty states and several territories, with the majority in high-poverty, segregated neighborhoods.[52] Most public housing authorities (PHAs) are agencies of the federal—not the local—government, despite confusing names like the Seattle Housing Authority or the Housing Authority of New Orleans.

These days, the United States' scarce, inadequate public housing is leased primarily to the lowest income households. Who are they? According to the Center for Budget and Policy Priorities, as of 2020, 56% of the households in public housing were headed by older adults or people with disabilities. Most of the other 44% included a working or recently unemployed adult. More than one-third of the people who live in public housing are children.[53]

Marital status doesn't matter as much anymore, but US public housing still screens tenants for more than just their income. Households must be able to prove an eligible citizenship status.[54] People with criminal records are not allowed, with a few exceptions in certain places. Housing authorities evict families for allowing a relative with a criminal record to stay with them. They force parents and grandparents in public housing to choose between leaving family in need on the streets or risking everything to let their teenage or adult child sleep on the couch while they get their feet under them.

Of all the forms of affordable housing the United States has attempted, public housing faces the largest political risk. Not any risk the projects pose to politicians during moral panics about civil disorder, nor during scandals over lead paint,[55] stolen funds,[56] or sexual coercion[57]—although yes, those too. I mean that public housing itself is especially vulnerable to shifting politics and extreme partisanship because it is almost solely dependent on the federal government.

Massachusetts Senator Edward Brooke spearheaded the federal legislation that changed how housing authorities charge rent. Prior to 1969, PHAs charged a fixed monthly rent, like fifty dollars per month. The Brooke Amendment instead set a tenant share of rent at 25% (now 30%) of each household's income. The households, of course, had very little income with which to pay rent. Tenant shares of rent systemically stagnated as the poor and working classes in the US experienced half a century of wage stagnation from the 1970s on and as social security and other safety net programs declined in purchasing power.

Congress, of course, did not appropriate more subsidy to make up for restricting the amount of rent PHAs could collect. Quite the opposite, over the last forty years, Congress cut HUD's budget by 80%, from $83 billion to $18 billion[58] before bringing it back to $52 billion—still 37% below peak despite many, many more Americans now needing housing assistance. As a result of the federal government's cuts, we lost a quarter million public housing apartments to deterioration. We left our public housing to rot until the prevailing academic, policy, and professional efforts began to focus on how to replace the "failed" projects, but we will come back to that later.

The capital needs of seventy- to ninety-year-old buildings that housed generations and generations of children would be high even with fastidious ownership and management. That's true for New Englanders living in triple-deckers. It's true for old farmhouses in the Midwest. It's true for Seattleites in Craftsman bungalows. It's true for our public housing. Sadly, most (not all!) public housing in the US did not have owners who invested in the care of their buildings over time. That irresponsible owner is us, by the way, US citizens and our federal government. We are shitty landlords.

Homes need tender, loving care, and our Congress's inadequate capital funding worsened the backlog of unmet renovation needs in public housing. "The most recent national assessment in 2010 estimated the backlog of unmet needs at $26 billion, but it excluded major categories of costs, and other data indicate that the need is likely considerably higher. For example, a 2017 assessment found that the New York City Housing Authority, which administers 17% of the nation's public housing, faced $32 billion in capital needs over five years."[59]

The status of public housing reached new lows—or was believed to have reached new lows—during a period when politicians of both parties competed over who was tougher on crime. The US largely gave up on public housing, as it had done with the earlier institutional and tenement strategies for providing homes to poor people. Congress last funded the creation of additional public housing in the mid-1990s. Then, Congress passed the "Faircloth Amendment," which prohibits HUD from funding the construction or operation of new public housing.

Simultaneously, our governments increased funding to build prisons and passed laws to evict public housing residents and disqualify people for aid if their landlord even so much as *believed* those households used drugs or allowed drugs to be used anywhere within blocks of the property.[60] A later chapter discusses the role of public institutions in housing the poor, but it is not a stretch to say that the United States began to replace public housing with prisons on a large scale under Presidents Reagan, Bush I, and Clinton.

Despite federal disinvestment, some highly successful public housing authorities kept their properties in relatively good condition, had decent management practices, and found alternative ways to find money from other sources. In my opinion, the best, such as the Tacoma Housing Authority, do all of that plus connect their residents to the other things that will help them survive and to escape poverty. These include deep and meaningful partnerships with local community colleges, school districts, early learning centers, health care systems, city agencies, emergency services, food banks, and more. Affordable housing can provide a wonderful opportunity to literally meet people where they are at—at home.

Sadly, those exemplary housing authorities are not the norm, and many of them evolved under exceptionally innovative and competent leaders who took risks that would drive most general counsels (counsels general?) to drink. Maybe all public housing in the US could improve to be as good as our best. Maybe we could have what places like Germany, Hong Kong, Vienna, and Singapore have—plentiful, well-maintained public housing that serves a large portion of our people. But in the US, we have one political party that has consistently attacked public housing over the last century and another party that has consistently failed to protect necessary funding for public housing.

The BHA and HUD allowed Bromley-Heath to fall into disrepair after its racial integration in 1954. The BHA and City did not provide basic services to residents, including trash pickup, mail delivery, and security. The buildings themselves were denied basic maintenance, repairs, and replacements. At the same time, highway planners drafted plans to construct the new I-95 Southwest Corridor Expressway along the east side of Bromley-Heath. Bulldozers left a swath of destruction five hundred feet wide and miles long from Bromley-Heath to the other side of Columbus Avenue and all the way up to Boston City Hospital, where a crescent of demolished land that is now Melnea Cass Boulevard stretched east to I-93.

One of Boston's most celebrated protest movements stopped the Southwest Corridor and Inner Belt highway projects. Then, coalitions of residents, professionals, and politicians shocked the nation by successfully transferring the money Congress appropriated for the highway to instead build the new Orange Line subway that you just rode to Jackson Square. That vacant land became a battleground between Bromley-Heath's young people and the Academy Homes' young people.

ASSISTED HOUSING - ACADEMY HOMES

For the next stop on our tour, let's head back downhill towards Columbus Avenue. Passing the Jackson Square T, across a still-vacant lot demolished for the highway project, you see the Academy Homes. The Academy Homes look less conspicuous than Bromley-Heath. Squat four-story mid-century apartments line Columbus Avenue and rise along the hill into Roxbury, providing homes to 202 households. They exemplify a historic change in the United States' approach to affordable housing.

In the mid-twentieth century, the US shifted away from purely public housing towards models that mixed public and private institutions and funding. While public housing has government as owner, manager, developer, and funder, these newer models of subsidized housing split those roles. Typically, this housing has a private owner, which could be a for-profit business, a nonprofit organization, or even a religious congregation. The owner may manage this housing itself, or it may contract with a third-party property management firm. Private entities develop this housing, but they do so with funding and incentives from local, county, state, and/or federal governments.

Rather than develop the site themselves—as would have happened in the public housing era—the Boston Redevelopment Authority (BRA) selected the Building Services Employees International Union Local 254 to develop the Academy Homes under a nonprofit satellite company. Rather than being built with direct funding from the federal government—as would have happened in the public housing era—the Academy Homes depended on a more complex capital stack of subsidized debt products.[61]

Section 8 vouchers created the rental income stream with which Academy Homes operated and serviced these mortgage loans. *Section 8* refers to the part of the Housing Act of 1937 (42 USC § 1437f) that authorizes the federal government to pay rent directly to a low-income household's landlord on their behalf. The National Low Income Housing Coalition counts 133 active rental assistance programs in thirty-eight states and seventeen cities, but three out of four lack long-term, dedicated funding sources.[62] These programs tend to mirror the federal program, with additional local priorities and compliance rules.

The Section 8 program as we now know it followed President Nixon's moratorium on all existing federal housing programs in 1973. He was responding to criticisms about cost, profiteering, and slumlord practices in federal housing lending and subsidy programs by developers like Fred Trump.[63] During the moratorium, Congress and HUD considered options for restructuring federal housing programs towards our publicly subsidized, privately owned model.[64] The Housing and Community Development Act of 1974 further amended the US Housing Act of 1937 to create three sub-programs that assigned subsidies to New Construction, Substantial Rehabilitation, and Existing Housing, with a fourth added in 1978, the Moderate Rehabilitation Program. The Reagan administration added the tenant-based mobile voucher program in 1983, but it cut funding dramatically and ended all new construction and rehabilitation activities. Our housing infrastructure collapsed.

In 1970, there were 300,000 more low-cost rental homes (6.5 million) than low-income renter households (6.2 million) in our nation, but by 1985 there were 3.3 million *fewer* affordable homes than low-income renter households.[65] By 1985, the number of low-cost homes had fallen to 5.6 million, and the number of low-income renter households had grown to 8.9 million, a disparity of 3.3 million homes. This was the situation my mother had to navigate as a newly single mother searching for affordable housing in 1988.

Today, Section 8 rental assistance comes in two basic flavors: tenant-based vouchers (aka mobile, aka housing choice) and project-based (aka Housing Assistance Payment contract). Project-based vouchers stay with the building; tenant-based vouchers stay with the household.

Congress appropriates money to HUD to administer the tenant-based *Housing Choice Voucher* program. HUD distributes that funding by formula to local Section 8 administrators around the country. The local administrator—often a Public Housing Authority or state Housing Finance Agency—assigns the Housing Choice Voucher to a low-income household. That household must then find an apartment willing to accept the price HUD pays in their area and willing to go through the additional paperwork and inspections required by the program. Landlords can (and do) refuse to lease to Section 8 households. Even in the few cities and states with laws prohibiting discrimination based on source of income, some continue to break the law with implicit or explicit source of income discrimination against voucher holders.

Approximately 2.2 million of the 5.2 million households (42%) that receive Section 8 rental assistance receive it through a Housing Choice Voucher.[66] People who advocate market-based solutions to social problems and people who wish to deconcentrate poverty both find much to like in mobile vouchers. When redevelopment projects displaced public housing residents, housing authorities offered mobile vouchers, and social scientists learned much through the resulting natural experiment.[67] They can demonstrate improvements in health for the experiment's children but may indicate that changing socioeconomic class takes generations.

The other 3 million households utilizing Section 8 lease their homes from landlords who have a project-based Housing Assistance Payment (HAP) contract covering their apartments. To those households, these project-based vouchers operate similarly to the tenant-based ones, except if the household needs to move, the assistance does not move with them. The next qualifying low-income household to rent that apartment would receive the benefit of the HAP covering a portion of their rent. To owners, and especially to developers, the project-based voucher program provides a major advantage over the tenant-based one because lenders view project-based vouchers as less risky and are willing to underwrite a loan based on them, as with the Academy Homes.

In 1961, the BRA began preparing this fourteen-acre site for the Academy Homes when its former owners—the Sisters of Notre Dame—announced plans to move their school to a wealthy suburb. The BRA and its director, Ed Logue, selected the architect Carl Koch to design affordable housing on the site, ostensibly as a place for people the City had displaced in other urban renewal demolitions. Koch was a Harvard Graduate School of Design alum who studied under Walter Gropius and worked with Ed Logue on New Haven's Urban Renewal program. He's been called the "grandfather of prefab" for his use of simple, repetitive precast forms to reduce construction costs.

The 221(d)(3) loan from the US Housing Finance Agency paid for about two-thirds of the project's total cost. The City of Boston contributed nearly one-third from the sale of municipal bonds, which the Commonwealth of Massachusetts matched dollar for dollar with off-budget infrastructure development in and around the site. The state also provided tax exemptions for nonprofit organizations engaged in housing production to reduce costs. The BRA reduced costs and risks for the developer by purchasing the site and completing many site preparation tasks—including building streets—before officially selling the site to the selected developer.

The union sponsor and its contractor, the Development Corporation of America, built Academy Homes in five phases over four years using Carl Koch's own Spancrete prestressed concrete plank and wall parts that were made in factory and delivered to the site. Building Department staff and the on-site contractors had trouble working with this brand-new product. The architectural community loved the Spancrete concept, and Progressive Architecture highlighted the Academy Homes in its 1965 issue. But the Spancrete failed, and structural problems plagued the Academy Homes for decades.[68]

A local Community Development Corporation, Urban Edge, acquired and rehabilitated the Academy Homes in 1998. They addressed structural and social issues, and today Academy is a far nicer place to live than it was in the 1990s. Urban Edge's offices and two additional affordable housing developments of theirs are on the block just north of Academy Homes, across Columbus Avenue from where you walked the stairs up from the Orange Line T.

CDCS – LIHTC DEVELOPMENT

If you looked forward across Centre Street when you exited the Jackson Square T, you saw a Jamaica Plain Neighborhood Development Corporation (JPNDC) building. You may have overlooked it, not even noticing it's affordable housing. It looks like any other early twenty-first-century apartment building.

Community Development Corporations (CDCs) like JPNDC and Urban Edge are nonprofits that develop, own, and sometimes manage affordable housing, as well as take on other community initiatives like food programs, social services, economic development initiatives, neighborhood organizing, and more. They include community representatives on their boards, typically alongside civic leaders, bankers, funders, and architects. Boston was an early adopter of the CDC concept, and to this day, it has a higher concentration of CDCs than most cities have.

After decades of blight and crime following the Southwest Expressway demolitions, local groups created a plan to redevelop Jackson Square. In 2005, the Boston Redevelopment Authority designated the Jackson Square Partners (JPNDC, Urban Edge, The Community Builders, and Hyde Square Task Force) to redevelop the area. The two CDCs, JPNDC and Urban Edge, have completed several Low-Income Housing Tax Credit (LIHTC) developments around Jackson Square, including Jackson Commons, 25 Amory Street, 75 Amory Street, and 270 Centre Street.

Those four buildings are medium-sized buildings that blend with neighborhood context and are each home to a few dozen low-income households and neighborhood small businesses. They are typical examples of affordable housing built with the LIHTC program,

which has been the primary method for creating affordable housing in the US since Ronald Reagan's 1986 tax reform. The National Multifamily Housing Council estimates that the LIHTC program has partially financed more than 4 million affordable apartments.[69]

"In conventional real estate, investors buy cash flow. In affordable housing, investors buy tax shelter." That's how The Community Builders' director of finance, Tom Buonopane, once described it to me. When a for-profit developer explores the feasibility of a development prospect, they calculate how much revenue the project could potentially produce, how much it would cost, and whether it can provide enough of a profit to attract funders. If the project can't produce enough revenue to provide a good return on investment, it doesn't happen.

But that no-return scenario is where we start in affordable housing. Because the whole point is to hold down rents and prices, we know that our cash revenue will be insufficient to provide a return on investment. The LIHTC, similar tax credits, and certain provisions of the tax code attract private investors to affordable housing by providing a return on investment through reducing their tax liability. Instead of giving a taxpayer's dollar to build affordable housing, the IRS does not collect that dollar in the first place. Other tax credits that might be utilized in the same project as LIHTC include Brownfields tax credits (to pay a fraction of the cost of cleaning up old pollution), historic tax credits (to preserve historic buildings), state Low-Income Housing Tax Credits, solar tax credits, New Markets Tax Credits (to attract private finance to projects that create jobs in certain areas), and more.

Each year, the federal government allocates about $6 billion of Low-Income Housing Tax Credits to each state and territory, plus a couple large cities, according to population. Local *allocating agencies* add their own rules about which projects to prioritize. The affordable housing proposals that are awarded these credits partner with an equity investor, who earns a return from dollar-for-dollar credits off their federal taxes plus additional tax deductions for depreciation and accounting losses.

However, in the unlikely event the property fails, the IRS may recapture the value of those credits from the investor, who in turn would require the developer/owner to pay the investor back what they'd paid the IRS.

Most LIHTC properties are fully occupied and financially stable with extremely low foreclosure rates. The respondents to CohnReznick's survey reported a cumulative 0.57% foreclosure rate, including only one new foreclosure in 2020.[70] That is roughly one-eighth the rate of market multifamily loans currently not performing.[71]

The Low-Income Housing Tax Credit comes in two flavors. The 9% credit is the more lucrative and scarce of the two and is limited by the federal allocation to each state. The 4% credit is less lucrative, more often paired with permanent mortgage debt, and is limited by each state's tax-exempt bond borrowing capacity.

The typical LIHTC investor is a bank with CRA compliance needs. LIHTC investments also qualify for CRA credits. Besides the banks, life insurance companies and large corporations like Google or Microsoft also invest equity in the LIHTC market.

To qualify for LIHTC, developments must commit to keeping rents on 40% of their homes at an affordable level calculated as no more than 30% of 60% of the Area Median Income (AMI).* Households who move into these homes must fill out a tremendous amount of paperwork to be *income certified* and demonstrate conclusively that they earn less than the required AMI. In recent years,

---

* Alternately, keeping 20% of the homes affordable below 50% AMI also qualifies for LIHTC.

the IRS and allocating agencies also began allowing *income averaging* so that developments could offer homes to a broader diversity of income levels while keeping the average affordability below 60% AMI.

Project-based Section 8 vouchers combine well with LIHTC developments to allow new affordable housing built with the Low-Income Housing Tax Credit to serve poorer households. In some cases, the rent that HUD will pay for a Section 8 eligible household is higher than the LIHTC rents. The additional cash flow enables developers to leverage more debt financing to build or rehabilitate more homes, to ensure quality maintenance and operations, and to fund resident services. Some Section 8 administrators (like the Seattle Housing Authority) and state programs (like the Massachusetts Rental Voucher Program) cap the rent paid to affordable housing developments at the lower LIHTC rent. Paying less per affordable home allows them to subsidize more homes. It is a difficult balance. There is no right way to divide a pie that is simply too small.

As you may imagine, the complexity of the LIHTC program—I've been told section 42 is in fact the longest section of the United States tax code[72]—means that for every development there is a team of lawyers, accountants, and other skilled professionals navigating the complex legal structures, complex financial structures, complex accounting structures, and actual physical structures. In recent years, the complexity has increased alongside an increase in the number of participating funders each LIHTC project needs.[73] By some estimates, for every dollar of Low-Income Housing Tax Credit the federal government provides, only an average of $0.66 goes to building housing for low-income people. The rest goes to investor profits and the expense of additional legal and accounting services.

Despite its inefficiency, the LIHTC program has consistently produced the best quality, best-performing affordable housing for low-income people in our history of affordable housing efforts. It takes a village. A typical LIHTC development includes a private investor that stands to lose many millions of dollars should the project fall out of compliance or into disrepair. It may also have a permanent lender with a thirty- to forty-year mortgage on the property that stands to lose millions of dollars if the property begins performing poorly and cannot repay its loans. Anywhere from one or two to a dozen or more public or philanthropic agencies may provide subordinate debt, each with its own compliance mechanisms to hold the sponsor accountable should the project fall out of compliance or into disrepair.

By contrast, only one or two agencies had their eyes on traditional public housing: the local Public Housing Authority and the federal government through HUD. During the heyday of Section 8-based construction, those developments would have HUD, often a lender, and perhaps a city agency looking. Those developments were more vulnerable to bad actors, such as Fred Trump, because oversight and accountability were limited compared with LIHTC development.

LIHTC—like most market-based programs—has another major weakness. Its affordability restrictions are temporary. In a 2022 report, Freddie Mac found that LIHTC properties generally maintain their affordability restrictions for at least thirty years, but as the program ages and more properties near the end of their compliance periods, more are at risk. Performance so far gives some hope for affordability, as 86.8% of LIHTC properties remain in the program and subject to rent restrictions.[74]

The LIHTC buildings in Jackson Square look nicer and less conspicuous than Bromley-Heath or the Academy Homes. You might even overlook them as you begin to eye the line of Dominican restaurants up Centre Street, but you have another couple stops on your tour around Jackson Square and the history of affordable housing in the US before lunch.

225 CENTRE STREET – MIXED-INCOME/FINANCE/USE

225 Centre Street rises seven stories above Columbus Avenue, across from the Academy Homes and Urban Edge's developments and over the tracks from the Mildred Hailey public housing. It is a mixed-use, mixed-income, mixed-finance development that represented the cutting edge of community development finance when it was built in 2013.

Developers Bart Mitchell and Dave Traggorth and The Community Builders, Inc. wove several legal entities into this one building so that it could simultaneously utilize LIHTC equity, private equity, New Markets Tax Credits equity, Brownfields Tax Credit equity, and at least half a dozen hard and subordinate loans from public and quasi-public agencies. The lawyers who worked it out got mugs that featured the spiderweb legal organizational chart with a caption reading, "Can your lawyer close this?"

The developers undertook that boundary-pushing level of complexity to fulfill promises to the well-organized Jackson Square community's demands for this corner to include households making enough to afford market rents, households earning low incomes, and households exiting homelessness, as well as residential amenities, parking, and retail spaces built in hopes of leasing to a chain drugstore, a local restaurant, and a local café—if possible. Additionally, the development mixed its various income levels within the building so that each floor included some of everybody.

In the late twentieth century, scholars across the political spectrum—from Charles Murray to Robert Putnam to William Julius Wilson—converged on a shared conclusion that proximity to upper-class white people is very important for escaping poverty in the US. From the Clinton administration onwards, the US charged affordable housing professionals with creating the neighborhoods where different classes of people could live in harmony, spreading social capital like apple seeds.

Early advocates recommended mixing incomes to avoid or reduce concentrated poverty in subsidized housing and to potentially give poor families access to safer neighborhoods, better schools, and more employment opportunities. They also saw it as a way to reduce subsidy costs (by shifting some costs to market units) and to promote better design and management (to attract and retain market-rate tenants). Since the tax reforms of 1986, it has also been seen as a way to bring *market discipline* to project planning and financing. Proponents also cite its potential to reduce opposition to affordable housing in low-poverty areas and suburban communities, as local officials and residents appear to prefer it as a social and fiscal model.

Overall, there is broad agreement in the literature that while there is little hard data on the benefits of mixed-income housing, it appears to be a useful vehicle for producing high-quality, well-managed housing. At the same time, there is agreement that the social and real estate benefits can also be realized in developments that do not include market-rate units so long as they include working households and are adequately funded and well managed. It also suggests that income mixing itself has limited power to provide upwards economic mobility. Finally, there is general agreement that the policies that promote mixed-income housing must include safeguards to ensure that government will continue to address the housing needs of the most troubled and disadvantaged households, as well as households who do not wish to move to low-poverty areas.[75]

Conceptually, there are only a handful of situations in which we can build mixed-income communities. We can try to convince wealthier neighborhoods to accept poorer neighbors, or we can preserve affordability for poor people in gentrifying neighborhoods like Jackson Square. We can also try to do it all in one development—like 225 Centre Street. That is often the politically feasible compromise.

In practice, there are a few ways to develop mixed-income properties. If affordable homes and market-rate homes are allowed to be built in separate buildings, the financial structuring is straightforward. One building can be built with private market equity and include some small portion of affordability based on the space between the construction rent and the market rent. Another building can be built with LIHTC equity and potentially still include a few market-rate homes outside of qualified basis.

But if the income mixing is expected to be within one building and expected to have relatively equal amounts of affordable and market-rate housing, find a talented lawyer. Market equity and tax credit equity are fundamentally incompatible. In one, the equity owner expects to profit from cash flows and sale after eight to ten years. In the other, the equity owner expects to profit from tax credits and tax-deductible losses over a fifteen-year compliance period. They cannot own the same property. They are oil and water.

How can investors define the portion of the property they own? Structurally separate buildings? Separately entered parts of the same structure? A collection of individual homes? Ultimately, local laws and regulations tend to dictate how finely grained income mixing can be achieved. Additional permitting, accounting, and legal work apply at each step, from fee simple titles to subdivisions to legally separating parts of the same building by structure, floor, or unit into condominiums. Some jurisdictions do not allow for so-called checkerboard condominiums like 225 Centre—where alternating units are owned by separate legal entities.

To actually achieve integration, we must keep in mind that future residents of these developments are people too. Where do you encounter your neighbors? Your hallway? Courtyard? Sidewalk? School? Gym? Local events? The pub? Church? Did I just repeat myself? Are there more opportunities for positive encounters like parties, happy hours, cookouts, classes, programs, gardening, snow shoveling, etc.? Or are there more opportunities for negative encounters like the dirty garbage room, the dreary laundry room, a tiny mailroom, snow shoveling, etc.? Well-designed, intentionally diverse, and connected communities depend on asking those questions of every segment of the potential resident population, and then designing places, running events, and setting rules in ways that are attractive to each group you expect to live there.

125 AMORY STREET – PUBLIC HOUSING REDEVELOPMENT

Just a block or so farther from the Jackson Square T stop, the 125 Amory Street Development represents the latest trend in the preservation of public housing.[76] Congress does not appropriate enough money to keep public housing in good repair, and our need for new homes far outstrips available resources. So public housing authorities have been finding ways to leverage what resources they have through joint ventures with private nonprofit organizations and for-profit businesses to preserve and create homes. For the Boston Housing Authority and many like it, the resource they have is underutilized land.

At 125 Amory, the BHA partnered with the area's two local Community Development Corporations and a national nonprofit housing developer to create new homes on the site's vast surface parking lots while also preserving the building's existing 199 residences for low-income seniors and people with disabilities.

The Community Builders, Inc., Urban Edge, and JPNDC are currently seven years into redevelopment with a long community process, several phases of development led by different partners, and many years of competitive funding rounds for Low-Income Housing Tax Credits and state and local subordinate loans. Within a few years, they will have created 305 new homes at various levels of affordability, preserved and modernized the existing senior housing tower for its existing tenants without displacement, introduced the latest in sustainable construction techniques to both, created this safe and attractive path to the T stop you are now walking from, and kept 208 automobile parking spaces to boot. The BHA maintains ownership of the land, and the ground lease payments from the new buildings provide funding for the BHA to renovate their existing building. But why should it all be so complicated and so slow?

The question of how to redevelop, fix, and/or eliminate public housing dominated affordable housing in the 1990s and 2000s. Some redevelopments were successful. Some were not. I recommend Professor Larry Vale's excellent series on public housing for highly detailed history and insightful commentary on public housing redevelopment. Once again, professionals, architects, planners, politicians, sociologists, and researchers of all kinds focused on the questions: What was wrong with these people and/or buildings? Who is deserving of help and how much? What is the proper mix of owners and renters, mix of income groups, and mix of household sizes? Which architectural strategies confer safety or community?

Which strict enforcement policies can evict the undeserving or dis-ruptive?

Three hundred years of experimenting with answers to those questions have not led to radical new answers. Each time an exper-iment or tactic fell short, a new round of social investigations arose to focus on how to fix poor people and how to split scarce resources among various classes of poor people, who, of course, must be pre-cisely defined through exhaustive research. It doesn't matter which way you serve it; a small pizza will still leave everyone hungry.

Tougher on crime politics coalesced with a new consensus on deconcentrating poverty and income mixing to create the HOPE VI program during President Clinton's administration. The program modeled the success of the BHA's redevelopment of its highly dis-tressed Columbia Point projects. The BHA and its private partner Corcoran Jennison transformed a place once notorious for having one road in and one road out that ambulances would refuse to enter into a more desirable waterfront neighborhood, primarily of market-rate households, with a portion that is affordable.

HUD awarded its first pilot grant for this strategy in 1992 to the Atlanta Housing Authority to redevelop Centennial Place. From 1992 to 2005, the government spent nearly $6 billion on HOPE VI developments that demolished or rehabilitated "distressed" public housing; added new infrastructure; broke up poorly executed super-block experiments; disposed of sites to for- and nonprofit private developers and owners to leverage the Low Income Housing Tax Credit and subsidized debt programs; built new, lower-density hous-ing reserved for people at a mix of incomes, including homes for sale; and funded several years of robust resident service programs. Tragi-cally, the program did not require one-to-one replacement of public housing apartments. Only 14%, about one in seven households, were able to return to HOPE VI redeveloped public housing.[77]

THE SWEET

Some HOPE VI developments are considered highly successful. They are neighborhoods where people are proud to live. Others are despised for having displaced poor people, spending scarce dollars to provide less housing to higher-income households than before. Twenty-some years on, the pastel-painted, low-density townhomes emblematic of HOPE VI redevelopments are as symbolic of public housing as the red brick high-rises they replaced. The low-density approach fell out of favor in growing cities, such as Seattle where three generally successful HOPE VI redevelopments favored townhomes, but the redevelopment of the Yesler public housing neighborhood is adding density. The mixing approach failed in HOPE VI developments in struggling markets like Chicago's South Side or Hartford, Connecticut, where empty lots still mark spots reserved for middle-class homeowners that never materialized.

President George W. Bush wanted to end the HOPE VI program, and Congress obligingly reduced its funding. President Obama later provided $120 million to HOPE VI in 2009 before shifting to a successor program called Choice Neighborhoods. Choice Neighborhoods attempted to redevelop distressed public and federally assisted (like Section 8) housing while avoiding some of the HOPE VI program's failings.

Choice Neighborhoods required one-to-one replacement of the original low-income homes plus the addition of moderate- and middle-income homes. It required the developers applying for funds to also evaluate non-housing problems such as public health, education, employment, crime, transportation, and food access. They had to partner with community groups, local government, and federal agencies to attempt to address those non-housing issues as part of the redevelopment. The program prioritized redevelopments that also included new nonresidential space to give residents better access to food, goods, and services. The Obama administration directed other federal agencies to establish sister programs (such as the Department of Education's Promise Neighborhoods and the Department of Justice's Byrne grants), and they encouraged local communities and developers to layer and coordinate all these disparate resources. Choice Neighborhoods brought loftier goals based on better information but with only a small fraction of HOPE VI's funding. Neither was available for this 125 Amory redevelopment.

The redevelopment you see happening on Amory Street required the creativity and resources of the BHA and dozens of funders and developers besides. In the absence of a real public commitment, we use what we got to get what we need.

TRIPLE-DECKERS –
CHEAP HOUSING AND REDLINING

All right, all right, we'll get back to the heart of Jackson Square and get that Dominican food you wanted before putting you back on the T. On the way, check out all these nice triple-deckers. Huh? Yes, some people do call them three-deckers. Dunks/Dunkies; tomáto/ tomâto.

These blocky, three-story wooden buildings with full-size decks in the front and back, standing mere feet from each other, are emblematic of urban New England, especially Boston. They're our version of Shenzhen's urban villages. Generations of immigrants, newcomers, townies, and students found homes in these triple-deckers. Much like the row houses of Mid-Atlantic cities or the six-flats of Midwestern ones, private developers built these relatively affordable homes for the influx of new workers arriving from the 1880s to 1930 or so.

As described in Sam Bass Warner's foundational urban planning text, *Streetcar Suburbs*, these developments accompanied rapid transit expansions.[78] Cities provided some combination of land, funding, and licenses to corporations to build rail extensions. Then, that transportation developer could build homes and/or sell land along the new line. The new public transit enabled many more people to live in these neighborhoods. That density in turn enabled housing development for these potential residents to become feasible at a much lower price point.

Triple-deckers were also renowned for the affordable homeownership opportunities they once provided to working-class families and immigrants. A more established family could afford a loan to purchase the triple-decker to live in by renting out its other two apartments, often to relations from the old country. Grandmy's parents fit this common story from their hats to their shoes, and they did it just three stops down the Orange Line from Jackson Square here, in the Forest Hills neighborhood, though it starts farther up the line.

Dances at Hibernian Hall in Roxbury must have been a rare escape from Mary's work as a household maid in Beacon Hill. Hibernian Hall was at the time a heart of Boston's Irish community, the place to go for recent immigrants to build community. That dance changed her life on the night she met Thomas Meehan. They were two Irish immigrants, both single and passing thirty, and they would spend the rest of their lives together.

Eighty-some years after that night, I would intern for Madison Park Development Corporation in Hibernian Hall. I celebrated retirements and birthdays in the top-floor ballroom at Hibernian Hall. I drank enough complementary Hennessy Black during the Roxbury Film Festival kickoff at Hibernian Hall that I did not drink Hennessy for fourteen years afterwards. What memories did my great-grandparents have in that same building? Did they walk to

Dudley Station and ride the El back downtown together? Did they hold hands?

Grandmy's father, Thomas Joseph Meehan, was baptized at the newly built Church of the Immaculate Conception in Curry, Achonry Parish, County Sligo on May 24, 1898. His parents spoke both English and Irish, as about half of the people left in Achonry did. His family were tenant farmers, like 70% of their neighbors. They practiced Ireland's native oral culture, being illiterate themselves. They and their parents and their grandparents lived their entire lives in Achonry Parish. Their ancestors lived and died there since time immemorial, in the northern reaches of Connacht at the headlands of the River Mhuaidh with its formerly abundant salmon runs. They survived foreign occupation and two genocidal famines.

So why did their children leave?

Terence O'Rorke published a detailed and comprehensive *History of Sligo: Town and County* in 1900, when Thomas was a toddler. According to O'Rorke, "flatness, poverty, and barren soil" defined Thomas's hometown, Curry. There were hardly any trees left, the grass could not support livestock, and potatoes were still the only root crops grown, five decades after *An Gorta Mór*.[79] Curry is the anglicization of Curraigh, which is an Irish word for swamp.

Our Meehans and their neighbors paid oppressive rents to one Colonel Cooper. His right to collect that rent began in blood. After conquering Connacht, the English granted most of the land in Curry to a Lord Collooney and his agent Jeremy Jones. English and Scottish settlers led a post-war population rebound in the more desirable parts of County Sligo, but Cromwell's 1659 census listed only twenty-six people—all Irish—left in Curry after his conquest.

O'Rorke wrote in 1900 that "the aim of the State, during the period, being to aggrandize the few—the descendants of Cromwell's settlers—at the cost of the many—the mass of the people; and the

173

means employed for the accomplishment of this gigantic injustice being, first, the sword, and, after the disuse of the sword, the law, and the tyranny practised under the law, by Cromwellian landlords." The laws the British passed and their practices in Ireland were prologue to the system we have in the United States today.

On the other side of County Sligo from the Meehan's, Sligo Town had grown into one of Ireland's most important ports. From 1834, shipping companies advertised "reduced rates of passage money to the United States and British America by way of Liverpool, with free passage to that port." Thousands were sailing. Thomas took that discount ticket via Liverpool, where, according to Grandmy, he worked a short stint in the mines before leaving for the US. He spent eight days on a ship called the Celtic before arriving at Ellis Island on July 8, 1923. He eventually made his way to Boston's South End, where he lived in a boarding house at 86 West Springfield Street and labored on a wharf nearby in Boston's now-filled South Bay. That is, until he met Mary Jane at Hibernian Hall in Roxbury.

After marrying, the young(ish) couple, Thomas and Mary, rented an apartment in Jamaica Plain's Blessed Sacrament Parish. Sadly, it was infested with bed bugs, and they were forced to burn all their possessions that first year. They moved in with Mary's Aunt Delia in her triple-decker—this is a song about triple-deckers—nearby at 43 Wachusett Street in Forest Hills, a growing streetcar suburb cradled between the Arnold Arboretum and the Forest Hills Cemetery. The home was newly built. The seller had developed it for his wife and family, but his wife died suddenly just six months before the building's completion. Mary's Aunt Delia bought the home through a connection, and she lived on the ground floor.

Thomas and Mary raised their four children there on Wachusett Street. She kept house while he worked maintenance for a building in Copley Square, then for a building at the Harvard Medical School until his retirement. The Meehans all lived in the first-floor apartment until their second child got older, and they moved upstairs to the second-floor apartment. They enclosed the front porch, and that's where the boys, Thomas Jr. and John, slept. Grandmy and her older sister, Alice, shared a three-quarters-size bed in a room with their mother's Aunt Delia Farrell until she died. They laid the body to wake at home in the parlor, just before Thanksgiving. "That's when I first smoked," Grandmy told me. "The undertakers placed cigarettes all around the parlor for the wake. Old Golds. I took a bunch. Afterwards, I'd take a cigarette and smoke in the bathroom with the window open, waving a towel to try to push the smoke out." She remembers she was fourteen years old because, "my mother had the first heart attack when I was thirteen."

Thomas Meehan survived his wife until 1979, when he passed an ocean away from his birthplace and ancestors, having never seen Ireland again. Grandmy's sister sold their old triple-decker home for $23,000 ($99,000 inflated to 2025 dollars). Did redlining contribute to this low price, about the same they had purchased it for four decades earlier? It's impossible to know for certain. But, yes. Yes, it did.

In 1937, the federal government, through the Home Owner's Loan Corporation (HOLC), described the Forest Hills area as "Grade 3: Definitely Declining" due to the "threatening encroachment of lower class occupants. Very congested." If that weren't bad enough, the people drawing the redlining maps wanted potential home lenders to know that the "foreign element is concentrated in the poorer properties north of Henly playground to Forest Hills station,"[80] which is where my family, the Meehans, lived. I like to tell Grandmy that she's a lower-class foreign element.

Residents and owners in places with low grades from HOLC, red or yellow on their maps, could not access financing to purchase or rehabilitate their homes. Or, if they were able to, they often fell victim to extractive schemes like contract purchases or usurious interest rate loans. This "redlining" is responsible for a major share of the racial wealth gap in the US, having ensured poor people and people of color would lose money in housing while white and suburban people reaped large profits on real estate with government-subsidized loans.[81]

But these triple-deckers you see here, they no longer serve Boston's new, working-class families. The next Meehans are unlikely to live in such a great location. Gentrification has put these triple-deckers out of reach, even for college-educated professionals.

Let's use the Meehans' place to consider the massive change. That Wachusett Street triple-decker most recently sold as three different condos for $640,000 in 2023 (#2), $435,000 in 2017 (#1), and $226,000 in 2002 (#3). Redfin estimated each condo would sell for over $650,000 in 2023. There's quite a gap between $23,000 and $1,950,000, but it says more about Boston's housing crisis than it does about Aunt Alice's real estate acumen.

In 1985, the City of Boston assessed the entire triple-decker at $50,600, plus $9,200 for the land, more than double the Meehans' sale price just six years earlier. It next sold in 2001 to a purchaser who converted the building to three individual condos. The condos sold for about $150,000 each, many times larger than 1979's price and yet a tiny fraction of 2023's. The exponential increase in price coincided with a proliferation of exclusionary zoning laws in Massachusetts and with Boston's economic rebirth as a financial, educational, and medical hub. Richard B. Freeman and Brian Hall accurately predicted the consequences of job growth exceeding housing growth in the National Bureau of Economic Research's "Permanent Homelessness in America?"[82] published when I was four years old, the year we first lost our home.

This story repeated all over Boston until the region lost huge swaths of once affordable housing. That is the risk that unregulated, so-called naturally occurring affordable housing poses, from trailer parks to triple-deckers. They can be taken away from the poor and working classes without much process or notice.

And we'll end our long-winded tour of this small neighborhood there, at the affordability crisis displacing millions of Americans in the present day. Enjoy the Dominican restaurant while they can still afford the retail rent. Ponder the absurdity of severe gentrification pressure in a neighborhood with thousands of low-income homes in public, assisted, and LIHTC housing, old and new. Pray the Orange Line gets you back downtown without derailing or catching on fire. I've got to get back to my job on the Campaign to Protect the Affordable Housing Law.

TWELVE

40B Campaign: Value Capture and Incentives

Whenever someone asked me where I was from, I could say Randolph, and then I would have to explain that it's a suburb, but that its demographics and problems were what everyone called "urban" at the time. What was Randolph really? By the time my last semester at MIT came around, I'd already earned enough credits to graduate and focused my thesis on exploring that question.

I coined Randolph Boston's "Gateway Suburb" and compared it to places like Upper Darby, Pennsylvania; Prince George's County, Maryland; Tukwila, Washington; and New Rochelle, New York. Not long after, Missouri gave me much easier shorthand to explain Randolph.

A *Boston Globe* reporter writing a "could it happen here?" story found my thesis online and called to ask whether Randolph was the Ferguson of Boston. My pride wanted to answer first, "That couldn't happen here! Surely, we are better than that!" And then I remembered our drug-dealing DARE officer who beat up teenagers in the Burger King parking lot. I remembered the Randolph Police who responded to a drive-by shooting by stopping the wrong Black man in an SUV of the wrong description. He turned out to be a Boston police officer himself, which shielded him from further consequences but not from the initial detention and humiliation. Now, when asked, I sometimes just say, "Randolph is like the Ferguson of Boston."

But before I'd even finished that thesis, I'd started a job. We were deep in the Great Recession, and there were not many jobs to be had, especially in housing. Although I'd gone to grad school in part to leave organizing, I enthusiastically told Karen Weiner and Aaron Gornstein *yes* when they offered me a job as the field director for the Campaign to Protect the Affordable Housing Law.

The Affordable Housing Law, Chapter 40B, is an older vintage of a genre of *value capture* policies. These policies, like inclusionary zoning requirements and linkage payments, attempt to induce the private sector to build affordable housing through requirements and incentives.

In 1969, in the wake of the civil rights movement, Massachusetts had passed Chapter 40B to manage bad actors who had begun abusing local zoning codes to keep all but the wealthiest out of their towns.[83] The law did two things. First, it set a goal for 10% of the homes in every municipality to be deed-restricted affordable housing.* Second, it established a *comprehensive permit* process that is simpler, faster, and more open to productive negotiation than the gauntlet of local approvals might otherwise be. If the local Zoning Board of Appeals rejects a qualified development proposal for no justifiable reason, *and* if that naysaying town hasn't met the 10%

---

* Towns with mobile home communities and cheap housing opposed the "restricted" part of that definition. The gentrification and displacement of the last couple decades demonstrates the danger in relying too much on unrestricted housing.

affordability threshold, *and* if that town hasn't even approved a plan to work *towards* the 10% goal, *then* the developer can appeal to the state. The state can overrule the local decision, unless the proposed development presents unmitigated health or safety concerns.

Between 1970 and 2009, Massachusetts used Chapter 40B to produce over 60,000 homes, of which 32,500 were affordable and 18,000 were homes for sale. Thirty-five of those new homes were in the Bittersweet Lane Apartments where I grew up. Randolph became spectacularly diverse in large part because its land use policies were less exclusionary than most Massachusetts towns. Public policy and my personal life joined up again.

Over the years, a few developers angered communities with inconsiderate development proposals. These bad proposals typically died on the vine. Nevertheless, 40B's passionate opponents collected enough signatures to put a repeal of the law on the 2010 ballot.

If the repeal succeeded, affordable housing construction would halt in most areas of the state. The law is responsible for about 80% of the rental housing and 80% of the affordable housing built in suburban and rural Massachusetts towns. One-half century in, a depressingly small number of Massachusetts towns have met the law's affordability targets. As of 2023, only 71 of the 351 municipalities in Massachusetts had met the 10% affordability goal, six fewer than in 2020.[84]

Back in 2010, there were approximately twelve thousand homes in the development pipeline that the ballot question could kill. The Commonwealth would have lost an estimated $10 billion in economic activity and thousands of related jobs. The next generation of children would not have the same opportunity I had, nor would retiring seniors, newly single parents, or returning veterans have opportunities to stay in their home communities. These were high stakes.

The campaign committee hired Megan Amundson, a seasoned environmental advocate, to be the campaign manager. I worked under her as the field director. We hired seven regional organizers, two support staff, and some energetic interns to pull together a statewide, nonpartisan coalition to oppose the repeal effort.

Before joining the campaign, I was doubtful that the repeal effort could be stopped. Scott "Foamy Stout" Brown* had just upset Massachusetts's Democrats, winning a special election for Senate after the passing of Senator Ted Kennedy. Then, the Republican Tea Party movement turned the November 2010 election into an ugly backlash election following President Obama's 2008 victory. Conventional wisdom held that Chapter 40B was wildly unpopular and that its opponents were the same constituencies who put Scott Brown in the Senate. The truth was that most voters had no idea what the law was or why it might be important to their lives.

Opportunities to educate and convince voters were limited because Massachusetts ballots were the most crowded they had been in decades. Voters were tasked with sorting out a four-way race for governor, competitive races for three other statewide offices, an open congressional seat, viable challengers in several additional congressional districts, the highest number of seriously contested races for the state legislature in memory, and two tax-related ballot questions besides the affordable housing repeal. Voters and the media have short attention spans, and November 2010 was legitimately a lot. The crowded political space also limited our resources as donors focused elsewhere. How would we be able to educate voters on a complicated issue, dispel the myths spread by proponents of repeal, and win over skeptical voters?

---

* See Chapter 1.

We focused our campaign on messaging and coalition building. We spread a simple message, "Protect *the* Affordable Housing Law for our seniors and working families." We succeeded in building the largest and most diverse coalition to ever come together in support of affordable housing in Massachusetts. More than 1,600 supporters signed on. Our coalition included civic, business, labor, and municipal leaders as well as elder, environmental, civil rights, human services, and housing groups across the Commonwealth. More than two hundred religious leaders joined in an interfaith statement of support. We earned endorsements from all four gubernatorial candidates, Democrat, Republican, Green, and Libertarian. After driving all over the state, my messy car demonstrated the proof of our campaign's nonpartisanship—empty coffee cups from Dunkin' Donuts, Starbucks, Marylou's, and Flat Black.

We couldn't afford to hire enough organizers to cover the entire state. With each new hire, I took a region off my own plate until my staff covered all the areas where we expected support. I left myself to cover forums and meetings in hostile parts of the state. I also kept Cape Cod, where the well-organized local affordable housing community ensured we would run up the vote in Barnstable County.

One cold autumn night, I attended a forum on our ballot question in a well-off seaside town. The organizers invited seven proponents of the repeal and just one affordable housing advocate, Aaron Gornstein. Local voters packed the library to standing room only.

It was not going well. The panel ganged up on Aaron. During Q&A, I used my personal experience for the first time during the campaign. I dropped my code-switched standard English for my natural Boston accent, and I asked what would happen to the next kid like me: "The affordable housing I grew up in was built with the Affordable Housing Law. Because of that, we were able to stay in our town even after my mother found herself alone to raise two boys. I got to grow up near my grandparents and family. A few months ago, I earned a Master's in City Planning from MIT, and my brother is serving in the 82nd Airborne. How can we make sure the next kid has the opportunities that we got?" I can't recall anyone's answer, but my question shifted the tone of the room. Stories and feelings can do things data and reason can't.

After the forum, our small team worked the crowd and then met up to go over the night. Karen Wiener told me she overheard some older women talking outside say, "Well, I was wholly against 40B until that nice young boy who grew up here spoke and changed my mind."

I most definitely did not grow up in that well-off town, and me being nice is debatable, but I was happy to take the win. I became more practiced at sharing my story and trying to get skeptical local leaders to see their own people through the story of mine. No doubt it helped that I am white and well educated, with an appearance that had made my great-aunts exclaim, "Well, isn't that just the map of Ireland upon his face!"

We turned the ballot question into a referendum on affordable housing, which turned out to be very important to Massachusetts voters after all. By its nature, news coverage skews towards the unusual and controversial. The opposition to 40B, shown through years of press articles about developers vs. current homeowners, turned out to not reflect the true sentiment of most Massachusetts voters. We won with 58% of the vote and earned majorities in 80% of the state's cities and towns. We won the ability to keep playing the game as it was, doing what we could do to create affordable housing in an extremely challenging environment.

THIRTEEN

TCB and the Development Cycle

I caught the break of my career when a former professor and a classmate each recommended me to Willie Jones at The Community Builders (TCB). Willie and I hit it off during my job interview, and he thought I would be a good fit for a new position funded with a $78.2 million grant award from HUD. The Obama administration funded the Neighborhood Stabilization Program (NSP2) through the American Recovery and Reinvestment Act (ARRA) stimulus to address the foreclosure crisis. Many of my MIT classmates who graduated into the recession also found jobs funded in one way or another by the stimulus. (Thanks, Obama!)

In that first role with TCB, I helped in the creation and management of a revolving loan fund capitalized with the NSP2 dollars. The goal was to preserve multifamily buildings or create new affordable housing in neighborhoods struggling with foreclosures and vacancy. That role gave me insights into how affordable housing development worked across all its phases, all its development types, and fifteen different states. The affordable housing communities in all those places felt familiar to me, different from Bittersweet Lane only by degrees.

This on-the-job education bridged my transition from grad student to developer and helped me into the forest and trees, broad and deep perspective that our work demands. I began to develop an understanding of the fundamentals of our system while also working through its detailed little tasks.

Remember, the fundamentals are place, permissions, and resources. We need a place to build, the permissions to build there, and the resources to direct materials and labor. The development process is the pursuit of those three fundamentals. The work moves in a cycle that I like to break down into ten phases:

1. Prospecting
2. Due diligence
3. Predevelopment
4. Closing
5. Construction
6. Lease up or sales
7. Conversion
8. Property management
9. Resident services
10. Preservation

Developers locate potential sites during the *prospecting* phase. During *due diligence*, we pursue preliminary answers to the questions: Is the site buildable? How much of what is allowed to be built on the site? Are the resulting possible development concepts financially feasible?

With good answers to those questions, we move into the *predevelopment* phase. The developer acquires legal development rights for the site; collaborates with communities and public agencies to shape the development into something they will approve; hires the necessary design, construction, and other specialists needed to develop construction plans; and achieves commitments of loans, equity investments, and subsidies to pay the total development cost (TDC) of the project.

Predevelopment shifts into *closing* mode once all the above have been achieved. All participants establish binding legal certainty in the development plan such that the lenders, investors, and public agencies are allowed to release the money that will allow the developer to begin *construction*.

Multifamily residential *construction* typically lasts twelve to thirty months depending on the project's size and complexity. As construction nears completion, the *lease-up* (or sales) phase begins with marketing and income certifications. After property management qualifies the residents and they move in, the property can be said to have "stabilized" when income exceeds expenses. An affordable housing developer can then complete *conversion* after the property is built and operating as promised. That is when funders release the final dollars, and the developer pays off its construction loan. At this point, firms finish transferring responsibility for the property from a development team to asset management and *property management* teams, which often include *resident services* as well.

Like all of us, buildings age. Over time, a *preservation* transaction will be necessary to keep the building in good operation and maintain its affordability restrictions. That preservation work begins the development cycle over again.

This long, complex process isn't easier for smaller projects than large. Ed Logue reshaped large swaths of Boston, New Haven, and New York City, but stated, "Nothing I've done was as difficult as building those two goddamn houses on Charlotte Street" in New Haven.[85]

At work, we rarely get to experience this cycle linearly. I'd usually have one or two prospecting assignments, one development in closing or construction, and a fourth finishing up at any given time.

PROSPECTING

In 2014, the Pine Street Inn approached The Community Builders, Inc. to explore options for a site they owned in Boston's Egleston Square neighborhood. TCB assigned me to explore the site's potential. I truly enjoy the work of helping communities create real estate. Development dreams are just a glimmer in the eye during the prospecting phase. It's the fun part for me. The job is to imagine what could be and then try to make it happen.

Real estate jargon discusses two general prospecting styles, "a use looking for a site" and "a site looking for a use." The "use looking for a site" business plan is more common among private sector developers who have a specific type of product for which one location is interchangeable with another. These developers search out sites with the best combination of low land prices, high rents, and future marketability.

By contrast, most nonprofit affordable housing developers follow the "site looking for a use" business model. We most often partner in some way with a local community that wants to transform a site in their neighborhood into affordable housing.

I like to visit a site on foot first. I took the Orange Line to the Stony Brook stop, a good eight blocks northwest of the site. Before the 1980s, I could have taken the Orange Line directly to Egleston Square, back when the trains ran along an elevated railway above Washington Street from Chinatown all the way to Forest Hills. After activists stopped the Southwest Expressway that would have run along the Bromley-Heath public housing community, the activists further succeeded by getting a new Orange Line subway built with the old highway money. Losing the El allowed Washington Street to see the sun again but took away its rapid transit.

The Pine Street Inn is Massachusetts's largest and best-known homeless shelter, primarily serving single men. Their main shelter occupies an entire city block in Boston's South End. It's a Boston landmark, a replica of a Sienese tower, visible from I-93 traffic. Fire-fighters used to practice jumping from its tower into a net below.[86] The Pine Street Inn bought the building when it was vacant and misused, just like its Dover Street skid row neighbors. However, times have changed in that corner of the world. As of June 2023, the building across East Berkeley Street (formerly Dover Street) from the shelter offered studio apartments for rent from $3,265 per month, $6.29 per square foot.[87]

Pine Street Inn repeated the strategy in Egleston Square. They purchased the site there back during deindustrialization and used it as a warehouse, office space, and woodworking social venture. Ending homelessness being their mission and all, Pine Street's dream for the site was to replace the existing building with a taller, mixed-use development with apartments for people exiting homelessness above space for Pine Street offices and social ventures.

During my walk in 2014, the obvious signs of gentrification—remodeled triple-deckers, expensive coffee, and oblivious suburban types—had just barely crossed the Orange Line tracks from Pond-side Jamaica Plain. As I walked closer to Washington Street, worn buildings, Latin music, street life, and the smell of Dominican food signified the last ungentrified corner of Jamaica Plain. The site deserved better than its nondescript warehouse with disruptive, difficult truck access.

I walked around the property. I took a note of the steep slope and the design opportunities and constraints it would bring. I looked at the neighboring lots; adding one of these little ones could make for a better development. Then, I went inside to find our partners from Pine Street, who toured me through the building. We could easily rule out building on top of the existing building due to its unworkable structure and footprint. So we had a blank—if constrained—canvas on which to work. During the visit, Pine Street gifted me a couple of the cutting boards made on-site by their clients at the Boston Handyworks social venture. I still use them.

Back in the office, I studied the zoning and drew some simple massing concepts, which is to say, I drew some boxes. From that, I could calculate roughly how many apartments an imagined building on the site could hold, and how much space could be provided for Pine Street's social ventures. My sophisticated wild-ass guess (SWAG) for prospecting purposes showed the site could house a couple hundred people currently experiencing homelessness with potential for some income mixing, plus provide the minimum of Pine Street's needs for parking and office/warehouse space. As is typical with affordable housing, the site would need quite a bit of subsidy to realize that vision, but not an unusual amount, and it might be able to use New Markets Tax Credits in addition to Low-Income Housing Tax Credits. That result was good enough to move this prospect forward and begin focusing on the partnership between the Pine Street Inn and TCB and then to begin conversations with the community.

When a site is looking for a use, it is in no way interchangeable with any other site. It is a unique and important place. I view prospecting as the stage where we create an idealized vision of a community's fondest ambitions for their neighborhood.

When I advise community groups and less experienced developers, I ask them to identify the two, maybe three, things on which they will not compromise. I advise them to hold those tightly but be willing to concede on everything else. We end up spending much of the rest of the development process compromising ideals to make the project feasible, to create real homes for real people.

Often, we affordable housing professionals do not get to close and finish construction on the developments that we ourselves prospected. The development process takes more years than most people spend in one job. I was in high school when TCB prospected the development that would eventually be the first project I got to manage, well after graduate school. Guess how long the Pine Street Inn Egleston Square site took! You will find the answer in a future chapter.

DUE DILIGENCE

I could hear the clacking of the Orange Line, the rolling thunder of the commuter rail, and the jet-like whoosh of the Amtrak trains as they passed outside my office window, but my mind was in Cincinnati. TCB was considering whether to purchase thirty-two of the worst buildings in that city. Fannie Mae had foreclosed on the New York–based landlord entity that had run this portfolio of housing into the ground while pocketing HUD subsidies. We had the potential to use our NSP2 funding to purchase the buildings out of foreclosure from Fannie Mae and preserve them for their residents. My Midwestern colleagues performed on-the-ground due diligence while I researched from my seat in Boston's South End.

Once a potential project has been identified, we pursue further feasibility questions in the due diligence phase. Is the site buildable? Are its size and dimensions sufficient? How much environmental contamination is on-site? Are the topography and soils structurally sound? What can we build there given its size and location? Does existing zoning allow for the necessary number of apartments, mix of uses, height, setbacks, parking, etc.? We answer these questions with the help of niche professionals such as a surveyor, licensed environmental professional, appraiser, title company, zoning attorney, and others.

In a preservation and rehabilitation project like this, we ask additional questions about the current state of the buildings and their residents. We order a capital needs assessment (CNA) to analyze and quantify just how much must be replaced or repaired to return the property to safe, modern standards. We perform hazardous materials assessments to identify any potentially dangerous contaminants from twentieth-century building materials, such as lead paint, PCB-laden caulking, leaking fuel tanks, or petroleum-soaked soil. We examine rent rolls and operating budgets to understand the financial position of the property and its residents. We hold resident meetings and surveys to understand from the residents—who, after all, know the property more intimately than anyone—what the community needs.

After purchasing this portfolio, our redevelopment plan expanded to neighborhood-scale improvements. We decided to apply for the Obama administration's new Choice Neighborhoods grant. Seven of those buildings TCB bought out of foreclosure were concentrated along Reading Road in Avondale, a chasm of vacancy and poverty resulting from decades of racism and disinvestment, sandwiched between famed institutions like the Cincinnati Children's Hospital, Xavier University, and the Cincinnati Zoo. We believed the Choice Neighborhoods grant would enable a partnership among community groups, churches, business owners, hospitals, schools, police, and TCB to rehabilitate those seven buildings, add new affordable housing serving a variety of incomes, increase fresh food access at corner stores, build a grocery store, address poor prenatal and childhood health, reduce crime, and improve life outcomes for our residents and their neighbors throughout Avondale. It was a tall order. I share two tragic anecdotes with you to demonstrate how bad the situation was for Avondale residents.

While I was writing up the application and my colleagues were doing the real and challenging work on the ground in Cincinnati, men shooting guns at each other outside one of the buildings killed a three-year-old child sitting on their stoop. That toddler died in front of their own home, a building address with the highest number of reported crimes in its police district, which in turn was the highest crime police district in Cincinnati, whose crime rate was in the top twenty-five of the United States' largest one hundred cities.

Avondale was a food desert. That was, sadly, not unusual. Avondale was also a *laundry* desert. None of our seven buildings had laundry machines, nor laundry rooms, nor laundry hookups in apartments. There was no laundromat in Avondale. If you lived there, you had to take one or two buses (depending on the schedule) out of the neighborhood to reach a laundromat. Or alternately, you could walk two miles, crossing Interstate Highway 71 with your clothes. Stop and ponder what your life would be like without access to laundry facilities.

From due diligence studies, we calculate the potential cost of a project, often with a rough dollars per square foot estimate plus any known special conditions such as adding laundry rooms. We put together a *building program* that sets out how many of which kinds of homes and other spaces we plan to build. We create a conceptual financial pro forma based on the emerging building program and design. We use that model to understand whether the project may qualify for competitive affordable housing resources and calculate whether the concept is financially feasible to build.

For Avondale, that required winning the federal Choice Neighborhoods grant, convincing HUD to agree to transfer project-based

Section 8 Housing Assistance Payment (HAP) contracts, winning Low-Income Housing Tax Credits, finding New Markets Tax Credits, leveraging debt, and garnering many local and state resources besides. After months and months of work, we assembled a team, finished the acquisition, and began securing these resources. After years and years of work, Avondale's redevelopment is ongoing. But those seven buildings have been rehabilitated, made energy efficient, and gained laundry rooms. TCB also built a brand new mixed-use development, adding homes and community-serving businesses. The Avondale CDC gave me a tour when I passed through Cincinnati years later, after I'd left TCB.

One important due diligence step is the title search. Title is the legal foundation for our entire real estate system. A clear title is proof that the entity that claims to own a property truly does so under the law and that it has the right to sell, mortgage, develop, use, or otherwise encumber the property. Title review is standard operating procedure for real estate transactions. No reasonable entity will lend or invest large sums of money to develop a piece of property without this proof of legal ownership. Lenders and investors also typically require developers to purchase title insurance, which would reimburse the policyholder in the rare event of a successful title claim.

Title review includes an examination of the property's chain of ownership to ensure no one else can make a claim on the property. Title review typically looks back as far as the property's last legal subdivision. Something we don't do in our day-to-day work is explore the origins of that chain of legal ownership, before the subdivision, before the incorporation. But this is a book, not a closing binder, so why not give it a try here?

FOURTEEN

Establishing Title: A Land Acknowledgment

My childhood home, the Bittersweet Lane Apartments, was built on the traditional lands of the
Massachusett people, just . . . not their best land. The better lands
were up the hill, in the river valley, or on the coast. The Bittersweet
Lane site was near the corner of two paths through a large cedar
swamp in the southern reach of Massachusett lands. The Cochato
people lived not far to the east, sharing their name with the Cochato
River that now forms the Town of Randolph's eastern boundary.
The Wampanoag peoples to the south likely also had influence over
the area. Massachusett and Wampanoag travelers probably passed
through what is now Randolph regularly, just as South Coast residents traveling Route 24 to Boston still do today.

Before the arrival of the English, the local Massachusett people
lived part of the year in summer homes along their eastern waters
and bays, where they feasted on seafood. During cold seasons, they
lived in their inland homes in Massawachusett, the Blue Hills,
which provided rich hunting grounds, granite quarries, berries, and
freshwater fishing. In between the two, the Massachusett farmed

large fields of corn, beans, and squash in the Neponset River valley, covering much of what is now Dorchester and North Quincy. The area's abundant and diverse natural resources sustained the people who stewarded them from time immemorial. Friendly settlers favorably compared the Massachusett way of life to English lords with their summer homes. By contrast, successful settlers used the Massachusett's seasonal moves as evidence that the natives were itinerant savages with no claim to their land.

According to early settler Thomas Morton, the natives built houses "much like the wild Irish; they gather Poles in the woodes and put the great end of them in the ground, placinge them in forme of a circle or circumference, and, bendinge the topps of them in forme of an Arch, they bind them together with the Barke of Walnut trees, which is wondrous stuff, so that they make the same round on the Topp for the smoke of their fire to ascend and pass through."[88] Another settler reported, "I have seen half a hundred of their wigwams together in a piece of ground and they show prettily."[89] He also admired the Massachusett use of controlled burns to manage their forests, saying that it was "the meanes to make it passable; and by that meanes the trees growe here and there as in our parks: and makes the Country very beautifull and commodious." Thomas described the Massachusett's leather clothing worn under large fur cloaks and mantles: "When they have their Apparrell on they looke like Irish."

European diseases from trade and from colonies on other nations' land reached the Massachusett in advance of the English settlers themselves. A great plague in 1616 killed nearly 80% of the Indigenous population along the New England coast. The settler Thomas Morton wrote, "They died on heapes as they lay in their houses; and the living, that were able to shift for themselves, would runn away and let them die, and let their Carcasses lie above the ground without buriall. For in a place where many inhabited, there hath been but one left alive to tell what became of the rest; the living being (as it seems) not able to bury the dead, they were left for Crowes, Kites and vermin to pray upon. And the bones and skulls upon the severall places of their habitations made such a spectacle after my coming into those partes, that, as I travailed in that Forest near the Massachusetts, it seemed to me a new found Golgotha."[90] Settler accounts state that only a few hundred of the Massachusett survived the plague.[91]

English settlers on Massachusett land named the area "Merry Mount" because they had such a good time there. The name survives to this day, if quietly and often overlooked. The settlement had changed its English name from Mount Wollaston to Merry Mount after their original leader, Captain Wollaston, fled to the Virginia colony. He'd lost a dispute over slavery with the rest of the Merry Mount settlers who may have been indentured but weren't so interested in being sold down south.[92]

Thomas Morton then led the Merry Mount colony, which maintained trade and friendly relations with the natives. After word reached the Puritan Plymouth colony that the Merry Mount colonists celebrated May Day by dancing around a maypole with the natives, the Pilgrims knew something must be done. In William Bradford's own words, Merry Mount invited "the Indian women, for their consorts, dancing and frisking together, (like so many fairies, or furies rather) and worse practises."[93] Or maybe it was the fact that the Merry Mount colony sold guns to the native peoples.

Either way, in 1628, Bradford sent Miles Standish and the Plymouth militia to remove both Morton and the natives. Standish exiled Morton. He then invited the Massachusett's warriors to a peace talk set up through a Wampanoag translator, whose daughter the English held to ensure cooperation. It was a trap. Standish and his men massacred the peace talk attendees and the surrounding villagers at Wessagusset, where my kung fu brother Kody grew up. Standish displayed a severed Massachusett head on a pole at his Plymouth settlement. The Puritans regarded the pole for the displaying of severed heads as more moral than the maypole. Dance bad. Beheading good.

These evil actions devastated the fledgling English colony's ability to trade with local tribes. Those who had previously been friendly with the Plymouth settlers could read the severed heads on the wall, and they decided to bond with other tribes in defense. The hostilities and rival alliances evolved into what was later called King Philip's War, during which the English settlers exterminated Massachusetts's Indigenous peoples.

The English proclaimed the land of New England, America, and everything in it to be theirs alone "by the grace of King Charles of England"—who may well have been distracted by the English Civil War that he was busy losing.

Around that same time, Britain colonized my own ancestors across the Atlantic from Massachusetts in Ireland using substantially similar tactics and only 25% as much genocide. The English evolved their civil, property, and poor laws to support these simultaneous colonial projects.[94]

The work of colony building necessitated treaties and land title that could be justified in England's legal system. One way to create that title was to insist that individual male Indigenous leaders had the authority to speak for their entire tribes and had the right to dispose of tribal lands in the same way an English Lord or Duke might sell or lease feudal lands. James Sullivan, in his 1801 *The History of Land Titles in Massachusetts*, stated, "The forms of government, the rules and regulations of the savage tribes, were of no moment to [the settlers] . . . There is one circumstance, which all the adventurers to these shores agree in; that is, that each tribe had a Chief, or a Sachem, to whom they [the settlers] paid peculiar honours, and whose authority they respected."[95]

As to how the English specifically established legal title over the Massachusett's lands, the English declared "the Indian chief Chickataubut in full possession of all this country," and that "it was never denied in his lifetime or that of his grandson that he held an undisputed possession," and that "in 1621 he went to Plymouth and signed a treaty with the English," in which "he consented to the occupancy of Dorchester."[96] The English, under their own law, believed that treaty legally transferred title from Massachusett lands to English colonists.

James Sullivan defended this title in his 1801 history, written and published while he was the attorney general of Massachusetts, stating, "Even there, the fields thus carelessly tilled [because corn, beans, and squash were grown together], did not seem to afford any evidence of an exclusive permanent claim in him, who expected to gather the promised harvest." He then went on to argue that the key ingredient the Massachusett farms lacked in order to be considered property under the law was . . . fences. "It is said that property is originated by separating something, not before especially appropriated, and annexing to it the labour of man."[97]

And if you do not buy James's legal reasoning, he'd also like you to know that "If the Europeans sought out this continent, and gained possession of it upon wrong principles, and under the influence of wrong motives, it will by no means follow, that the act was in itself, simply considered, an unjustifiable act." He then spends several chapters arguing that land title in Massachusetts was valid because the English Crown had declared it on behalf of Christendom and because the English created some of the bedrock of capitalism in this period by assigning various forms of title that worked better for corporations than the feudal system. He wrote the most honest statement about law I have ever read from a lawyer: "The people ardently wished that it might be true, and therefore believed it before there was any evidence to support the truth of the fact . . . What happened . . . is of more consequence to the historian than to the lawyer."

Chickataubut had indeed signed a treaty consenting to "occupancy." One may reasonably wonder whether the Massachusett people intended to allow the English to use their fields but did not intend to confer exclusive control of the land. By custom, they'd allowed other native nations to hunt on their land occasionally. I'd wager they'd never once heard of an easement. Plague and conflict had recently deprived the Massachusett of enough people to maintain their farms, so why not let these new people join in the land's bounty? The English conception of land title was an alien concept to the locals, but sharing and hospitality were not.[98]

In this way, the English in under forty years reduced the Massachusett to less than 5% of their pre-contact population and reduced their territory to six thousand acres of the least valuable parts of their ancestral lands, area the English considered frontier at the time anyway. The English deprived the Indigenous people of their better agricultural lands, their quarries, and their access to the ocean, leaving the families at Ponkapoag to survive on freshwater fishing, hunting, trapping, and cultivating inferior land. The survivors made a living cutting down their cedar swamps—likely the very land that Bittersweet Lane now sits on—to sell off their trees as clapboards and shingles for the growing English settlements.

Chickataubut's grandson Josias Wampatuck understood that the English required paper records for land control, and so he requested a deed for the six thousand acres remaining to the tribe. Over the next fifty years, the colonizers repeatedly removed, interned, and returned the Ponkapoag. Ebenezer Billings took control of an esti-mated half of the remaining six thousand acres of the Ponkapoag Reservation from the natives in 1687. Colonial guardians continued to take away land by giving other settlers "leases" on the reservation. These settlers' surnames are familiar to anyone who has spent time in the area, adorning streets, parks, and schools to this day. By 1760, the Ponkapoag were down to 710 acres.

After King Philip's War, the English parceled out most of the area of present-day Randolph and Holbrook, around the east edges of the Ponkapoag's reservation area and on former Cochato land. In 1700, citizens of Braintree paid the citizens of Boston to release their claim on title over lands in this area. They divided the territory into three parts, one of which would become the present town of Randolph.

Settlers in Randolph learned the hard way what the Massachusett could have told them: this part of their lands was rocky, swampy, and much less suitable for agriculture than the fields around the Neponset River. European settlers in Randolph supplemented meager farming with shoemaking, which over the years developed into shoe and boot factories.

When they gained a town charter, they decided to name the new town after Peyton Randolph. Massachusetts places named after the American Revolution tended to avoid the traditional English and Indigenous place names in favor of honoring leaders of the revo-lution and their fledgling nation. Peyton Randolph's grandparents were among the founders of the English Virginia colony. His father was a public official and the only person born in the Virginia colony to receive an English knighthood. Peyton served as speaker of the Virginia House of Burgesses, president of the Virginia Conven-tions, and the first and third president of the Continental Congress, which technically made him our first president. Peyton Randolph also enslaved African workers on a plantation in Virginia. He wrote in his 1774 will that the people he enslaved were to be inherited by his wife, Elizabeth, and other family members, or, if necessary, be sold to pay off his debts. The will was timely. Peyton Randolph died in a fit of apoplexy just the next year, while dining with his distant cousin, Thomas Jefferson, in Philadelphia for the Continental Congress.

By 1827, the guardians sold off the remaining few acres reserved for the Ponkapoag. In 1857, the guardians reported, "Punkapoag [sic] tribe of Indians is nearly extinct; only some fifteen or twenty and those mostly of mixed blood, remain." In 1869, Massachusetts passed an Act of Enfranchisement, making all Indians citizens and terminating the tribes.[99]

The United States replicated this strategy across the continent to move Native Americans away from collective land ownership into the more individualistic economy and culture of European settlers, and of course, to gain title over more land for themselves. That's how land became a commodity that could be owned, bought, sold, and developed.

And that is the story of how the land on which I grew up became entitled such that it would—eventually—be developed into homes.

FIFTEEN

Predevelopment

I n-unit laundry? No, you have to take that out." We'd brought together our public funders to discuss the path forward for a mixed-income development across from the Forest Hills MBTA terminal. Their director of design and construction had some opinions on our architect's plans. In fairness, her job was to have strong opinions on design, but the condescending air was extra flair. Ever since serving coffee to grumpy people in a chain bookstore, I've tried to react in a conciliatory but firm manner.

"I hear you. The thing is, our directive from the community, the City, and the MBTA is for this building to be mixed-income. To achieve market rents on the unsubsidized apartments, we need in-unit laundry."

"Well, we aren't paying for them, and you need to value engineer, so take them out."

"You're asking for us to redesign the entire building: removing in-unit laundry; removing the associated plumbing, electrical runs, and venting; and changing all our layouts to reduce space in each apartment to gain the space for laundry rooms. Is that going to save us money at this stage?"

"Maybe they can leave them for just the market units?" someone suggested.

"No, the affordable and market units must be identical," someone else reminded.

I did my best to keep my patience, but I'm sure my irritation showed in my body language. What can I say? Laundry triggers me. "So, here's the thing. There are absolutely compromises to make in value engineering. But I'll die on the hill of laundry. I grew up in affordable housing with a dreary laundry room where I had to babysit my clothes. They occasionally got stolen when we didn't. Our affordable apartments in this development are mostly family-sized. I don't think it's fair to ask families with children to go without laundry if we have any choice, and we can't achieve market rents on the other apartments without in-unit laundry. Without those rents, we can't achieve as large a permanent loan on this development. So if we remove laundry, we end up with a larger funding gap on a less desirable building."

The head of the agency—whom I'd always had a good working relationship with—came back into the conference room before our argument devolved into a shouting match. We tabled the laundry issue and continued on with an otherwise productive meeting.

The predevelopment phase is stressful. We have to mold and shape that idealized development proposal from earlier in the prospecting process to fit into a variety of constrained, sometimes conflicting boxes required by public funders, private lenders and investors, community groups, city permitting processes, state regulations, and federal rules.

Later in my career, I was tasked with creating a visual chart to explain affordable housing predevelopment. I ended up with a triple helix. Look, making things simple is hard to do.

I illustrate the predevelopment process with three strands: design, finance, and community. Each strand intertwines with each other one through an iterative process that transforms ideal dream concepts into feasible development projects.

DESIGN

The milestones along the design strand begin with a *conceptual design*, basic drawings of building and floor layouts, which are used to begin gathering community input and to begin a funding plan in a basic pro forma. That evolves into *schematic design*, during which the building program and its financial pro forma become more precise and have responded to requested changes from the community and funders. From schematic drawings, your architects and engineers draw up the *design development set* that begins to integrate building systems into the layout of hallways and apartments.

Ideally, there's a partner from the construction world during the predevelopment phase who can review these early plan sets, estimate pricing, and suggest potential alternate methods and materials to ensure your project's feasibility. After completing the design development set of drawings and refining the financial pro forma (and at this stage probably having achieved funding awards from a couple of your major funders, if not all of them), it is time to direct the architects and engineers to create a *bid set* of drawings. Also referred to by other jargon like 95% design set, the bid set is almost buildable, includes a book of specifications for materials and methods, and provides a basis for potential general contractors to bid for the project. The contractors' bids detail how much time and money they would ask to build the project and under what terms. At this point, it's likely in affordable housing that the project will cost more money to build than its funders are willing to pay. Another round of input, edits, feedback from the selected general contractor, and likely value engineering—like the meeting I recounted above—follow to transform the bid set into the final set of *construction documents*.

Value engineering is a set of difficult compromises. Funders, engaged community members, approval agencies, and bosses each have strong feelings about what can and cannot be taken out of the project to save money. Those nice balconies you wanted to give residents? Nope, change it to useless Juliet balconies. That large solar array that required extra structural costs on your roof? Poof. Gone. Beautifully landscaped edible plant garden? How about drought-resistant grass instead? Sometimes, their requests even contradict each other.

On this same project, the City staff who review sustainability elements told me to put stairs front and center in the lobby to disincentivize elevator usage, and they liked the external stoops and stairs designed for the ground floor apartments. Their colleagues in the department who review for accessibility told me no extra outdoor stairs would be allowed, and they required the main entrance to be universally accessible with the elevator front and center. Both worthy goals, but impossible to satisfy both. So the work becomes negotiating trade-offs and navigating politics to develop consensus among contradictory perspectives. Elected officials can help sometimes, but agency staff rarely appreciate when politicians check their work. Afterwards, they may treat an offending applicant accordingly.

FINANCE

The financial strand of predevelopment begins with iteratively improving the pro forma spreadsheet model alongside the evolving development concept as it moves through design and community processes. The goal is a balanced pro forma. The total costs of the development must match the total funding sources available to pay for it. And the design and program must fall within all applicable guidelines to be eligible and competitive for the intended funding sources.

From the business perspective, predevelopment is the riskiest phase of the development process. During several years of predevelopment, firms put large sums of money at risk to pay for architecture, engineering, survey, environmental assessment, market study, community process, funding applications, and many more necessary items. All along, almost anything could happen to kill the project.

As a result, predevelopment funding is both rare and expensive. Private lenders perceive predevelopment lending as overly risky to participate in, except at very high interest rates and over short terms. Public funders are hesitant to put public resources at risk for homes that might never get built. Quasi-public lenders often combine public or philanthropic dollars with private investments or loans to offer predevelopment loans. The cost of money in a predevelopment loan may be as much as three or four times the cost of a permanent loan.

In the present, nearly every affordable housing development must complete an application to the Low-Income Housing Tax Credit allocating agency in its jurisdiction and submit four to twelve additional applications for subordinate debt, grants, or other types of tax credits to any number of public agencies at the city, county, state, and/or federal levels. If the development pro forma predicts adequate cash flow, developers also apply to lenders for construction loans, a permanent mortgage loan, and others. It is common for affordable housing developments to have a dozen or more financial participants. Each one of those funding sources has its own set of competitive scoring criteria and its own set of strings attached.

Some funders are willing to be the first to commit to a project, while others insist on being "the last money in." It is not uncommon for several intransigent bureaucracies to each insist their funding be the last money in. Not everyone can be last. Two agencies can't occupy the same space at the same time. It's against the laws of physics. So we convince these agencies we already have all commitments. It's a game of spinning plates.

When the financial pro forma just won't balance or isn't competitive, then the finance strand of predevelopment needs to inform the design strand to redesign the project for additional efficiency, feasibility, and competitiveness—the aforementioned value engineering.

Because available resources are far below demand for them, it often takes multiple years of repeated applications to finally receive affordable housing funding. Low-Income Housing Tax Credits in hand, developers then invite syndicators to bid on becoming the equity investor in the project. Developers compare the investors' proposed deal terms and their implications for long-term affordability and feasibility, but the number everyone will ask about is, "How many pennies?" The amount the investor is willing to pay per dollar of tax credit associated with the investment is the headline. It commonly varies between $0.80 and $1.05 depending on market factors. The amount of corporate tax liability in the economy creates demand for the credits. Congress fixes the supply.

A Boston project I worked on that closed in 2011 and had intended to close in 2009 faced the headwinds of the Great Recession straight on. The core of the LIHTC investor market—large banks—put up some of the largest losses in that recession. Without Community Reinvestment Act–motivated investors and with the number of corporations losing money and thus not generating tax liability, demand completely fell out of the LIHTC market. That project eventually selected an investor who paid $0.73 per dollar for the credits. The investor corporation got a fantastic return on a recession-era investment.

By contrast, that project where I argued over laundry closed in 2017's hot market and received $1.20 per dollar for the credits. How does that work? Why would someone pay a dollar twenty to get a dollar in return? Many LIHTC developments, especially of the 4% flavor, also generate accounting losses from depreciation of the physical assets, from the accumulation of interest on subordinate debt, and through other accounting mechanisms. The tax benefit of those additional losses, plus the benefit of the Community Reinvestment Act points, plus the dollar of credit added up such that this investor could pay $1.20 on the dollar and still receive a profit over ten years.

But no one will invest in a development that a jurisdiction will not allow to be built, and that's where the community strand of predevelopment comes in.

COMMUNITY

The laundry argument wasn't nearly as challenging as the community meetings on that Forest Hills project. I'd dress nice—but not too nice—to attend maybe a dozen meetings in and near Forest Hills. The approval of community groups was required—both officially and unofficially—to achieve City permissions to build. Forest Hills is the neighborhood where Grandmy grew up. My close friend Kate was living in Forest Hills, and I'd stayed there with her for a while as well. I knew and loved Forest Hills. Yet I did not feel comfortable in the community meetings. I tapped and swayed with nervous energy, forcing myself forward into conversations with crucial community members. But to be fair, I've never been wholly comfortable in predominantly white, professional-class spaces.

Land use meetings tend to be dominated by home-owning, older, higher-class, white people. Like any creation, projects benefit from multiple perspectives, including those of renters, people who don't speak or read English well, people with disabilities, younger people, and people who don't live there *yet*. However, outreach and organizing work are staff-intensive and difficult to fund. I don't always adhere to my own ideals in situations where time, money, or politics mean doing so would unravel another crucial predevelopment strand. Time is of the essence. Yet more diverse community input results in a better-designed project and a more resilient path through the community process. It's a challenging balance to maintain. For Forest Hills, I did as much outreach as I could, with some marginal success.

I did my best in the meetings. I asked good questions. I was respectful to a fault. I made responsive changes. I used charts and graphs to allay their fears of *those* people by showing the apartments would be available to the average current residents of Forest Hills. I took it when people yelled about parking, about density, about the old days in a neighborhood where they themselves could only remember five years back. I even listened to a libertarian talk my ear off after a meeting, first complaining about the exclusionary zoning and NIMBY committees but then telling me he opposed my project because it included affordability restrictions and public subsidies. I'd crash at Kate's place in the neighborhood after those late evenings. Eventually, we emerged successfully and received all our necessary permits and entitlements with community assent.

To get these land use approvals and/or because it's the right thing to do, developers undertake intense community processes involving all nearby or relevant community groups, public commissions, neighbors, local business owners, unions, and politicians. I like to involve the community at the earliest possible stage in predevelopment, so there's room to hear their concerns and modify drawings while doing so is still convenient, before the design development and construction drawing sets. For public meetings, I bring drawings that look less complete and less precise to make it visually clear to the community that their input is necessary and valued. Neighbors sometimes make incredibly constructive suggestions, for pedestrian traffic circulation perhaps, or for the massing, or for what types of people their community most needs housed.

We create allies by sharing the development concept, providing meaningful opportunities for feedback, and enabling people to feel ownership in a shared development vision. Or we at least avoid vocal opposition.

Community opposition can kill a development proposal, especially in jurisdictions with restrictive zoning codes. Developments are more likely to survive the community process when people feel heard. And it is about feelings, not facts. I have never witnessed a community process for affordable housing in which NIMBY activists did not complain about parking, traffic, property values, and crime—no matter where or when, no matter the facts and data. Empirical research has not found that affordable housing reduces neighborhood property values; quite the contrary, studies consistently show that new affordable housing development is associated with increasing nearby property values.[100] And studies consistently fail to convince NIMBY activists. No matter how much parking, there has never been enough parking to satisfy a community meeting.

I also invested the time to sit down with the city councilor, state representative, state senator, mayor's office, congressperson, or whatever other relevant elected officials cared about my project's neighborhood and its people. An elected official's opposition can sink a project. Their support can keep it alive. In the city of

Chicago, there is a long-standing practice dubbed *aldermanic privilege* that denies a development proposal if even one alderperson says no. New York City Council also practices a tradition in which individual members have veto power over zoning approvals within their districts. Even in less extreme cases, elected officials are chosen by their neighborhoods and usually care deeply about shaping their districts. Their support is important for working with community, obtaining government approvals, and assembling funding. Turning an elected official into a strong proponent of your project can make a large difference in moving it towards being a reality.

I want to be very clear here; I am not talking about bribery, pay for play, or any illegal practice of any sort. Affordable housing developers take special care to maintain squeaky clean business practices[101] because they face frequent audits from independent firms, federal agencies, and state and local funders. Owners invest in catching any potential malfeasance to avoid having the IRS come knocking. Affordable housing developers also depend on being in good standing with the agencies that award competitive funding. One or two bad audit findings could devastate business for years. In our highly regulated multifamily world, corruption doesn't pay.

In addition to neighbors and their elected officials, early partnership with building trade union leaders can result in better outcomes for the community process, for the entitlement process, and for finding the best-fit contractors to work on your project. In strong union cities, conversations with the trades are a necessary step of the process. For example, Boston restricted its zoning so severely that virtually every project must go to its Zoning Board of Appeals (ZBA) for relief. The ZBA always includes a representative of the building trade unions. In most of the ZBA meetings I attended, other building trades staff quietly questioned developers in the hallway or at the back of the room about which general contractor they intended on using, whether they pay union wages, and so forth. I have watched other Zoning Board of Appeal members look to the union representative for the final yay or nay on whether projects should be approved. As with organizing to reduce opposition by bringing neighbors in and maintaining good relations with their elected officials, growing a partnership with the building trades can make or break your project. Unfortunately, trade unions and affordable housing professionals occasionally end up opposing each other. The dollars our governments make available for building affordable housing are not enough to pay union wages. So affordable housing developers become incentivized to sidestep unions, and the unions work to keep job sites organized.

A last, often overlooked, target of community outreach is the development's potential future residents and workers. To improve lives, buildings must meet future residents' needs. Every development—affordable or market-rate—designs to appeal to real estate market niches. What makes residents feel safe in terms of lighting, entryways, or windows? Does this market want larger closets or larger bedrooms? Just how important is in-unit laundry here, or can a laundry room save money? What amenities are important—a gathering space for seniors, a playground for children, a coworking space? How do we ensure residents and visitors from marginalized communities feel welcomed? Architectural trends follow the top of the market, not the bottom. In affordable housing, our future customers—our residents—tend to be furthest from the process and often unable to easily access it. So it takes extra work on our part. Very few people with lived experience of poverty manage to attain the educational and career successes necessary to put themselves in a position to lead affordable housing development proposals. Our residents and our property management staff must live with the decisions we make during the development process. Please collaborate with your residents and your property management staff early and often.

The goal is consensus, but people rarely ever unify around a single vision, do we? The compromises necessary to move a project through its community process often leave both residents and developers frustrated. And sometimes there is simply nothing we can do. Even after years of community outreach and earning approvals to build, lawsuits create further delays.

In January 2022, eight years after I performed the due diligence phase, Pine Street Inn and The Community Builders (TCB) began construction on the Egleston Square site. Eight years is on the fast side in our world.

Three years after that, Mayor Wu wore her St. Patrick's Day green dress to the grand opening in March 2025. More than a decade after I participated in the prospecting and due diligence for this project, it became home to sixty-two moderate-income households and 140 individuals exiting homelessness. In the end, it took $105 million from federal and state Low-Income Housing Tax Credits and city and state subordinate loans, as well as $6 million in corporate donations.[102]

That development could have housed an additional twenty-three moderate-income households, and it could have opened years earlier.[103] During the community process, the developers lost twenty-three homes to reduce the building from six stories to five stories. Every development proposal in Massachusetts seems to lose a floor or two during the community process. I always feel shame that my people have this fear of heights. Many Boston-based developers responded by routinely proposing taller buildings than truly intended so their proposals could survive the community process with a feasible building after inevitably giving up a floor or five.

Developers who start out asking for only as much height and density as they need—like the eejit writing this book—must make herculean efforts to keep projects feasible.

Further delay at Egleston came after Monty Green, the landlord of a new craft brewery across the street from the site, filed suit to revoke the site's zoning approvals. Clearly, gentrification had made its way over the tracks to Washington Street by then. This landlord argued that sixty parking spaces would not be enough for the approved development, despite its short walk to the MBTA, the bus stop on its block, and the fact that most residents would be coming out of homelessness. Monty claimed his tenant's customers would lose access to the public street parking on which they depended for visiting the brewery.[104] He filed a lawsuit to ask the City to officially prioritize public land for the convenience of driving drinkers.

I would like to never experience one night of housing insecurity ever again. I dread it. My childhood anxiety still haunts me. At least 140 Bostonians spent more time homeless than they should have, not nights but years. For a lawsuit about parking. To spend years satisfying neighbors so they can feel good after cutting twenty-three homes. I hate these trade-offs.

Community. Design. Money. It all intertwines. Community demands change design. Design changes costs. Funders change the design again, which must then be communicated to the community. This iterative process cycles back and forth throughout the predevelopment phase.

Bring your best communication skills, be honest, and discuss conflicting values and priorities. Closing and construction are still to come, and they are stressful enough without the many partners in a project holding over grudges from predevelopment.

SIXTEEN

Closing

Closings are to real estate developers what wins are to pitchers, what album releases are to musicians. There are other ways to quantify outcomes, but if you interview for a development job, you will get questions about your closing record. Good developers close.

The closing process is the last stage of development before shovels hit the ground. We enter the closing process with funding, entitlements, construction documents, and a general contractor. We are working with a firmed-up development vision. Now it's time to resolve every tiny detail needed for investors and lenders to become comfortable putting tens of millions of dollars at risk. Typical LIHTC developments include a construction lender, a permanent lender, an equity investor, and several public subordinate lenders.

Lenders focus on identifying and minimizing risk, since their upside profit is relatively fixed. They analyze development proposals against their underwriting standards (or the standards of the secondary mortgage market). They look towards the experience and financial strength of the borrower and their development team, the value of the land, building, or other collateral, and the validity of the assumptions in the development proposal. The lender will also analyze the terms of other funders' subordinate loans or invest-ments. The permanent lender will insist on first position—being the first in line to be paid in the event of a default. The closing process typically includes much negotiating among funders to remove con-flicting terms.

Investors undertake a similar process analyzing the development proposal, though with a greater focus on the deal terms that affect the timing and size of their required equity pay-ins.

Public agency funders focus on regulatory compliance and minimizing public dollars per unit in their reviews. Our field's cut-ting-edge innovations over the last century have been reactions to funders' esoteric, byzantine rules. We dance between the raindrops of conflicting requirements from each different funder, regulator, and influential interest group.

I have closed deals with creative, collaborative public servants who see their role in their funding agency as ensuring the housing gets built well. I have also become infamous with my coworkers for the creative strings of expletives I release after holding my tongue in calls with the other kind of bureaucrat. Too many cannot see the forest for their own trees, treat the public's money like it's theirs per-sonally, embark on power trips, are blind to nuance, and work only so much as necessary to cover themselves.

Gently pressing these folks to deliver the paper for closing is an art I'm not sure I'll ever master. Several years back, a client asked me to get badly needed official letters of their funding awards from an individual who had been holding them for unnecessary months. I tried polite emails, about one or two a week. I tried voicemails, maybe once a week. She never picked up my calls, but she did call me back on her long commute home from the office once.

"Look, I know you don't like me very much, but you have to

trust we're going to get this done. It is our job to create housing too you know."

"I don't dislike you. I don't know you. We haven't worked together before. And honestly, I don't care one way or the other about that. I've a job to do, and I'm just trying to get it done."

Maybe misinterpreting, maybe bullying, she squealed, "You *better care*. You shouldn't be doing this work if you don't care . . ." and continued to upbraid me. I bit my tongue and let her finish.

"OK, let's hold on right there, since we don't know each other yet. I grew up in not very nice affordable housing in Randolph. I have family and friends who experience housing insecurity and homelessness still. I care. I care too much for the good of my own mental health. So that's the one thing I need you to never accuse me of, not caring about creating affordable housing. What I truly don't care for is playing games and making the work unnecessarily personal. Can you *please* deliver the letters by the end of the week? Your agency made the award four months ago, and we can't move this project to the next steps without them." She got my Irish up, and I'd let my temper get the better of me again. Two years later, she did the same thing to my client on another project. After one solitary, polite email from me, she made false accusations about me, cry-bullying as a form of CYA* before I could even begin to complain.

Affordable housing development timelines are long, but they are made much worse by that behavior. Often, the timelines stretch long enough that costs rise, and our projects begin to approach closing with a new funding gap. Occasionally, it happens to the entire system at once.

Abt Associates issued a study in 2022, "Filling Funding Gaps," which reported that nearly all projects that received Low-Income

---

* Cover Your Ass

Housing Tax Credit between 2019 and 2022 faced unexpected funding gaps of 30% or more. The entire affordable housing industry was knocked back by the combined forces of the Federal Reserve's choice to raise interest rates repeatedly; labor shortages due to a combination of high construction activity, the pandemic, and the Obama, Trump, and Biden administrations' hostility towards immigrants; rapid increases in materials costs due to the supply chain disruptions that first emerged during the pandemic and remain unresolved; increases in the price of fuel; a sharp rise in lumber costs due to a Trump administration tariff on Canada; rising insurance premiums; and a reduction in the value of Low-Income Housing Tax Credits due to Trump's corporate tax cuts. Rising insurance costs put massive strains on housing development, and they will only get worse as climate change progresses. The New York Housing Conference released a study that showed insurance premiums increasing an average of 26% annually. Despite that additional cost, owners report receiving less coverage with more strings attached.[105]

I worked with a client to close on thirty-nine new affordable homes in Mashpee, Massachusetts, at the time. Between a November 2021 pricing estimate and May 2022 bid prices, the cost of construction had gone up 30%, despite the design team having substantially simplified the design during those six months. I had a second client on the opposite coast, in Bremerton, Washington. Costs for their project had gone up about 25%, and we spent a year moving the project two steps forward and one step back. We closed the gap eventually, with the generosity of State of Washington and Kitsap County funders, plus the patience and price-holding of BJC Construction.

To keep building during this period of rapid inflation, developers and funders responded with our limited set of tools. Funders made more money available, often by borrowing from future years. Developers value engineered, deferred developer fees, and negotiated hard with contractors. According to Abt, "Even when these strategies have filled funding gaps and enabled projects to proceed, they have often come at the expense of the current and future production of affordable housing."[106]

The closing process is always fast-paced, usually fraught, and typically frustrating for all involved. The lawyers will nitpick every document. Funders will demand changes without due consideration of budget, operations, or design. We will edit and prod and beg up until the last moments.

The closing checklist tracks the items that must be signed, sealed, and delivered. The appendix includes a list of the fifty typical items needed to close a deal, alongside concise explanations of the purpose behind each. My editor wouldn't let me insert a big, boring list here. I tried. She was right.

That list was too long for a book, which is my point. The long closing checklist represents many months of work from dozens of professionals, and it also functions as index to the closing binder. During guest lectures and trainings on affordable housing development, I include a photograph of the closing binder for the Charlesview Residences. Binder may be a misnomer. It is a shelf of eight six-inch binders stuffed full, not even counting the architectural plans and specifications book. Charlesview was complicated, but not unique.

It is the developer's job to hire the consultants needed to generate most of the tremendous amount of information listed in the appendix, to assemble the final, signed versions for each of the items in the list, to communicate those documents to every party to the deal, to answer their questions, to negotiate among conflicting requirements, and to generate a final consensus among all parties to formally execute the many agreements. Then, upon closing, funders begin sending money as agreed, and the developer releases the general contractor to begin construction.

SEVENTEEN

Charlesview: Construction, Lease Up, and Sales

Now you break ground! First, the funders, politicians, and executives who were even peripherally involved in the project put on clean white hard hats and hold golden shovels to throw a little bit of dirt in the air after the speeches at a ceremonial groundbreaking. I've spoken from a podium and held a golden shovel for projects I barely touched. I never did on the projects that took months and years of my life. Regardless, after years of uncertainty, groundbreakings truly are a milestone to celebrate. Then, your general contractor breaks ground for real to begin site work.

We talk about construction projects *going vertical* after site preparation, excavation, and foundation pours give way to framing up the structure. The underground stage, before going vertical, might be the riskiest stage of construction. During predevelopment, you will have surveyed the land, gotten soil samples, and completed geotechnical explorations, but it's impossible to truly know what's underground until you dig. Most developers I know have some funny or horrible story about what construction revealed in the ground. One friend undertook a gut rehab of a triple-decker for the South Boston Community Development Corporation in the 1980s, but she had to pause construction when workers found a body buried under the basement. That same friend dealt with an indigenous archaeological find on a Martha's Vineyard project. On a third, she was left with a room full of cremated human remains while redeveloping a former funeral home site in Roslindale. Another friend found a large underground tunnel with somebody living in it.

More commonly, digging may reveal an underground fuel storage tank or undetected contamination. Or perhaps the soil turns out not to be as structurally sound as your geotechnical report would have indicated, resulting in an expensive change to your foundation design. You will have budgeted construction reserves to pay for these unknown circumstances. But when these unexpected costs exceed your reserves, you end up with an additional round of value engineering compromises on the landscaping or the building itself.

When my colleague and former classmate Jeff Beam left Boston to open an Ohio office for TCB, Bev Bates and Willie Jones made it my job to project manage the under-construction Charlesview Residences development to completion. But let's begin at the beginning with the Charlesview story.

A rabbi, a priest, and a minister walked onto an urban renewal site in a neighborhood once called Barry's Corner. They created an ecumenical group to organize opposition to a Boston Redevelopment Authority (BRA) demolition and urban renewal plan. A well-connected development partnership had purchased six acres of the neighborhood and planned to build a hotel and/or luxury apartments. Despite homeowners placing their bodies in the way of bulldozers, the City demolished forty-one homes and several small businesses.[107] When BRA director Ed Logue prepared a list of his greatest mistakes for a planned memoir, this urban renewal demolition was number one on his regret list.[108]

The ecumenical group continued organizing after the demolition, and they won the right to redevelop the site. They formed a nonprofit, Charlesview, Inc., and they developed the Charlesview Apartments. They utilized a 221(d)(3) loan and a significant Housing Assistance Payment contract from HUD to create 213 homes, 200 of which were affordable under Section 8 rules. From its opening in 1970, generations of families lived at Charlesview, which was isolated from other housing but did provide the services and stability that helped its families thrive and its children accomplish social mobility.

However, the Charlesview Apartments' brutalist poured-cement buildings surrounded by surface parking lots were no longer in decent shape after thirty years. So Charlesview, Inc.—still a volunteer group composed of leaders from St. Anthony's Catholic Church, Oak Square Methodist Church, and Congregation Kadimah-Toras Moshe synagogue—procured an affordable housing development partner to attempt to rehabilitate Charlesview and preserve its affordability for its residents.[109] I was in high school at the time, and that developer was my future employer, The Community Builders, Inc.

As the development team moved through the predevelopment process, they determined that bringing the aged concrete buildings to modern standards would be more expensive than simply demolishing them and building new. The team also knew that their land was far more valuable than their buildings to one specific buyer. They controlled the corner at the heart of Harvard University's planned new Allston campus.

They approached Harvard to engineer a sale and land swap. In exchange for their current site, they would receive a larger piece of land a half mile away and resources for a development that would enable Charlesview to include more housing and to expand into other crucial support services. Involving Harvard complicated the community process as the University had angered Allston over its campus plans. After several extremely contentious years of community process with no shortage of bigotry from neighbors, Charlesview and TCB planned to break ground on the first of three phases in the Charlesview redevelopment in 2009. Then, the recession took the bottom out of the LIHTC market just as a building boom in China also sent construction materials prices skyrocketing. After several years of value engineering and innovations in leveraging scarce housing resources, the team closed on the largest loan in MassHousing history in 2011 and began construction.

Then, TCB assigned me as Charlesview's project manager after Jeff Beam. The first phase at Charlesview included five new city blocks hosting 240 new rental homes in three mid-rise buildings and nineteen townhome buildings. The project also created a new 10,000-square-foot community center and one-acre public park, reconnected the historic street grid, and created 25,000 square feet of retail space. My first PM assignment was for the largest and most complex construction start in Boston since the 2008 recession.

Thankfully, TCB also hired a mainstay of the Massachusetts affordable housing community—Bev Gallo—to train and mentor me as I got up to speed. She has been a dear mentor and friend ever since. Over four years, I had the responsibility of shepherding the multiphase Charlesview redevelopment. Along the way, I had to manage affordable rental, affordable homeownership, market homeownership, and retail phases; with steel, wood frame, and hybrid low-, mid-, and high-rise building types; with entitlements and politics; with environmental remediation and Brownfield Tax Credits; with debt and equity closings; with 4% LIHTC, tax-exempt bond

226

financing, subordinate debt, land sales, and creative legal structuring to utilize losses; with tenant relocation (199 families in eleven weeks!); with mixed-income leasing; with intentional community building and resident services; and with working in close partnership with a smaller, ecumenical organization that had lost trust in us.

I boiled all that down to seeing my role during the construction phase as about connecting and problem solving. I had to understand the needs, goals, and issues of our residents, our nonprofit partner, our general contractor, our unionized workforce, our elected officials, our lender, our investor, and our property management firm. When problems arose, I had to balance all their interests to advance compromises in the project's best interest.

CONSTRUCTION

Every developer I know has some esoteric knowledge they acquired because something went wrong on a construction project. My first biggest learning curve was environmental remediation. Charlesview, like most urban sites, was a contaminated brownfield. We had to test, characterize, and properly use or dispose of several different grades of dirty dirt, plus our buildings required vapor barriers and exhaust systems below their foundations to prevent volatile organic compounds in the groundwater from ever entering living spaces. I learned a tremendous amount from our environmental consultants, but then, I also had to get up to speed very quickly on design for acoustic separation.

After tenant complaints identified construction defects in a recently finished development, TCB invited acousticians to train us on proper construction methods to reduce the sound transmitted between floors and between apartments. They didn't want to see us make the same mistakes on any of our projects. Since I was a child, playing music and attending concerts helped me keep my soul alive. I was absolutely fascinated by the acoustic science the experts shared with us—the different types of sound transmission, the methods that work to acoustically separate and isolate different rooms and floors.

When the acousticians projected photos showing what *not* to do, my construction manager Doug Tierney and I flashed each other *oh shit* looks.

"Do those look like . . ."

". . . what's happening on our site?"

We talked to our bosses about it after the training. We rearranged our schedules to make a site visit the next day. I reviewed the construction budget. How much money did we have left in the construction contingency fund? I hoped the problem wouldn't be that large.

Sure enough, the carpenters at Charlesview had been drilling fasteners straight through the resilient channeling. The key to soundproofing is separation. You want to interrupt the sound waves. Resilient channels are a method of doing that, but the metal fasteners going through them directly connected floor and ceiling assembly. That creates a sound bridge which helps your upstairs neighbor's footsteps carry through to your bedroom below. In six or so buildings, our contractors had already made that crucial mistake, and we had to decide how to proceed to fix the ceiling assemblies. On another ten or so, the problem was caught early enough to be addressed with new shop drawings pointing out the correct method. Problem solved, but at a cost that had to be dealt with in the project budget.

Another morning, I met the local city councilor's staff person at a diner in between the old and new Charlesview sites. She and her sister both grew up in the old Charlesview, and both grew up to get law degrees from prestigious schools. I remember describing my job to her as "putting out fires." Every day, new, urgent problems arise in construction and development.

The next morning I received a call that there was an actual fire on the Charlesview construction site. Worse yet, Father Mike—the kind, unassuming Catholic priest who chaired our ecumenical partner organization—was the first to see the fire and call it in. I no longer say that the job is putting out fires. I fear the phrase turning literal again.

Our fire at Charlesview was minor. The fire at a nearly complete seven-story affordable housing development next to the Ashmont MBTA terminal in 2017 was not. The sprinkler system was not yet operational, and the building burned to the ground. Its developer was able to raise the funds from insurance and elsewhere to rebuild. However, the fire likely caused an additional two years of housing insecurity for the people who would otherwise have moved in.

Construction safety must be paramount, for our workers and our eventual residents as well as for developers and our funders. It takes work to balance the best safety and most inclusive labor practices with the pressures to build as quickly and cheaply as possible.

There's usually a rush towards construction completion, which is defined as the receipt of Certificates of Occupancy from the local government. Developers plan lease up or sales schedules with the construction schedule—aiming for an August finish for September 1 leases in student-heavy areas, for example. Perhaps you are signing leases during the last few months of construction and now must be ready for your tenants to move in. Additionally, the LIHTC program requires projects to be *placed in service* by December 31, or else your investor cannot claim tax credits for the year and might expect millions of dollars in return from you for the profits they lost due to project delays.

In the last month or so of construction, you begin *punch listing*. You as owner/sponsor, representatives from your general contractor and architect, and representatives of your various funders walk through the completed construction, put up little blue squares of painter's tape, and take notes on a tablet to mark everything that needs a fix to be considered complete. You must get the building ready for the many final inspections it must pass, such as those from the fire department, the building department, and any required by funders. If the project includes certain HUD funds, it must pass another quirky inspection called the REAC (Real Estate Assessment Center) inspection. Did a paint chip end up on a sprinkler head? Is a ramp too steep to be ADA compliant? Is water coming down from the pitched roofs in a way that lands on the doorstep and will create ice for residents to slip on? Any number of things may need to be fixed at this point. The expense of time and money to complete fixes often pits the interests of the general contractor, the architect, and the developer/owner against each other.

Several of those routine final tests became high drama at the Charlesview Residences. When you construct a new building, most cities require noise testing to ensure that the building's machinery doesn't make the area any noisier. The tests are performed at night to avoid contamination from construction and traffic noise. Our noise testing at Charlesview occurred the night of a shootout. Just over the river in Watertown, the Boston Marathon bombing suspects opened fire on police. In a seven-minute shootout, they fired fifty-six rounds. Police from five departments fired an additional two hundred or so bullets. The suspects also threw a pressure cooker bomb and crude grenades at the police. We verified that the condensing boilers and other rooftop machinery at Charlesview were not louder than sirens shrieking up Western Avenue or the bombs and gunfight barely a mile away across the Charles River in Watertown (or the actual ambient noise, which there were short periods of that night).

Sung's family came into town two days later. My Monday morning walk to work was my one chance to get her father alone and ask for his blessing to propose. We stopped at the Public Garden and sat together on a bench where he gave his answer. Picture the scene from *Good Will Hunting* filmed on a bench in that same park, but replace Robin Williams with a slimmer, beardless Korean man. Pastor Kim went on at length about his views on life, marriage, and Christianity while we sat there. He gave me his blessing. Now, I needed to find the right time and place to propose.

On the way home from work, I stopped at Savenor's to buy Sung an Iggy's Bakery baguette. When I got home, Sung was in the shower, relaxing after the end of her family's visit. I hid the ring on a high shelf in a kitchen cabinet and started preparing dinner. Sung joined me in the kitchen after her shower.

I was too excited, and life is too uncertain. While Sung was mincing garlic, I pulled out the baguette and said, "I bought you bread . . ." Sung reacted to the baguette with the excitement she saves for truly good bread. Then I said, "and this!" pulled the ring down from the cabinet, and asked her to marry me. She reacted to the ring with confusion. She stood in stunned silence for thirty seconds that felt like thirty days to me, believing my life was about to shatter again, before she screamed yes and hugged and kissed me. No construction problems could take the smile from my face the next day.

LEASE UP

That same summer, we faced the challenge of successfully moving the 199 households left at the old Charlesview into the new building. We had just a thirteen-week window because we'd promised Charlesview's families that the moves would not take place during the school year. TCB, Charlesview, and their residents had been preparing for this moment for years, ever since early in the predevelopment phase.

Once we were a few months out, our relocation consultant met with every one of those 199 households to plan their moves, sometimes multiple times. The Universal Relocation Act details residents' rights very specifically, and hiring a specialist was important to ensuring we didn't accidentally step outside the law. Months of meetings, paperwork, and filling dumpsters turned into packing, moving, address changes, and new tenant income qualification paperwork as we reached summer.

The residents were ready to go; the buildings, not quite as much. The new Charlesview's three mid-rise buildings and nineteen townhome-style fourplexes each completed and received Certificates of Occupancy at different times. Some construction schedules slipped due to errors like the acoustic separation discussed earlier. The natural gas utility, electric utility, tel/com utilities, post office, fire department, and building department each added their own bit of chaos and heartburn to the construction schedule with slow responses, missed dates, and requested changes.

That all added up to scheduling the 199 moves alongside the shifting schedule of building completions. On any given day that summer, Charlesview would have moving trucks on some blocks and construction vehicles on others. The majority of the households had requested "reasonable accommodations" for minor health-related renovations to their apartments, such as grab bars or alternate flooring materials. I think our general contractor got flustered that a grab bar in a random unit might be the most crucial item in our view when they believed there were bigger problems, but the relocation schedule was of the utmost importance to us. By the start of the 2013–2014 school year, all existing residents were happily in their new homes. Then, it became crucial for our property management firm to lease up the other forty-one apartments—some of which had obscure tenant screening requirements—in the last few months of the year to meet our December 31 deadline. And we had to find a way to pay them . . .

The old Charlesview relied on a two-hundred-unit Housing Assistance Payment (HAP) contract to fund operations. During Charlesview's predevelopment phase, TCB's then general counsel, Karen Kelleher, led an effort for HUD to experiment with a section of the law—Section 8(bb)—that allows project-based HAP contracts to be transferred to new addresses. While leasing up and relocating, I was also focused on completing HUD's checklist of milestones and documentation to *port* the HAP contract from the old Charlesview to the new.

But residents were already living on-site, and the contract would not transfer until everyone had moved. So every time we moved a household from the old to the new, we lost the subsidy portion of their rent. September was the crucial month before the new Charlesview would be running in the red. I aimed to be ready in August. New England regional HUD staff tried to reassure us on the schedule while simultaneously discouraging us from believing that the porting was a done deal. HUD reserved the right to reject the request, which would have sent the new Charlesview very quickly into foreclosure with its lender, MassHousing, whose loan was insured by

HUD. Charlesview's equity investors had insisted on funding a $2 million reserve at closing in case the HAP contract transfer failed to occur on time. It caused a not insignificant amount of value engineering for what had felt like not much risk at the time.

Then the government shut down. HUD couldn't approve our HAP porting because HUD staff couldn't go to work because HUD couldn't pay them, or us. Charlesview operated off that reserve month after month until the federal government reopened in November, and then it dug into the reserve month after month after month until HUD had approved each and every little bit of paperwork. The federal government was generous enough to provide back pay on the subsidies from November to January. Charlesview was SOL for the months of losses from July to November. That reserve turned out to be a clutch idea. The negotiators were right to create a backup plan in the case of the United States government failing to function.

Charlesview was an odd case, but aren't they all?

Ideally, your property management team markets the new homes to potential residents during construction, with lease-up and move-in scheduled with a completion date well in hand. Typically, the law and funders require affordable housing developments to perform their marketing and tenant selection in very specific ways to further policy goals. The Tenant Selection Plan is an important closing document, and funders often pay close attention to it. Among other things, affordable housing must market to media sources aimed both at general populations and towards those in underrepresented demographics considered "least likely to apply" in order to "affirmatively further fair housing."

Potential tenants fill out burdensome rental applications that include everything a private market lease application would, plus all the information needed to qualify that household for the subsidies attached to the project and to assign that household to a preference category in the lottery or waitlist.

Property management must complete income certifications, background checks, asset checks, and other qualifications with the information from those burdensome applications to ensure the applicants are legally allowed to lease those affordable homes. Income certifications are relatively easy with households whose income comes from regular salary or benefits and slightly more complicated with wage earners. But households with seasonal, irregular, inconsistent, and/or cash incomes present challenges to the system. Staff and applicants both spend hours chasing down paperwork and statements from various employers and agencies.

There are several methods for selecting tenants. Households may be able to lease on a first-come, first-served basis. That becomes unwieldy when there is overwhelming demand for the homes, as there often is for affordable housing. So you may employ a lottery that rank orders applicants according to a fair housing compliant process or complete some other fair and legal method memorialized in the Tenant Selection Plan. Once selected, tenants must sign leases, place deposits (if applicable), and schedule move-ins. Then, the manager must complete certification paperwork to prove to the funders and relevant authorities that the development is serving only who it is intended to serve and nobody else whomsoever.

SALES

The Charlesview Residences' second and third phases were both for-sale housing developments. The Town Homes at Brighton Mills would provide twenty new affordable homes. The Telford Condos would be a tower with ninety or so condos, 15% of which would be affordable.

The sales period for an affordable housing development is not especially different from a lease up. Marketing and sales must comply with affirmatively furthering fair housing rules. Community outreach is of utmost importance. There are reams of paperwork to qualify the homes for the mortgage lenders and to qualify the purchasers for the homes. There are last-minute requests and changes and small crises that threaten to derail everything.

That said, first-time homebuyers' success at closing a mortgage loan on a condominium purchase is a much more legally involved and risky process than a renter signing a lease. And the deadline to sell the homes is driven by the project's need to pay back its construction lender.

The Town Homes at Brighton Mills arose from abutter demands during Charlesview's entitlement and permitting process. The City of Boston required The Community Builders to build twenty homeownership units for sale to middle-class households—ten at 80% AMI and ten at 100% AMI. (That 100% always struck me as unnecessary, but is it weirder to say "at the AMI"?) Half of each were two-bedroom and half were three-bedroom. The townhomes were to be built where the five-city-block Charlesview redevelopment faced existing homes across two narrow side streets. They were meant to "buffer" the incumbent homeowners from "those people" who would be living in the Charlesview Residences.

The federal government spent $25 billion to subsidize homeownership for wealthy households that year,[110] but none of it was useful for us. The Home Mortgage Interest Deduction has been, by far, the largest housing subsidy in US history. That subsidy transfers money to homeowners well-off enough to itemize their income taxes, and it even subsidizes summer homes and pieds-à-terre besides. The US has been far less generous to lower-income people and renters, and there are few supports to build affordable homes for sale.

At its core, developing for homeownership adheres to the same principles as for rental. It is still a matter of whether the construction rent can be met by the price that households are willing and able to pay for it. Of course, in affordable homeownership, the answer starts from a "no." The mortgage that low- and moderate-income households can afford to pay for the home is lower than what it costs to build.

However, ownership housing is considered far riskier than rental housing because the financial moves occur over a short time frame. Owners, developers, investors, and lenders of affordable rental housing plan their financing based on fifteen to fifty years of performance. If there's a bad first year, say because a large employer leaves, or, I don't know, maybe a pandemic occurs, rental developments can still meet their financial obligations over time if they can weather the storm with reserves or other savings. But a bad first year or two can put an ownership development into foreclosure. Paying back the construction loan depends on successfully selling 70–80% of the homes, and construction loan terms are typically only two to three years. What happens if there are fewer people willing and able to purchase those homes in that place at that time than the number of homes you built there and then?

Homeownership developers are wise to study their target market(s) very carefully and design to the needs of that market segment. Developers of homes for sale often bring their developments to market in small phases of a dozen or twenty or so homes to manage the risk that there may turn out to be too few buyers that year. Also, buyers will not be able to get mortgages for developments that are less than 70% sold or committed.

The Brighton Mills Homeownership development sold townhomes for an average of about $200,000, while they each cost $400,000 to build. The community development specialists at Eastern Bank offered a construction loan, but I had to search for gap money. There were not many possibilities at the time, not all that long after the 2008 foreclosure crisis. The Federal Home Loan Bank system has the Affordable Housing Program (AHP) that can provide grants for affordable homeownership, but it required deeper affordability than the middle-income homes the City wanted.

Even if I were allowed to change the agreement with the City, the cost of compliance and the loss in sales revenue from targeting the lower-income households would cost the project as much money as the grant put into it. That is hypothetically good if it directs scarce resources to households in greater need. In my case, it would only ever be hypothetically good; no money to build meant no homes built. Nobody at any income level would benefit from a project that doesn't get built.

Similarly, the Boston Department of Neighborhood Development was willing to extend funding, but the requirements attached took away most of the value of the award, reducing $1 million to just $300,000 of value for the project. Some of the familiar affordable housing subsidies used in rental housing—the HOME Program, CDBG Community Development Block Grant), local Housing Trust Funds, and even creatively structured LIHTC or NMTC (New Market Tax Credit) investments—can be used for affordable homeownership. However, the complexity and requirements to do so may not pay for themselves.

Luckily for me and twenty first-time homebuyers, the rental phase of the Charlesview Residences was about to come in three months ahead of schedule and $3 million under budget (thank you, John Moriarty & Associates construction and a mild winter!). We convinced the relevant funders and regulators to pay those savings to The Community Builders as a developer fee, which TCB then invested as owner equity to subsidize the ownership development.

I had the enviable ability to complete the Town Homes at Brighton Mills without outside funders beyond the construction lender, which is extremely unusual for affordable housing developers.

But that didn't mean we developed the Town Homes at Brighton Mills without close coordination with City government. The agreement with the Boston Redevelopment Authority required us to sell the units via a lottery process that we were to administer under City guidelines and in coordination with City staff. We looked closely at the market study and local demographics and held meetings and conversations with potential first-time homebuyers in the neighborhood. We advertised in the places that could reach those deemed "least likely to apply" under Fair Housing Act rules, including the newspapers serving Boston's Black, Chinese, Haitian, and Spanish-speaking communities. We distributed and collected applications online and in person. We held a lottery in the Fiorentino Community Center at Charlesview. We got three different mortgage lenders to pre-underwrite our development so that potential buyers had a choice of lenders who were familiar with this odd project and its exotic bureaucracy.

My construction period luck at Charlesview seemed to repeat with the Town Homes at Brighton Mills. As 2014 turned to 2015, we experienced an unusually warm and snow-free winter, which allowed our general contractor, NEI, to get ahead of schedule and under budget. We were prepared to begin our marketing in February, with sales a few months after, per statutory requirements.

Then, a blizzard slammed into the Boston area at the end of January, halting work. A week later, we watched the New England Patriots win the Super Bowl while a second blizzard raged outside. A third blizzard hit the following weekend too, and would you believe it, a fourth blizzard came on the fourth consecutive weekend. The snow continued through the end of March, and temperatures never rose above freezing. By April, Boston snow totals set a four-century-long record at 110 inches.[111]

My luck had turned. Our completion and sales were delayed by several months. We spent $25,000 on snow removal alone. Again, I was thankful for funding reserves. Our plucky sales agent, Tamela Roche, found the silver lining by taking absolutely gorgeous photos of the snow-covered homes underneath crisp, freezing, blue skies.

Over the course of the spring, we sold the twenty homes to twenty first-time homebuyers. Every household had been renting in the city of Boston at the time, but they came from around the world and around the city. Our ceremonial first buyer was a life-long Allston resident who'd raised her son in the neighborhood even as her friends and family left. She cut the ribbon alongside Mayor Menino. Tamela gifted me a framed photo collection of the buyers receiving keys to their new homes alongside those snowy marketing photos. The Town Homes at Brighton Mills had been the smallest development I'd worked on, but I am very proud of it. I've kept that photo collage on my office walls for inspiration, the individual smiles providing the flip side to Ed Logue's "two goddamn houses on Charlotte Street."

Advocates of homeownership tout its potential wealth-building effects, especially for African Americans and other communities who have been excluded from wealth-building homeownership through redlining and other practices. They also cite ideological beliefs about the benefits of homeownership, like the feeling of control, matching a lifestyle to the American ideal, and correlations with higher voting rates, more participation at community meetings, greater social capital, and commitment to a neighborhood.

Skeptics point out that homeownership still includes many of the same payments that make up rent—taxes, utilities, insurance, security, maintenance, mortgage interest, and capital replacements. The wealth-building effects are lower for the 90% of American households who earn too little to itemize their taxes and are thus unable to collect the Home Mortgage Interest Deduction. Homeownership is risky. If a household falls on hard times and misses mortgage payments, tax payments, or homeowners association payments, they could lose their home and their savings both. Maintaining a structure is hard work, and not everyone is cut out for it, enjoys it, or has the time for it.

Affordable homeownership is a place where America's double-think on housing—refusing to choose sides in the conflict between homes as wealth and homes as shelter—creates real problems. Affordable homeownership can be a contradiction in terms. To maximize the wealth-building effects of *homeownership*, buyers must be able to sell at a significantly higher price or to rent it out above the costs of their mortgage, taxes, insurance, maintenance, etc. To maximize housing *affordability*, buyers must be required to sell at a restricted price that will be affordable to the next buyer.

Affordable homeownership professionals and regulators thread the needle by attaching compromise restrictions to a mortgage note, deed restriction, or other legal vehicle. For instance, many will allow buyers of affordable homeownership to sell with 5% annual price appreciation, or maybe 10% or 3%. Or they might require the home be sold to an income-qualifying household, which de facto restricts the sales price and therefore the wealth-building potential. Some require regulators to approve sales, but sales can be awfully hard to track many years after an agency's involvement in a development. A quick Google search can pull up any number of stories about affordable homeownership units being sold against the rules for a profit and the problems those scandals caused for housing programs and politicians.

THE SWEET

Don't believe brokers who say homeowners "pay themselves" and renters "pay a landlord." The total costs that make up the "ownership rent"—nondeductible mortgage interest, property taxes, closing costs, mortgage insurance premiums (MIP), HOA fees, maintenance costs, replacement costs, and extra utilities—can be twice as much as principal over the term of a conventional mortgage. Homeowners don't "pay themselves" with those costs; they only keep payments on principal, and even then, only if they eventually sell at a profit. Once you have calculated the true ownership rent, you can make a fair comparison with renting. Rent is the shelter cost of housing, and this method allows you to compare whether renting or owning truly costs more in a given situation. You don't get that money back, but you do get a place to live.

It might be that renting a home while investing money in tax-preferred investment vehicles like a 401(k) retirement account, Roth IRA, or 529 education plan, plus maybe other investments like index funds, investments in stock, or investment in a small business would have provided a higher return on your money than putting it into principal in your home would. Keep in mind that higher-income households are more likely to have maxed out those tax-preferred savings accounts than low-income households, so the calculation is significantly different for our higher-income readers. It could also be that homeownership is in fact the better investment than whatever else you might do with that money.

If (years of ownership)*(nondeductible mortgage interest + insurance + utilities + maintenance + repairs + replacements + landscaping + taxes + MIP + other costs of ownership) + (predicted return on sale) > (years of ownership)*(projected mean annual rent) + (alternate investment returns), then homeownership is financially better than renting. If it is less than, renting is better financially.

EIGHTEEN

Conversion and Operations

The CFO kept casually dropping by my office, casually asking, "How's the Charlesview closing going? Will it be done this week?" His job was to keep our organization operating well. My job was to finish the final perm loan closing and conversion on the Charlesview development. TCB was due to receive more than $10 million on the other side of the conversion from the final tranches of investment from our tax credit investors, plus the release of the $100 million guarantee on our outstanding construction loan. The CFO felt the stress. I felt the stress. Our colleagues inside the investment syndicator and certain public agencies were in no particular hurry.

Besides being large—the largest lending package MassHousing had done to date—this conversion was especially complicated, unprecedented even. As discussed in the lease up chapter, this conversion from development sources to permanent operating involved: 1) relocating 199 households and leasing up an additional forty-one apartments; 2) collecting positive cash flow for three months; 3) achieving HUD sign-off on the first ever project-based Section 8 porting, without which the cash flow wouldn't exist; 4) satisfying laundry lists of requirements and inspections from our investor, MassHousing, the IRS, and HUD; and 5) completing the final closing on the permanent mortgage to pay off the construction loan and developer fee. Did I mention the federal government shut down for three months in the middle of all this?

The final closing, aka permanent loan conversion, typically occurs a few months after both construction and lease up are completed. Before final closing, the developer must provide documents showing that the building is fully leased up, that its monthly revenue exceeds the debt service coverage ratio (that is to say, the property earns 20% more than its monthly mortgage payments) for at least three months, that it passes an independent audit's cost certification, that it has filed the appropriate paperwork (8609s) with the IRS to place the buildings in service and thus allow the investor to file for its tax credits, and that the development passed every relevant inspection and certification. The investor typically makes its last equity payment at final closing. Some public funders hold back money until final closing. The lender closes a new permanent mortgage and uses the proceeds to pay off the construction loan and any other outstanding debts, such as a portion of the developer fee.

Conversions can be as suspenseful as construction loan closings. Charlesview's conversion earned me my first gray hairs. I recall airport-style security on the way to Boston's HUD office for meeting after meeting. Weekly job site visits began to focus on the odder nitpicks in HUD's REAC inspections, and I had to hold some subcontractors hands through work they believed to be ridiculous. I managed the justified suspicions of Charlesview's board members and made clear how, when, and where the dollars would be flowing in this complicated transaction. I used carrots and sticks to encourage work from our third-party property manager. Professor

Marchant used to refer to project management as "polite nagging." And in the end, everyone got it done. The Charlesview Residences completed construction three months early and $3 million under budget. We relocated 199 households over thirteen summer weeks, and property management filled the remaining apartments by the end of December. HUD came through on the porting. The equity investor made their payments. MassHousing and the state Department of Housing and Community Development each collaborated with us to achieve perm loan conversion. The CFO stopped casually dropping by my office.

By this point in the development cycle, that early development concept has transformed into real homes. That's the end of the development cycle for people playing the development project management role. Property and asset management teams have taken over responsibility. People are at home now. If we've done a good job, they love their new homes. Without the constant worry about shelter, they can turn their attention to the other needs and wants of life.

Life never stops, and I felt like I was living two of them. My professional life stayed north of the Neponset River, and my old life stayed south of it.

"Kelly's wake is Thursday 4-8 at Hurley's in Randolph, and her funeral is at 10 on Friday at Saint Mary's in Randolph." [112]

A Facebook message from a cousin I hadn't seen in close to fifteen years. Received in the middle of an out-of-town business meeting. Her sister, Kelly, my oldest cousin, finally succumbed to multiple sclerosis, twelve or so years after collapsing on her way out of an exam to become an MBTA cop. Associate's degree in hand, she was the most educated one in the family at the time, young, pretty, and ready to build a life. She'd have been the first. I last saw Kelly before my father dropped my little brother and me off saying, "Don't call again until you're ready to give me the respect I deserve as a father."

"You heard about Kelly, right?"

A text from my brother. He always held a little tighter to romantic notions of family and loyalty and Boston-Irishness than I did. It's the buoy we both tie up to, but I like to sail out of the harbor more often. The right thing to do was to go to the wake. That was *coir*. So we would. Together.

A flight back from out-of-town business, a walk to the office, a ride to my job site, two buses home, and a drive through the clogged southeast expressway to meet my brother. A quiet drive through the hills of a state park, a drop down onto the main street of my hometown, a ride past the same old shit, some new vacant lots, some changed storefronts. A slide into an unnecessary on-street spot across from the funeral home. We crossed South Main Street, opened the doors together, and stepped into this funeral home for not the first time. A felt sign with stuck on letters:

Kelly Madden Sullivan ←

Sean and I turned ← into a room of sitting and standing, of rarely worn formal clothes, of freckles, wrinkles, and tired eyes. We shook uncles' hands and hugged aunts, unseen for many years. My brother the veteran brought easy admiration. No one would know what to do with me, so when asked, I left it at "Life is good," which seemed an odd thing to say at a wake but the most honest answer to the question. Through the handshaking and hugging, a gaunt, aged figure glowered from a corner but made no move to greet Sean and me.

We turned to the next room, scanning for faces that might be familiar underneath the years. Seeing none that would acknowledge us, we walked to the closed casket with an unfamiliar but unmistakable photo on top. We kneeled, touched forehead, heart, and shoulders, spoke to Kelly or God or ourselves in silence, touched forehead, heart, and shoulders, and rose in unison. Two brothers, twins four years apart, still together alone among these faces.

This was as much as I had signed up for. This was the part where I was supposed to walk back out. So far, so good though. For the first time in many years, I wanted to see the rest of them.

We found our aunt, Kelly's mom, hugged, and said condolences. She repeated how good it was of us to be there enough times for me to doubt her sincerity. We left in search of our cousins, who could only be found outside smoking.

Out back, I hugged women who looked like my aunts but I knew as the girls I'd searched for Easter eggs and built sandcastles and had snowball fights with all those years ago. They spoke in accents that I'd learned to forget and often try to remember. They talked about their kids—noticeably absent—and about where we all were in life.

"Russell's doing good. Got out of the Army. I wish he didn't live so far away."

"Yeah, and now he's moving to fucking Oregon or somewhere."

"Colorado, I think."

"And Mikey's clean now. He's out at a sober house in Pittsfield. They let him out to be here. He should be inside somewhere."

"Are you married yet? Kerry and I have been through a couple between us."

"Have you seen the photos of my kids?"

We passed around cell phones with pictures of little kids who looked much more like the cousins I remember than these women I was talking with.

"Hey, where is Abby?" I asked.

"Abby's not here."

Silence.

I'd thought Abby was sober now too. I didn't ask.

"Have you seen the video inside? They've got pictures of Kelly when she was young and shit."

Sean and I went back inside the funeral home to see the video and say a few goodbyes. We chatted with our uncles about work and Sean's hope for a union job. Aunt Nancy nearly bowled me over with a hug, proclaiming, "Jamie! It's Nancy!" Of course I recognized her, and I felt a pang of guilt that she assumed I hadn't.

As we talked, the gaunt figure in the corner got up and circled the crowd. He never made eye contact. He never moved in. He circled and walked past. He walked out the back door.

Sean and I chatted more and said warm goodbyes to our uncles and aunts. We left in search of a beer and a whiskey and some South Shore bar pizza. We tried Lynwood first. We sidled up to the bar, and as we began to order, a woman came up and said, "I saw you at the wake. I'm your second cousin I think."

"Well, hi, nice to meet you."

Meanwhile, the bartender refused to serve my brother because he only had his passport for ID. His argument, "They accept them the world over," did nothing for them. I wonder how many miles anyone in the bar had ever been from that room. We left the bar and our mystery cousin to go to a nearly identical Irish pub up the road. We spent long-overdue time catching up. I'd been working and traveling too much lately.

A quicker drive up a darkened Main Street, through an open expressway, down the parkway to Wolly Beach and my brother's place.

I followed Sean in and spent some time catching up with his roommate—my former roommate—Irish Jay. A friend of his came by after his day in court to see Jay. Whitey Bulger and a couple of South Boston's other well-known gangsters had murdered this friend's father years ago. He never imagined he'd get justice. Now he was spending every day in court searching for some redemption, for his father's ghost. He told us about witnesses' bullshit lies and about the reporters who wouldn't leave him alone. "Diane Sawyah wanted me on her show last night, but I told her no. My mom was like why, and I was like, 'Ma, the B's are on tonight.'" He said his family felt more respected by the defense attorney than the federal prosecutors.

I sat on the couch, watched Jay's friend hit the bong too hard and have a coughing fit. I wondered what he would give to see his father again, to have a chance to look him in the eyes. I thought about the gaunt shadow I saw at the funeral home and the eyes that wouldn't meet mine. I had to get up for work in the morning. I decided to leave.

PROPERTY MANAGEMENT

Connecticut's rolling hills were pretty enough to make up for the couple hour drive from Boston. My colleague and I were driving down to visit a housing development in an isolated old mill town. It had been built in the 1960s, not well managed, then purchased, renovated, and preserved by a local organization and our employer, TCB. Twenty-some years later, it was time to give the development new roofs, boilers, windows, flooring, landscaping, and paving, as well as preserve its affordability restrictions. We met the local architect team there, inside the property manager's small office.

The property manager was clearly unwell, said some things they shouldn't have, and snuck swigs from a bottle of Dayquil. We hurried the architects out of their office and met up with the maintenance supervisor for a walk-through of the site and buildings. He pulled me aside and begged me to do something about the property manager. "I've got compassion for that problem, but they swerved all over the parking lot on their way in this morning. It happens all the time. Someone is going to get hurt."

My colleague and I carried his message back to HQ. In my heart, I felt like I was betraying someone, snitching on their addiction, their disease. But like the maintenance man had said, someone could get hurt. Kids played in those lots, just like Sean and I had played in our parking lot. Finding the property manager help and finding a person to be a helpful property manager were the right things to do.

Property management is a very stressful, challenging job. Property managers are responsible for the day-to-day operations of the housing, including marketing, qualifying applicants, leasing, collecting rent, paying bills, maintenance, utilities, repairs, cleaning, emergency management, enforcing rules, mediating resident disputes, carrying out evictions, and coordinating periodic inspections for fire, sprinkler, elevator, HUD, and others.

In owner-occupied detached homes, owners are their own property managers. Condominium owners typically share some property management costs through a homeowners' association. In affordable housing, local power rests in property managers' hands.

In affordable housing, property management is additionally responsible for getting applicants and existing residents both to satisfactorily complete stacks of eligibility documents. This includes a review of tax returns, pay stubs, and other records of income to ensure an applicant makes enough to afford the rent but not so much that they are above the income limit prescribed by the housing's funders. It includes an examination of a household's assets, criminal record, citizenship status, credit score, references from past landlords, evidence of homeless status, and more. If the property manager makes mistakes on the resident certification process, the IRS or other funders could require the owner to repay millions of dollars to the government, for which the equity investor(s) and lender(s) would in turn require the developer to repay them. It's high stakes for the owner firm. It's high stakes for the residents. Property managers catch stress from both sides.

Management practices can make or break a firm's reputation. Mission-driven affordable housing firms that develop, own, manage, and provide resident services to properties often use consistent branding so that residents know that they live in a property built, owned, and maintained by The Community Builders, Preservation of Affordable Housing, the Tacoma Housing Authority, Community Roots Housing, or Winn Communities, for some examples. If everyone is performing their job well, those residents and neighbors will be generally happy with the development. By extension, their elected officials and the funders of affordable housing are then more likely to look favorably on the firm's next development proposal.

Of course, the opposite is true as well. From a resident's perspective, property management is the face of the entire housing system. We know what we write on the rent check, whose name is on a maintenance vest, and who to ask if something breaks or we get locked out. Before working at TCB, my only real experience with property management staff was with the maintenance man who stalked my mother. Property managers usually occupy a low position in their corporate hierarchies, but their power over tenants has life and death consequences. The power imbalances are clear, and many people interact with property managers with the same sensible, wary deference we do with cops. Experience preempts trust.

Many owners hire third-party management firms that may have their own company branding and presence, which sometimes obscures accountability. As a small child, I knew that "MB" managed the Bittersweet Lane Apartments, but I had no clue whatsoever who owned or developed it or even what MB stood for. I just knew they weren't good.

251

RESIDENT SERVICES

"Excuse me a moment, I need to ask him something." Jo-Ann turned to a boy walking towards us. "Hey, did you finish up your report in the computer room, or do you need the room again tonight?"

"Um, yeah, I'll be back." The middle schooler glanced up at Jo-Ann and smiled, then looked back at the floor and walked down the hall of the Fiorentino Community Center at Charlesview.

No matter what kind of day I was having at work, Charlesview could cheer me up. I was back on-site to meet with Jo-Ann about the vacant retail spaces we were still trying to fill. Otherwise, after many years of work from many people, the Charlesview Residences had completely transformed from construction site to community. I loved seeing the kids there, kids like me but living in a much nicer place. And I was lucky enough to have helped play a part in creating the place. Jo-Ann helped build the community.

"Hola!"

"*Hola!Hola!Hola!Hola!Hola!*" responded a class of toddlers from the bilingual preschool at Charlesview. Jo-Ann paused our conversation again to engage with them.

Children growing up at the Charlesview Residences got to see that the people running that place cared for them. Jo-Ann, the volunteer board, the resident services staff, and visitors from other nonprofits or from the local universities were there and would reach out to ask how they could help.

No one cared about us at Bittersweet Lane, unless you count the stalker maintenance man.

Some version of resident services is common at most nonprofit affordable housing developments. From small, culturally competent organizations to national firms partnering with government and academia to deliver on theories of change, nearly all mission-driven affordable housing developers invest time, energy, and funding to help their residents succeed in life.

Resident services often include some mix of programming, affinity groups, and individual assistance. They help residents move into a new home and neighborhood, navigate bureaucracies, pursue education, work on their health, and ensure the basics—food, safety, shelter—are covered. Helping residents succeed makes good financial sense for property owners and managers. Evictions cost money in legal fees, vacancy loss, repairs and maintenance, and marketing.

Nonprofit and government agencies often struggle to provide services because they struggle to connect to the people who need those services. Willie Sutton robbed banks "because that's where the money is." Affordable housing is where the poor is. Good resident services programs in housing developments bridge the professional silos and gatekeeping among social services. They help people access health insurance, health care, education, voter registration, childcare, transportation, food, financial planning, and more, all right at home.

During the Barack Obama administration, cross-sector partnerships became required for new federal funding from HUD's Sustainable Communities program, HUD's Choice Neighborhoods, the Department of Education's Promised Neighborhoods, the Department of Justice's Byrne Public Safety Grants, and others. The administration encouraged the staff running these programs to coordinate across agencies, and the funding competitions required grant applicants to establish partnerships across sectors to address demonstrable community needs.

More advanced resident services programs understand that residents have both gifts and needs. They gather neighbors and assist them in sharing their skills and passions with each other, from dance troupes to self-defense classes, from barbecues to voter registration events. There is dignity in exchange, in mutual aid. One-way help is not a relationship.

I am personally thankful for the people who dedicate their professional lives to maintaining supportive communities. Poor people often are. Supportive, that is. At Bittersweet Lane, we always helped each other when we could because we all needed help sometimes. We babysat, shoveled snow, jimmied locks, gave rides, rescued people from the elevator, and looked in on the elderly. Organizations that view residents as whole people with both gifts and needs, organizations that think about homes not units, they help the next kid have it better.

NINETEEN

Homeless Services

I'm not thinking of you
when I swing left onto Massachusetts Avenue.
It's just the way the traffic moves . . .

My mother called in a panic on a Tuesday night in 2012. "Kevin is at Boston Health Care for the Homeless, and they won't let me in to see him. I don't know what to do."

I'd just talked to him the week before. Things had seemed more stable. What happened?

"Security wouldn't let me in. Was a big clusterfuck. Tom is going in tomorrow to see what the hell is going on. Will let you know as soon as I know. I'm really pissed at the people who let this happen."

I called Kevin and talked with him for a bit. He was utterly confused about where he was. He tried to tell me the hospital was in Cambridge. He was still on "Albany Street" after all. He had no idea he'd been moved three miles across the river to Boston, that he was sitting just on the other side of the expressway from the D Street projects he'd once lived and worked in. I packed a bag of clothes to bring him, mostly his own clothes that he'd given me over the years.

Kevin had been sleeping at a homeless shelter on Albany Street, Cambridge, around the corner from MIT. He was stabilizing and hoping he could get off Cambridge's long public housing waitlist. On Monday night, Kevin passed out at the shelter. Alcohol? Diabetes? No one knew. While Kevin was out, other shelter guests stripped him of everything but the clothes he was wearing. They took his bit of cash, his knife, his cigarettes, his wallet with his driver's license, his MBTA pass, and everything else. Kevin woke up in a hospital bed on Albany Street, Boston, around the corner from Mass and Cass.

"Mass and Cass" is where addiction and homelessness show themselves most vividly in Boston. The intersection of Massachusetts Avenue and Melnea Cass Boulevard separates an industrial district from a hospital area. A two-block radius includes a prison, an immigration detention facility, a food bank, a clinic for the homeless, a sketchy motel, methadone clinics, a hospital, and Boston Health Care for the Homeless. The land use around Mass and Cass is a recipe for mixing poverty, addiction, and disease among vulnerable people.

Mass and Cass is the city's scar tissue from the Inner Belt/Southwest Expressway highway project. Melnea Cass Boulevard traces the route of what would have been the Inner Belt highway. Organized communities had stopped highway construction in the 1970s, but not before demolition crews turned a large swath of Dorchester, Roxbury, and Jamaica Plain into rubble. The Inner Belt Project created an eight-lane boulevard instead, a surface highway by the standards of Boston's narrow streets. The demolition created vacant parcels that remain vacant until this day. It destroyed the real estate value of its neighbors.

In the US, we choose to place public institutions and services for poor people on vacant, publicly owned sites because services for the poor do not generate revenues that can pay for land on the open market. We demand our government choose the lowest upfront cost for public capital projects, heedless of consequences. We stuff the poor in leftover places because we are cheap.

When homelessness began racing the opioid crisis for worst crisis award, more tents than Boston had seen in a century popped up on the neglected bits of land around Mass and Cass. Tent encampments in places like these are familiar to anyone who's lived in a West Coast city in the last couple decades, but they were vanishingly rare in Boston until the Trump administration and pandemic.

The staff at Boston Health Care for the Homeless have a difficult job, and they keep very strict visitor policies. Poor people know poor people. Addicts know other addicts and dealers. People in difficult and extreme circumstances are prone to extreme behavior. Trauma alters the brain, and decades of traumas can break a person's ability to respond to threats and stimuli appropriately. So the staff treated visitors with a level of suspicion and intrusion reminiscent of a TSA agent having a bad day. That's how they treated my mother, anyway.

Wednesday morning, I wore a nice suit to work. I asked my boss, Willie Jones, if I could skip out to go to the midday visitation opening. "It better not be no fucking job interview," Willie joked before turning serious. "Of course. Put family first."

I rode the 10 bus from one edge of the South End to the other and walked briskly the last couple blocks to meet Tom standing outside. Tom trained with Kevin and with some of Kevin's teachers for years. When Tom visits, my wife plays a game of "try to come up with something Tom has never done." He's been everything from inmate in a Greek jail to biotech executive. He's made shoes, and he built a cabin in the deep woods from scratch. One of the things Tom had done along the way had earned him a Boston Medical Center ID card, which dangled conspicuously from a BMC lanyard over his suit. We walked into Boston Health Care for the Homeless' lobby, suitably armored for a confrontation with the system.

We arrived at the right time, but we weren't on the list to be let in. Tom explained the situation, and security searched us and my duffel bag of Kevin's clothes before they let us in with an "Of course, Dr. Dahl." Tom was not a doctor and hadn't claimed to be. We didn't correct the guard.

The elevator opened to the lobby and visitation area at the center of hallways of inpatient rooms. Kevin had already charmed everyone in the place, patients and staff. The staff took his charm with a polite smile and laugh but loosed an eyeroll when they turned away. Two patients, fifty-something women, hung on his every word and laughed at every joke. Kevin exclaimed to them, "This is my son!" and gave me a huge hug.

Kevin greeted Tom with a hug too, and then we walked over to an isolated corner to catch up and to hear Kevin's account of what had happened and what was going on. A social worker on staff joined us and then talked to Tom and me separately. We reviewed potential next steps, discussed care plans, and got clear on rules for visitation and belongings. We asked the social worker what bureaucratic wheels he needed turned to get Kevin what he needed—most pressingly a home—and the social worker pointed us in a couple directions where we could try to be helpful. But he also told us that they were having trouble finding somewhere for Kevin to go after discharge. The few available beds were in strictly dry shelters over an hour's drive away, and Kevin refused them on both counts.

I was putting in long hours at work to try to build affordable housing, but I couldn't get my own family housed. I'm not sure how much more I could have done in this system we have, but I feel guilty to this day.

Before I left, Kevin asked me the questions he'd been asking me for years, even when I was an embarrassed teenager. "Has anyone told you today how awesome you are? Has anyone told you they love you? Well, you're awesome, and I love you."

. . . But then I pass the last place I saw you alive[113]

TWENTY

Preservation

Buildings need tender loving care, plus the occasional new roof, boiler, windows, and so on. TLC comes at a price.

Because our housing strategy in the last half century focused on leveraging private equity and debt, much of our current affordable housing is only temporarily restricted as affordable, for terms ranging from fifteen years to ninety-nine years, depending on funding sources and location. As a result, each year we risk losing approximately one hundred thousand affordable homes to market conversion.[114]

There is an entire specialty within the affordable housing world focused on preservation. Highly skilled specialists like the nonprofit Preservation of Affordable Housing (POAH) utilize a range of financing tools to purchase, recapitalize, resyndicate, rehabilitate, and ultimately preserve both the physical homes and their affordability restrictions for decades to come.

Sometimes, building rehabilitation can be completed while leaving tenants in place in their homes, with assistance and consideration from the project team. Other times, we must relocate tenants temporarily for more extensive rehabilitation work. One-to-one replacement policies for affordable housing alongside the strong tenant protections in the Universal Relocation Act help ensure tenants are consulted, given options, and compensated for temporary or permanent relocations. There are firms that specialize in helping coordinate and perform these relocations on behalf of developers/owners. While by no means perfect, the current system protects residents from the abuses suffered from slum clearance, market conversion, and the early generation of HOPE VI developments.

Preservation tools resemble those for new construction, including subsidized debt products that provide low-cost acquisition, bridge, construction, and/or permanent debt; Low-Income Housing Tax Credit and other tax credit resources to attract equity; and public subordinate debt. Preservation also tends to dive into esoteric sections of law and policy, such as Section 8(bb) porting, Section 8 Mark-to-Market, and the Rental Assistance Demonstration project, to better leverage existing rental income streams into capital financing to pay for rehabilitation.

The Obama administration introduced the Rental Assistance Demonstration (RAD) to preserve public housing using a discrepancy in federal law between public housing funding and Section 8 Housing Assistance Payment (HAP) funding. The Section 8 program did not fare well through repeated cycles of budget cutting and sequestration, but it remained much better funded than public housing. The federal government was willing to pay more to an apartment subsidized with a HAP contract than an apartment subsidized through public housing funds. HAP subsidies go to private entities (both non- and for-profit), which in turn take their HAP contract to the bank to underwrite a mortgage loan and further leverage both by introducing LIHTC equity from private investors.

Public housing cannot mortgage itself or admit the *investor limited partner owner* necessary to use LIHTC resources. So the RAD program allowed housing authorities to convert their public housing developments into HAP-funded developments. The extra revenue helped, but it was the ability to leverage other private and public debt and equity that enabled housing authorities to repair, rehabilitate, or redevelop their properties and to responsibly fund operating and maintenance into the future.

As with HOPE VI, LIHTC, and other affordable housing programs, RAD's success varies depending on who was involved, where the project is, and what your definition of success is. Success for existing residents? For poor people generally? For moderate-income households needing housing? For the neighborhood and abutters? For people driving past? For energy savings and the environment? For universal accessibility? For the removal of hazardous contaminants, including lead, PCBs, asbestos, and volatile organic compounds (VOCs)? Many tenant groups and housing advocates have approached RAD conversions with due skepticism. It technically privatizes public housing, even when it's structured in a way to give the Public Housing Authority ongoing control.

That question—what is it all for?—should be asked throughout the development process, from a home's conception to birth to life to rebirth. Creating affordable homes is ultimately a circular process. It takes ongoing work to create, use, and preserve our nation's housing infrastructure.

To sum up the development cycle, that ongoing work includes prospecting sites, performing due diligence, creating development concepts, and nurturing them through predevelopment to closing and construction. Then, permanent loan conversion clears the way for ongoing property management and resident services. When we fail to create enough homes, we rely on shelter, services, and streets. When the homes we created age, we must work hard to preserve their physical structures, their finances, and their affordability.

That's as linearly as I can describe the phases of the development cycle. I envision the development process as a triple helix of finance, design/construction, and community—circling back on itself ouro- boros-like. At work, we experience these phases simultaneously or vicariously. Many firms consider an ideal workload for development project managers as having one project in construction or conver- sion, another moving towards closing, and another one or two in predevelopment. Some professionals only ever experience one phase of the process. It's a relative rarity to shepherd an affordable hous- ing development the whole way from prospecting to operations. We accomplish our work together, hundreds of individuals from dozens of professions.

We can fix this housing crisis. We know how, you and me. We can create enough homes of the right kinds, in the right places, with sufficient subsidies such that every person in this country has a home. We just need places, permissions, and the resources to orga- nize the people and materials necessary.

We know how to identify sites for new homes. There are more sites ready to go right now than we have resources for right now. Some of them are existing affordable housing facing the expiration of their use restrictions or the deterioration of their buildings. Some of them are permitted sites whose owners would rather sell than develop. Many are spelled out in official City and Town plans. We have inventories of surplus property that we the public already own. Advocates across the nation know the places in our neighborhoods left neglected, needing redevelopment. Even in the most expensive downtowns in America, there are large amounts of paved, vacant land used for car storage.

We know how to get permissions to build on those sites, where jurisdictions have not banned housing through restrictive zoning and land use codes. Currently, this is the most restrictive phase of the process, and unnecessarily so. We cannot say honestly that we have decided every person should have a home until we have done away with these exclusionary zoning codes.

With sites and permissions in hand, we know how to organize the people and materials necessary to build. We know how to create effective capital subsidies for affordable housing, from public housing to project-based vouchers to subordinate debt products and tax credits. Those methods have their relative advantages and disadvantages, but if we chose to adequately fund them, they would work. There is a strong industry of developers who can direct those resources such that designers, builders, lawyers, accountants, managers, and the rest can do their jobs to create homes. Are there enough of us? If not, we build more slowly and we create more jobs.

If you are one of those people working away at this crisis, thank you. Truly. If you would like to improve your practice or join our ranks, I hope this book provides useful tools and insight. Technical appendices further detail the affordable housing system's roles and programs plus the developer's primary tool—the pro forma.

Knowing how is half the battle—and thankfully, it's the half we have won. But we cannot stop there. In Part 3: The Laneway, we'll look at how we got here, how this system became so entrenched, and—more importantly—what is necessary to take the solutions the rest of the way.

What if we fix this housing crisis? Can you imagine the creativity and energy people could have if none of us had to worry about losing our homes? Do you understand how much healing we could all do? Can you envision the art, entrepreneurship, music, cooking, and caregiving we could all enjoy?

What would you create, dear reader, if you didn't have to worry about survival?

PART 3

The Laneway

TWENTY-ONE

How Did We End Up Here?

I wrote this book in part to ask that question. How did we end up here? Yes, the big "we" of the United States of America, but also my own small "we"—my family. How did we end up in affordable housing? How has our country managed housing for poor people throughout our history? The research for these separate questions collided, and it changed me profoundly.

By now, we've explored the current state of affordable housing and its impact, but this isn't just about policies and programs—it's about the deeper, underlying beliefs that have shaped them. The English-speaking world, particularly, is an outlier in how few affordable homes it has produced compared to other nations.[115] And over the centuries, the one constant in how we've approached housing for the poor isn't the policies themselves but an ideology: a commitment to separating the worthy from the unworthy. To truly address this crisis, we need to understand how this ideology has permeated every level of housing development and what it will take to break free from it.

MCGONAGLE

She walked down to Tullagh Strand, fourteen-year-old Theresa Grace McGonagle did, to take a moment away from her family's worries. The beach faced the wild North Atlantic, waves kicking up. The wind carried a frigid mist to mix with Grace's tears.

Grace's family eked out a living on a small plot between the beach and the Urris Hills in this remote northern townland called Clonmany, located in the remote northern peninsula called Inishowen, in the remote northwestern County of Donegal, on the remote northwestern island of Ireland. They farmed potatoes and spun wool, as they had there for a few generations, but not forever.

Most of the families working this poor soil had once worked greener fields or practiced trades in Derry. The O'Dohertys had even been aristocrats. Then, one of them had the bright idea of aiding the English invasion, thinking the English would allow him to keep his lordship as they had with collaborator lords in Scotland and Wales. They did not. The English gave themselves title to the Doherty lands alongside the rest of the island, just a decade or so before creating title from Massachusett lands on the other side of the Atlantic.

The British truly colonized Ireland around the same time they colonized America. Often, the same people took property and exploited labor in both places. The Raleigh and Chichester families were both involved in the Irish plantations of Munster and Ulster (respectively) and Virginia (together). The Carews, Grenvilles, Gilberts, and Courtenays who planned a great colonizing expedition from Somerset and Devon into Ireland were the same men who invested in the earliest attempts to colonize Virginia.[116]

English legal innovations in the Plantation of Ulster, the Protestant Ascendancy, and the penal laws prohibited native Irish people from owning land. They removed the Irish from their ancestral homes to these poorer corners of the island. Not that the land came cheap even then.

Grace's family paid rent to a middleman, Thomas Douglas Bateson, who managed the property for his cousins, the Bateson Harveys. The "rent" was about equal to all the food Irish tenant farmers produced, even then, after *An Gorta Mór*. The Harveys had purchased the right under English law to demand rent from native Irish farmers. In their own words, the Harveys viewed Grace and the rest of the people who lived on their investment as "uncivilized, ignorant and barbarous," so the Harveys "tamed them and introduced order, settling more difficulties by the whiskey bottle and horsewhip."[117]

Officially, the English Lord George Chichester maintained title. Cromwell himself had granted the Inishowen peninsula to George's ancestor, Lord Arthur Chichester, to repay a loan that funded the Cromwellian conquest. Cromwell, in a brilliant colonial innovation with absolutely no present-day parallel to be found whatsoever in sales of Palestinian land in Brooklyn, funded his invasion by selling plots of land to aspiring settlers before he conquered them.

A few generations after the conquest, this George Chichester loved to gamble, bad as he was at it. He gambled away £50,000 he'd borrowed using the Inishowen properties as collateral. To pay back his lenders, he sold thousand-year leases. Harvey was just one of the investors looking for a good return by purchasing this future stream of cash flow from a motivated seller.

Grace's neighbors, the most optimistic, hardest working ones, they paid twenty pounds in rent to Thomas Bateson for a near useless plot at the foot of the hills. They worked hard to improve the land up the foothills, and they cultivated it well enough to pay the rent with the food they produced while they themselves lived almost exclusively off the potatoes they grew in the worst parts of their plot.

When the landlord's son went up the hill and saw how well they'd improved the land, he raised the rent from twenty to forty-two pounds. The twenty pounds already took all their efforts; coming up with forty-two was unimaginable. So, as reward for improving the land, the Bateson-Harveys served them with an eviction notice. Now they'd be leaving, like so many others Grace had known, off to America, or maybe England, or, if they resisted, on a prison ship to Australia.

But any tears Grace might have shed on the strand that morning were not for them but for her own family. Thomas, the middleman, paid them a visit to deliver a notice on John Harvey's behalf. This John, born in Russia to parents who were first cousins and wealthy English traders, he had the right to demolish Grace's home to force them out.

Clonmany is known in history for two things. The first was short-lived independence as the moonshining "Poitín Republic of Urris."[118] The second was violent resistance to evictions. And they were all out of poitín.

The English ruling class exerted control over Ireland's countryside through a system of land titling, tenancy at will, and eviction.[119] Forceful resistance to evictions in Inishowen began in the 1830s but grew in the 1850s following the landlords' and government's deadly inhumanity during *An Gorta Mór*. Landlords forced their tenants to hand over the food they'd grown, and they then exported it off the starving island.[120] The British government insisted the Irish must pay cash for food—even food donated from other nations for famine relief—and that landlords' right to export the food produced by their Irish tenants would not be curtailed in any way. As a result, Ireland lost half its population to death and emigration. The survivors in the Inishowen peninsula organized to physically stop these deadly evictions. Here is a local account, one of 497 eviction stories to be found among The Schools' Collection of elder interviews:

> There is a place in the townland of Carrohugh called Murderhole. It is said that bailiffs came to evict a family at this place. The neighbours all gathered to try to stop this eviction. It resulted in a fierce fight, in which one of the bailiffs was murdered, and the place is known as Murderhole ever since.[121]

But there would be no group of strong neighbors assembling to protect Grace's family. The landlords began to bundle many evictions in a single day rather than trying to evict one family at a time. This prevented the community coming to their neighbors' defense. To expedite the eviction process, landlords and British soldiers began to simply burn their tenants' thatch roofs to render the homes uninhabitable in the cold, wet climate.

Grace wondered what choices her family had left. Without warm, dry shelter, her family would not survive the winter. There were no factory jobs or even workhouses for her. Ireland's role in the British Empire was breadbasket, producing food for the English factory workers who'd given up farming for labor in England's new industrial centers.

Grace's parents faced a brutal decision: use the food they grew to feed their family or to pay the rent. Starvation or eviction. Here they were, again facing the quandary they had back when blight took the potato crops when Grace was born.

In November 1846, when Grace's mother was pregnant with her, the parish priests of Clonmany and Donagh and other notable men of the area sent a letter to the local government at the Barony, attempting to establish a famine relief committee. That letter was forwarded to a higher government office at Dublin Castle. The British government made no reply.

So in January, these local leaders again forwarded the request with a new cover letter politely begging for help, comparing the unfolding tragedy in Clonmany to the famous mass graves in Skibbereen and outlining how easily food could be brought to their "safe little bay" only two short miles from the parish center.

A bureaucrat at Dublin Castle responded with a letter in late January, but it only acknowledged receipt of the request. Hearing no substantive response as tragedy deepened, the men of Clonmany sent another letter to Dublin Castle in late February: "The Committee beg to state that the unaccountable harshness and cruel procrastination . . . may [be] the prolific parent of starvation, disease and death." They pleaded their "sanguine hopes that Government will in its wisdom and feelings of philanthropy grant them . . . a soup kitchen."

The final correspondence came in a letter of one sentence: "Sir, In acknowledging the receipt of your letter, I beg to state that I am directed . . . to inform you that they are determined not to establish a soup kitchen in this locality, having formed a depot in this town for the sale of cheap meal to the destitute."[122]

I came across the above correspondence during my research into why my second great-grandmother, Grace, left Ireland at fourteen. I physically shuddered as it called to mind the scores of similar letters, binders, emails, and speeches I'd read or crafted in my own career, begging American bureaucracies for approvals and funding, to be allowed to create affordable homes to stop our own evicted neighbors dying on the streets. The banality of evil is right there in black and white.

Today in the US, we use that same fundamental legal basis and body of English case law for land title, leases, and eviction. Most parts of the United States still allow evictions to occur at any time for any reason. Some places have passed just-cause eviction laws, establishing the circumstances under which an eviction may occur, such as illegal use, destruction, or failure to pay rent. Like many today, my Irish ancestors had no such legal recourse or protection. To survive, they had to leave home.

And *An Gorta Mór* wasn't even the only great hunger created by this system. The British—through their East India Company and through the Crown both—created massive famines in India and elsewhere in the same way they had in Ireland. While they oversaw the death and emigration of half the Irish, they built the physical and legal infrastructure to extract resources from India. They introduced inedible cash crops that couldn't grow without large-scale irrigation. The cash from the crops was, of course, used by the farmers to pay the British rent and taxes.

There had been famine in India before, but there was never a famine that had not been covered by good crop yields in other parts of the country, nor did any famine last for years on end. For centuries, local leaders created, and villagers managed, local water storage systems and food distribution networks that helped keep famines rare and brief.

The British ended all that. They had claimed their railroads and other infrastructure would render aid more effective by moving food more quickly, ending famine forever. Then, in 1876, they got a chance to prove it after back-to-back monsoon failures precipitated famine. The British used their infrastructure to take grain *away* from areas experiencing the famine, just as they had in Ireland one generation before. The food did move more quickly, just in the wrong direction.

So, as Mike Davis asserted, "the combination of all these things— private grain market, a reluctant and eventually destructive system of outdoor relief, and the fact that the villages no longer possessed the same infrastructure or resources—led to a famine that grew out of a drought, which ended up killing somewhere between eight and twelve million people." That is at least four times the body count of *An Gorta Mór*. Then, the Brits did it again in India in the late 1890s with as many deaths for the same reasons, having learned nothing, transforming bad weather into mass death.

In India and Africa, the British Empire's use of property laws and poor laws proved even more than their use in Ireland that the British goal was resource extraction, not nation building. Restrict the natives' ability to access basic human necessities—food, water, shelter, care—so that they must work themselves to death to survive.

I look out my window at downtown Seattle and wonder how different things are here and now.

HOW HAVE WE HOUSED OUR POOR FROM THE START?

Indigenous housing advocates like Seattle's Colleen Echohawk like to point out that "we housed 100% of our people" before colonization. Even if the historical facts were more complicated, it is simply true that the Indigenous peoples of the places that created me—the Massachusett, the Coast Salish, the Gaels—all created homes for kin and community, not as individual commodities for investment. Cultures around the world have operated on a principle that housing is both a right and responsibility. British and American cultures are not among them. We hold to a different ideology.

The US has always focused instead on defining whom the public should and should not help. From settler charity to industrial-age institutions to public and affordable housing, we have stuck to that

English colonial value. During the same period that English lords developed the conquer/entitle/rent/eviction form of social control on my ancestors in Ireland, English colonists did the same and worse on America's East Coast. Across the empire, they created and refined the English Poor Laws to manage poverty in contexts of colonial and racial-religious persecution.

The English tradition initially put the responsibility for social welfare on churches and "overseers of the poor" rather than on public institutions. Puritan colonists understood charity to their neighbor as a religious obligation, with emphasis on the words "to their neighbor." They defined "neighbor" as white Protestant landowners who were officially accepted into their town by a vote of the town meeting or board of selectmen. They did not consider indentured servants, the enslaved, non-whites, Catholics, Jews, natives, and unmarried women worthy of English Christian charity.

To help the neighbors they did deem worthy, Puritan settlers gave direct assistance or took the indigent into their own homes. They treated poverty relief as a face-to-face encounter among neighbors. If you were a person in need in seventeenth-century Massachusetts, you would be required to appear before the annual town meeting and publicly state your case for charity in front of your neighbors. Then, town leaders would decide whether you were worthy of help, what help they were willing to give you, and for how long. I, for one, would be horribly embarrassed and might even begin to associate charity with shame.

Despite their extraordinary limitations on charity, the Puritans still feared charity's costs. They put decades of effort into further specifying who counted as a neighbor worthy of assistance and who did not. Larry Vale's *From the Puritans to the Projects* demonstrates that throughout US history, our government's attempts to help people have always been caught in our debate over what the obligations of the public are to its members in need and who even counts as a member of our public in the first place.

The traditional English and American answer to housing shortages is simply "go away." They said that to the castoffs of northern Europe who colonized America, to homesteaders moving west, to the twentieth century "drive till you qualify," to your author's own move from Boston to Seattle. The genius author Octavia E. Butler spoke compellingly about our society's "myth of 'away,' as in 'I'll throw it away.' Where's that? There's no such place. It's going *somewhere.*"[123]

"Just move away; just go somewhere else" is a housing solution that devastated the people who already lived wherever "else" is, whether in Ulster, in Massachusetts, on Salish lands, or in Palestine. John Winthrop—a member of England's landed gentry and a leader of the Puritan colonization of Massachusetts—wrote, "God hath consumed the natives with a miraculous plague whereby the greater part of the country is left voide of inhabitants."

Pardon my harsh language, but John bore some false witness there. He knew well the land was not vacant. John himself kept captured Indigenous women as slaves, and he traded other Indigenous people to England's Caribbean colonies as slaves.[124] Whether a plague can be "miraculous" I'll leave to the theologians, but we know that the plague that decimated the Massachusett people spread from England to the Plymouth Colony on Wampanoag land to the Massachusett. Still, these English colonizers justified taking possession of the Americas by claiming the land was empty, *vacuum domicilium.* Their evidence for this farcical conclusion included cultural differences around housing. While the English built detached homes and enclosures, the "savage people ruleth over many lands without title or property; for they inclose no ground, neither have they cattell."[125]

The Massachusett people did not parcel land to individuals and track it with written title as in the English system. There was no need as land had not been commodified. The Massachusett lived with extended family, splitting the year between a summer home near the beach and its bounty of seafood and an inland winter home near quarries. By contrast, Winthrop's settlers in the 1630s separated each family into one of seven hundred individual, detached houses, each with its own garden. The Massachusett practiced agriculture collectively on vast fields of corn, beans, and squash across what is now Dorchester and North Quincy, much larger than the English settlers' gardens and small farms. As to the cattle, cows are an alien species in the Americas.

It would be nice to say the past is passed, but colonial England continues to set legal precedent in the United States today. No less an authority than Supreme Court Justice Samuel Alito in the year of our lord 2022 based his decision to outlaw abortion on the writing of the seventeenth-century Chief Justice of England, Sir Matthew Hale.[126]

After Alito's citation, I went searching for a Hale quote about poor people. I imagined there must be something as brutal and discriminatory as his treatment of women. This was the man who created the legal theory supporting marital rape and who sentenced two women to be burned at the stake. I was sure whatever he said about poor people would give me something punchy for the book. I was wrong.

Matty boy published "A Discourse Touching Provision for the Poor" in 1683. Hale argued that we have a duty to help the poor and that the criminalization of poverty is counterproductive for society unless and until all able-bodied people had opportunity to work and all those unable to work had access to care. "All the Laws against Vagrants, Beggers and Wanderers will be then Effectually put in

Execution, when we may be sure they may be imployed if they will: But till that, interdicting and punishing of the Beggars and Givers, seems to me a most unreasonable piece of Imprudence as well as Uncharitableness." That is to say, criminalizing poverty is wasteful, self-defeating, and immoral.

The marital rape guy appears to have been more progressive about poverty and homelessness than present-day elected Democrats in cities across the United States. Matty valued prevention over remedy: "The prevention of poverty, idleness, and a loose and disorderly Education, even of poor Children, would do more good to this Kingdom than all the Gibbets, and Cauterization, and Whipping Posts, and Jayls in this Kingdom, and would render these kinds of Disciplines less necessary and less frequent."[127] Our nation's liberal party today governs somewhere to the right of a seventeenth-century witch burner.

We continue to debate criminalization of poverty versus charity. Professor Larry Vale concluded that "the unwillingness of the American public (acting through its government) to commit to a large-scale program to house the country's low-income residents is both a product of ambivalence and a source of further contestation over which of the poor should be housed in the limited supply, what form this housing should take, and where it should be located."[128] We can't agree on who, what, or where, because we can't agree on *why*.

By the second quarter of the nineteenth century, the scale of housing needs in America's growing, diversifying towns and cities overwhelmed the colonial-era reliance on individuals and the Church to manage. Leaders began to create a variety of new institutions to sort and classify people in need and to help or punish them accordingly. Their laws and practices evolved until the question of "How do I help the poor (or not)?" subtly transformed into "How do we solve poverty without direct aid?"

For the poor, almshouses and workhouses came first. Boston built what was probably the first almshouse in the colonies on the edge of the Common in 1662, which at the time was the back of town, within the stench of the Back Bay's low tide. Even then, people disagreed on the almshouse's purpose. Some wanted a house of correction for the "debauched and idle." Some wanted a home for "honest poor peoples." They both got their way. Widows and their children, the elderly, the disabled, the mentally ill, and criminals lived together under the roof of the Boston Almshouse. City leaders put the able-bodied among them to work in an attached workhouse and later built larger workhouses where the conditions were designed to be a punishment to deter the poor from living in Boston. The model spread quickly and remained the cutting edge of housing the poor for centuries.

In the United States, leaders continued to create new categories of poverty to sort into institutional housing. Almshouses continued to house the poor who were unable to work while workhouses took the able-bodied poor. Penitentiaries housed people convicted of crimes. Slave plantations housed captive Africans and their descendants in minimal accommodations, including as sharecroppers after legal slavery. Asylums housed the mentally ill, as well as women simply declared such by their husbands. Orphanages housed homeless children who behaved; reformatories took children who misbehaved. Magdalene laundries kept poor and "fallen" women. Leaders of the time believed these institutions—even the chattel slavery—could improve the people suffering them. They took pains to disconnect their clients from their cultural heritages in favor of the "superior" white, Anglo-Saxon, Protestant culture. Architects with this belief experimented with form and structure in attempts to make the buildings' designs themselves help correct their residents' perceived deficiencies.

When the United States expanded westward, settlers behaved like the Puritans of the 1600s. As Josephine Ensign put it, "The pioneer settlers of what became Washington State carried the Poor Laws with them across the prairies from places like New England and the Midwest."[129] In 1854, when Seattle was home to just two hundred settlers, the Washington Territorial legislature adopted a poor law modeled on the same English Poor Laws that the Puritans utilized in Massachusetts two centuries earlier. Josephine Ensign documents the use and influence of those Poor Laws in Seattle in *Skid Road: On the Frontier of Health and Homelessness in an American City*. She also relays the story of King County's first official homeless person.

In 1854, Seattle settlement leaders found a thirty-two-year-old sailor from Boylston, Massachusetts, living in a tent nearby the residences of Indigenous Duwamish people living on their ancestral land—in violation of a City of Seattle ordinance that forbade them from residing within the newly declared city's limits. City officials amputated his frostbitten toes with an axe, as there was no hospital. They deemed him insane and incapable of caring for himself. They engaged in a long legal controversy over whether the King County public had any responsibility for this man from Massachusetts, and then they auctioned him off to be cared for by the lowest bidder. By 1856, the white leaders of Seattle raised private donations to ship him back to Massachusetts.

Twenty-one years later, in 1877, King County established its first institution for housing the poor. Rather than being shipped away or contracted out to the lowest bidder, poor people in King County would now be sent to work in the King County Poor Farm and Pauper Cemetery, located on what had been an Indigenous Duwamish settlement along the river.

The growth of institutions moved the poor and marginalized farther away from their communities and moved the responsibility for their care from face-to-face local interactions to more distant bureaucracy. The US abandoned the intimacy of the Puritan approach to managing poverty but maintained the Puritan obsession with separating the moral and worthy from the damned and contemptible.

In 1736, officials reported that only one-third of the eighty-eight people in the poorhouse were born in Boston. Outraged homeowners complained that money was spent on people "who are crept in among us." In 2023, the *Seattle Times* invited readers to ask questions about homelessness and seventy-five of its five hundred responses were some version of "why do people move here to be homeless?"

For at least four hundred years—four hundred years—American conservatives and liberals alike have complained that money should not be spent on the poor because they are outsiders. No matter that it is not true. The *Seattle Times* reported that studies here and across the nation consistently show only one-eighth to one-third of homeless people last lived out of state.[130] Most people who end up on the street end up on the streets nearby their last home. Time after time, this question is raised and answered, and then the answer is disregarded until someone asks the question again. Then professionals like me get paid to study the question again.

I wonder whether some people are mentally incapable of getting it. Is this othering a mental defense when people do not want to acknowledge their neighbors' suffering? When people move due to becoming homeless, we usually stay close, perhaps moving to the nearest larger town or city. The United States' urban dwelling taxpayers spend a disproportionate amount on homelessness as compared to their suburbs, but we still spend it on people who were from nearby.[131] They are our neighbors. We are their neighbors.

The US relied on institutions to house our poor throughout the eighteenth and nineteenth centuries, and in the twentieth century, partially shifted towards creating affordable housing as you learned in our Jackson Square tour in an earlier chapter. Yet those institutions persist to this day, including immigrant detention centers, locked wards, prisons, and congregate shelters. Prisons deserve a special look as a tool for housing our poor, one we have utilized at a large scale since the earliest days of colonialism.

In the 1600s and 1700s, Britain "transported" its convicts to colonies in the Americas, Australia, and Indian Ocean islands. British courts convicted some of those people of crimes like robbery, perjury, and forgery. But many of these convicts would be today regarded as political prisoners or people experiencing homelessness instead of as criminal rebels and vagrants. The colonies provided an excellent opportunity for the British to send their impoverished elsewhere, save money on both charity and prisons, and make a profit on the back end from indentured labor. One in four British immigrants to the Americas in the 1700s were convicts.

This convict transportation, indenture, and leasing existed alongside the far more brutal British system of African chattel slavery, which eventually replaced indentured servitude as the preferred form of forced labor in the Americas. Slaves and indentured servants both would have been housed in minimal accommodations on plantations and estates.[132]

As the United States evolved, penitentiaries and prisons grew up as parallel institutions to labor camps and plantations. In fact, the line between the two is blurry. During a cotton crash in the 1840s, Louisiana looked to its criminal justice system for profit. The state privatized its penitentiary and leased it to the McHatton, Pratt & Ward company, which transformed the penitentiary into a textile factory whose prisoners worked from dusk to dawn under threat of beatings and death.

In 1848, state legislatures across the South declared that all children born in the penitentiary to African Americans would become property of the state. Imprisoned women raised their children inside the prison until the age of ten, at which age prison officials would then auction the children off at the courthouse steps. Many of the buyers at the auctions were also prison officials. These being gender-segregated prisons, we can reasonably assume that prison officials provided the sperm themselves. In addition to the self-dealing in the prison system, proceeds from selling imprisoned Black children were used to fund public schools for white children.[133]

After the United States emerged victorious from the Confederate insurrection and declared chattel slavery illegal, former Confederate states replaced the chattel slavery system with sharecropping and convict leasing. Many non-Confederate states followed suit. The state would arrest Black people, lease them out to plantations, mines, and construction companies as forced labor, and take a neat profit for state government. The system was no less brutal than the chattel slavery it replaced; annual death rates ranged from 16–25%. There was no incentive to care for the person's health or well-being. Owners had the attitude of, work 'em to death and get another. Convict leasing provided as much as 10% of the Tennessee state budget. By 1928, the state of Texas would be running twelve prison plantations.[134] The City of Atlanta and private firms in Georgia profited from the Atlanta Prison Farm, which is currently being developed into an urban warfare training center.[135] Arkansas empowered inmate guards to practice whipping as late as 1967. Even in the Pacific Northwest, settlers established these types of state institutions to inter the impoverished for profit.

The practice continues today. The United States prison system spends $74 billion annually, more than the entire gross domestic product of 133 nations. We house more than 2.1 million people behind bars at a cost upwards of $50,000 per person per year. Publicly traded corporations like Corrections Corporation of America and GEO Group generated over $2.53 billion in revenue from taxpayers as early as 2012, and they represented only about half of the private prison business.[136]

Compare that to the 2.2 million people with housing vouchers, 3.5 million in LIHTC homes, and 970,000 in public housing.[137] Prisons are on par with Section 8 as a housing program and more than twice as large as public housing. And yet the most expensive permanent supportive housing only costs about $12,000–14,000 per person per year.

In addition to our couple million people residing in prisons, we have an estimated 4.5 million more people on probation and parole. Seventy million people have criminal convictions. All these millions are barred from affordable housing, among other necessities. When people leave prison and ask themselves where they will sleep at night, they may be unable to stay with their families without risking their family's eviction.

Here is a place where white privilege made a massive difference for my family. Because my grandparents got subsidized mortgages in an era when Black people were typically denied them, my grandparents were able to safely take us in when we were homeless. For the many Black and other families in public or subsidized housing, taking in their children and grandchildren is against the rules.

On the flip side from punishing and "reforming" poor people, American institutions have also consistently rewarded upwardly mobile, assimilated, white households. Larry Vale described this system of public rewards as "premised on the belief that good citizens require good homes, and the good home is one that is owned, not rented; an abode earned through hard work. From the Land Ordinance of 1785, inspired by Jefferson, through the various nineteenth-century initiatives to provide bounty lands to worthy veterans, to the Homestead Act of 1862, federal public lands policy advanced the ideological preference for single-family homes."[138] Twentieth-century American leaders built on this tradition. They invested in and spread the belief that detached, owned homes were morally superior and more patriotic than our traditional human tendency to live in community. The policies and laws governing housing today descend from this framework rooted in English, early capitalist culture.

So how did we end up here? My we, that is.

I grew up in affordable housing because my mother was poor. My mother was poor because she was raising two kids on one income in the United States. But well before she was a mother, she was a child born in the isolated Orient Heights public housing projects. Then she was a Dorchester teenager who—much like our pandemic's teenagers—lost her opportunity for a decent high school education due to adults' policy choices. Her mother, my Grandmy, had her first two children in public housing. Grandmy was lower class because her parents were lower-class immigrants. Her parents were lower-class immigrants because they were born with few rights to people who had barely survived a colonial system of no rights and crippling rents. Grace, James, and my other Irish immigrant ancestors arrived in the mid-nineteenth century, fleeing that same colonial system and its deadly famine, its poverty, its cultural destruction, and its forced labor. And that's why I am here.

Why are you where you are, dear reader? It's worth pondering, for better and worse. Who's your "we?" What's your collective story? It's easy to forget history in our culture, or to think we got to where we are on our own, that we're somehow exempt from the bigger picture. But the truth is, we're all part of this massive, tangled web, spun from history, inheritance, policies, and choices. No matter whether they were ours to make, we live the consequences and pass them on.

So take a minute and ask yourself: what stories, what systems, what luck or lack of it brought you to where you are now? Once we understand how we got here, maybe—just maybe—we can start to fix it.

"Maddens, Maddens, Maddens. I'm sick of hearing about these Maddens!" I looked up from the bar. Sean whirled around to yell, "Who the fuck said that?"

I can tell how drunk Sean is by how loud he gets and how many times he repeats himself. And even I was getting tired of Sean talking about Maddens, much as I can understand why. But seriously, who wants to hear anyone talk about us this much? It'd be like asking someone to read 120,000 words about us. It's absurd on its face. In fairness to Sean, this might have been his last chance to ask some of these questions. But so loudly? And here? Of all places? We're probably related to half the bar, for fuck's sake.

I took another sip from my first bottle of Budweiser heavy in many years—not because I got sober but because I got snobby—and I used it to push the laughter back down into my chest. Because I'd seen what Sean hadn't.

"The fuck you mean who the fuck am I? I'm your uncle! And who taught you how to talk like that?" It had been decades, but damned if it wasn't Danny Sullivan, our Aunt Susan's husband. Uncle Tommy and I started laughing at Sean, who'd gone from aggressive veteran to respectful nephew quicker than the Bruins could blow a Stanley Cup run, and we raised a toast up to Danny Sullivan and started explaining why we were talking endlessly about Maddens. Uncle Tommy had just made us Maddens again.

I'd been expecting the call the month before, if only because Sean got it first. My heart still raced when I saw the name Tommy Madden appear on my phone. "I wanted to call to say sorry," he said. "What happened to you wasn't right. And we're family, and we should've done more. And I'm not going to make any excuses or talk about why or anything. Just. I'm sorry," he told me.

He also told me he'd recently been diagnosed with stage four lung cancer. How'd he get diagnosed? When he was in the hospital for a heart attack. When'd he have the heart attack? A couple weeks after he'd retired from four decades of work as an auto mechanic. He'd just turned old enough to collect social security, and his sister-in-law, Aunt Nancy, had given Tommy $15,000 to retire on after Uncle Bobby passed. Put together, it was enough to pay rent for a room in the building next to the old Minihan's store.

Once we got past the necessities, we just talked, grown man to grown man. We chatted about family and history, Boston and Ireland, the Church and the war. Tommy was following the Russian invasion of Ukraine with an attention to detail on the level of a four-inch-thick hardcover history of World War II battles. It occurred to me I'd never had an adult conversation with Uncle Tommy. Last I saw him, I was fifteen and angry and he was drunk and meek, a real life Barney Gumble. But here we were, and I felt the weight of being told I belong to a family—to the Madden family—and the weight of the decades I'd thought I wasn't. I thanked Tommy for reaching out, for being the first Madden to reach out to me in seventeen years. He apologized again, and I told him he shouldn't worry, that this phone call earned forgiveness. Then I ugly cried the rest of the afternoon.

And that's what I told Danny Sullivan too. Not the uncontrollable sobbing part. I told him that Tommy, the runt of the litter, Brendan Behan minus the writing and singing, was the best of them.

And we all drank and ate our bar pizzas. We caught up, and we shot the shit with the bartender, who pointed to my late Uncle Bobby's empty stool farther down the bar. I felt at home, there in an unironic dive bar on the outskirts of Boston.

And that was as much home as we could gather in anyway. Tommy was renting a small room from an old townie. He would go to his grave never having had a bathroom or kitchen of his own, only being able to afford to stay with his mother or rent a room through the townie word-of-mouth network. My biological father also lost his housing after Nana and Grandpa passed and their house was sold. He now lives bitter and alone in Randolph Housing Authority senior public housing. He'll probably die there. Their father had enjoyed homeownership and a pension—a white boomer even if Irish—but their grandfather grew up in a Roxbury Irish slum and was born in a South End Irish slum, one that was demolished, memory-holed, and eventually transformed into early twentieth-century public housing. I've got degrees, a condo, a retirement account, and my own washer and dryer. Uncle Tommy never had his own bathroom.

We were poor because we were poor because we were poor because of racialized colonialism. It's the American story. And we didn't even get the worst of it us, not even close.

If the emerging science on trauma holds true, my and my relatives' struggles have roots not just in our own personal traumas but in our ancestors'.[139] We inherited the behaviors that helped our ancestors survive—our shared adaptations, even if they harm us now. Our mental health is inherited.

Wealth and poverty are also inherited. Inherited wealth decides who will always enjoy secure housing and who must worry about keeping a roof over their heads. Income pays the rent, but wealth handles the worry. It's nothing to do with who we are as people.

Poor people in the United States are not allowed to make mistakes. Class mobility requires near perfection and/or tremendous luck. My parents and grandparents made some bad choices. I'm sure of it. All of us have. Do we deserve the credible threat of homelessness as punishment?

The Puritans believed we deserve it. Do you?

TWENTY-TWO

Limbo

I had thought that my class background would be respected in the affordable housing field, or at least not be the liability it would be in market real estate.

I love the Chinese word *yiwei* 以为. The English "was mistaken" or "had thought" come close, but neither quite grasps the concept.

When another word became popular, it allowed me to name what happened to me at a Matt Desmond book talk. I hadn't understood "triggered" before. The stories from Matt's excellent book *Evicted* hit too close to home for me, for the child I was and for the people I loved. *But for the grace of God go I*, I thought. *I'm in danger*, I felt. Dressed nicely, sitting on a plastic chair at an 8:00 a.m. Boston Foundation breakfast, I was nowhere near danger. I felt the fragility of my path. I tried to share a story of mine that closely paralleled one in the book to demonstrate what it all meant to me, and I felt brushed off. I walked back to my office with my characteristic anger-motivation to do my job, to help the next kid. It was useless. I just couldn't concentrate on my work. It was all I could do to avoid sobbing.

I called Grandmy when I got home to thank her for all she did for me. I can do the math on what would probably have happened had Grandmy not taken us in whenever we faced housing insecurity during my childhood. It feels like a miracle that I have college degrees instead of a criminal record. Grandmy seemed nonplussed. "Well, what else would I have done? Don't you worry about it." The tears I held back all day broke through while I was on the phone with my Boston Irish grandmother, the woman who'd given me gems of wisdom like, "She's not depressed; she's just lazy" and "I never had time for that anxiety stuff; I had four kids to raise." I think she appreciated my gratitude but was confused by my emotion. The word "triggered" made sudden sense to me.

Feeling out of place in the professional class world, I kept searching for myself in other people's eyes. You never can know how you look in someone else's eyes, but I needed to try, to guess how I should behave. Somehow, it only got harder over time. In my personal experience, people who grew up in the padding of privilege cannot handle a direct look at the traumas of poverty in a colleague. It was true when I would show up with visible injuries to Board of Education meetings as a teenager, and it was true for failures to code-switch and shows of emotion in professional offices or higher education.

I found it increasingly difficult to code-switch and to assimilate as I got older and logged more years as an educated professional, surrounded by people who did not share similar scars to ours. I felt pressure from the professional class to forget whatever struggle I'd had before. Being in the room means I made it, right? Traumas and disadvantages due to race, social class, citizenship status, gender, sexuality, and so on should be hidden, forgiven, and forgotten, lest anyone ever be made uncomfortable by their own privilege, by the terror of learning what this world is about. Ironically, my worst social class gaslighting came from the same people who won large grants to develop "trauma-informed" approaches to our work. They tossed around the acronym ACEs without considering for a second that Adverse Childhood Experiences might matter for coworkers too.

Plentiful research concludes that even short spells of home-lessness are damaging, especially to children, who will carry the consequences the rest of their lives. A range of negative outcomes haunt us, including anxiety, poor health, inadequate medical care, emotional and behavioral problems, developmental delays, and lower educational attainment.[140] I'm four for six on the ACEs quiz, by the by.

Sometimes I found it impossible to concentrate on my job. Our painstaking, incremental change felt more and more like losing a class war day by day. Most people mean well, but the narrow pri-orities and self-interest of their employers cause them to delay and defer the creation of homes. How could we ever hope to fix it? Was I doing enough? Was I doing the right things?

I wondered whether I should have joined a building trades' union instead of going to higher education. Could I have accomplished more with my time, tuition money, and expertise as an electrician? We need more builders, not more regulators.

These are the sort of thoughts that haunted me during the most healthy, beautiful commute I could hope for, my daily walk from East Cambridge, looking down from the Longfellow Bridge at morning scullers and afternoon sailors on the Charles River, shop-ping like Julia Child in Beacon Hill, pausing in the Public Garden's peacefulness, observing the South End's palimpsest sharing my city's secrets. Two miles of Bostonian heaven, fearing the hell glimpsed in sleeping bags in the park or on winter sidewalk grates.

But it was through the phone it came. You know that moment, or you have yet to. On the morning of July 4, 2014, my mother called, early. Maybe that was the warning. I felt it coming from her breathing, that instant before she sobbed the news. But nothing could prepare me for it, her voice on the other end.

"Kevin died."

I'd expected it, but the grief tore the ceiling down on my head all the same. The heavens opened, and it poured rain on Boston. Of all the ways I've lost people, addiction has been the worst. It's the slowest suicide. It robs us of our loved ones long before their bodies give out. We spend years trying to help, trying not to enable, contemplating what-ifs, and grieving someone we used to know, all while their addictions eat them alive.

I'd planned to go watch the fireworks over the Charles River with friends that night. They called me to question going after the morning's thunderstorms, but hearing me, they decided to meet me there after all. I never missed the Boston Fourth, even when I was sick with heartbreak. How many years was it since that Fourth of July Candice and I broke up? Seven years? Or was it eight? When grief knocked me down back then, Kevin caught me. This time, he was the hole torn out from my reality. I walked down to the river in a daze, my wife Sung looking after me. I watched fireworks with water in my eyes, and then nature provided its own thundering booms, and the rain came in a weighty downpour. On the Boston side of the river, people sheltered in a Storrow Drive tunnel until it began to flood. On the Cambridge side, we went into MIT's student pub to wait out the storm.

Kevin's death was hard on all of us whose lives he'd changed. He'd given us the tools to survive and grow, then addiction and chronic illness set fire to the bridges that connected us, one by one. His passing devastated Mom and Sean. Mom drowned in tears and booze. Sean held back his tears with the booze, as far as he could anyway. I got busy, which if you haven't noticed by this point of the book, is a trauma response of mine. I went into caregiver mode. I did my best to help Mom and Sean, emotionally, financially, whatever was needed. Our cousins at Funerarias Multi Culturel in Brockton took care of Kevin's cremation and funeral for us. Kevin's families packed the funeral; his blood family despite strained relationships, his kung fu family mourning our Sifu.

The next morning when I walked to work, I paused and looked over the Charles River. I'd begun looking for two names in the obituaries each day. More than once, I'd imagined he'd be found washed up on the banks of that river.

In my heart, I couldn't separate my work in affordable housing from my personal life. When bureaucrats held back approvals for asinine reasons or when NIMBYism and bigotry took over community meetings, it felt personal to me. It was not just that people were making my job harder. It felt like they were complicit in the housing insecurity and displacement my own family and I experienced, that they were accelerating the housing crisis and the gentrification rapidly sweeping away the people I grew up with. It was hard not to be angry all the time. And in professional-class America—especially where I now live in Seattle—anger is simply not acceptable.

An employer sent me to a two-day convening on "economic mobility" strategies. The icebreaker the first afternoon was, "Share your name, position, where you're from, and your own family's experience with economic mobility." I thought, OK, a bit personal for an icebreaker, but I like to keep it real, right? Then, one by one, my colleagues told their ancestors' stories of hard work and sacrifice so that their grandparents could enter the professional class into which my colleagues were born. For some, it was even a parent who was first-generation. For most, these old stories inspired them to pursue a career in affordable housing to give back. That's wonderful, it truly is. I felt alone.

After listening to twenty or so stories of privilege built on the shoulders of ancestors, it was my turn. "I'm James Madden. I grew up in Randolph, Massachusetts, in affordable housing and experiencing housing insecurity and poverty. I was my high school's valedictorian, went to college at Swarthmore and then grad school at MIT. I'm sitting here, and that's mobility. But my family is still poor, and I'm still trying to help my mother and brother get stably housed, so um, I'm really not sure about economic mobility." I got dirty looks. It seemed to me as if no one wanted to hear it. One well-meaning colleague tried to connect with me by equating their childhood anxiety about money—in a well-off household in a famously well-off area—to my own experiences. I know they only meant well, but it was so off point that it left me feeling even more estranged. I thought about Black friends sharing hurt from liberal betrayal, and I searched my memory for times I may have hurt others. I hate being a hypocrite.

Another time, HUD rejected a submission and asked me to add additional data, primarily data HUD already had as their agency had generated it in the first place. But I needed to find it and adapt it to this form of theirs. Specifically, they asked for more data on the demographics and service needs of veterans experiencing homelessness and of people fleeing domestic violence in and around Seattle. I worked into the night to turn the application back to HUD immediately. The millions of dollars it would unlock were desperately needed to complete a purchase of an apartment building to house people coming out of homelessness. I couldn't let myself be the one to hold that up, knowing every extra day of delay is an additional traumatic night on the streets for the hundred or so people this building could house. I began typing the extra information into the HUD form's box for causes of homelessness among veterans:

"Veterans most often report alcohol and drug use (13%) and mental health issues (13%) as the reasons they are homeless. Illness or a medical problem was reported as the main reason for being homeless by 10% of veterans."

I stopped. I thought about my younger brother's recent struggles. PTSD from his two deployments with the 82nd Airborne Division occasionally manifested in panic attacks and deep depressive episodes. He had just lost a girlfriend after having a panic attack at a crowded Pats game. He lost jobs when he couldn't get out of bed or explain what was happening to him. His union suspended him and pointed him towards services. But none of the services were actually available to him unless he said he was at imminent risk of suicide, which he refused to do. He could not get access to the mental health care he needed. Booze is much easier to find. It works OK for keeping down PTSD symptoms, until it doesn't. I wondered if Sean needed help with the rent that month.

I turned my attention back to the screen and added, "However, post-traumatic stress disorder (PTSD) often results in substance abuse and other mental health issues, which then create these precipitating events that cause veterans to lose their housing."

I continued, "Across almost all health challenges, veterans fare worse than the nonveteran population. Most notably, veterans have an overall rate of psychiatric or emotional conditions of 70%, and 55% report experiencing PTSD."

Then Kevin popped to mind. What would his life have been like with access to health care and stable housing? Surely, he'd be alive anyway.

I added, "Veterans attempting to get help with their mental health—a condition that makes doing anything more difficult—are often faced with challenging bureaucracy and a severe shortage of VA and other resources."

I turned my attention to relaying what is known about people "fleeing, or attempting to flee, domestic violence" in our city. I copied from the most recent "point in time" report on homelessness:

"A total of 10% of the 2020 homeless population, or 1,211 individuals, report experiencing homelessness because they are fleeing domestic violence or abuse. This includes dating violence, sexual assault, and/or stalking. About 69% of these individuals are unsheltered . . ."

That didn't sound right to me, a percentage of humans. I thought I should at least count the people, instead of leaving it like this. So I added, "(836 people), and 15% (182 people) have children with them. This is likely an undercount. Due to the associated stigma and fears, survivors of domestic violence may not choose to report abuse during face-to-face surveys with volunteers."

I stopped to think about my mother. I wondered if all that counted. Then, I forced myself to stop thinking and just get back to it. Time was passing, and I wanted the bureaucrats to wake up to an email giving them what they requested. I ignored the electric current of neuropathic pain racing up my hands and arms. Work to do. The same pain woke me up in the morning, so I got to work early.

Decades of working through pain had earned me a modicum of economic mobility. Then, continuing to work through pain wrecked my body. After two years of physical therapy, medication, and surgeries, I still couldn't really use my hands. So I decided to finally act as if I were a responsible adult and go see a doctor, while at the same time making the irresponsible decision to write this book. "Have you ever broken your wrist?" my hand surgeon asked me when the problems persisted post-surgery.

"Not to my knowledge. But, I, uh, didn't always have access to health care as a young person."

They took X-rays of my left hand, and I was only surprised at how upset the results made me, not what they showed. Two old breaks. One left a bone chip floating on its own. The other led to a mild deformity but with care wouldn't have. I am lower class. It is in me. No amount of gaslighting, no amount of personal social mobility, can remove the evidence of poverty from my body. My wrists, my knees, my ankles, my mental health, they force me to acknowledge this truth. My childhood experiences began delivering serious consequences once I entered middle age. The research could have told me it would.[141]

"My rage has ancestry," wrote Cathy Park Hong in her earthshaking book *Minor Feelings*. She described the concept of minor feelings as "the racialized range of emotions that are negative, dysphoric, and therefore untelegenic, built from the sediments of everyday racial experience and the irritant of having one's perception of reality constantly questioned or dismissed . . . Minor feelings occur when American optimism is enforced upon you, which contradicts your own racialized reality, thereby creating a state of cognitive dissonance."[142]

Cathy says that her minor feelings give her a double consciousness, as she understands herself as both oppressor and oppressed. She explained how the resulting inability to trust one's own senses "engenders the minor feelings of paranoia, shame, irritation, and melancholy."

I snapped to attention the first time I heard Cathy read these words of hers. I felt she had also accurately named the dislocation of being lower class in upper-class spaces and workplaces. Alfred Lubrano's journalistic inquiry into class-straddlers, *Limbo: Blue Collar Roots White Collar Dreams*, is riddled with descriptions of minor feelings if not the phrase itself.

I realized how incredibly fortunate I'd been early in my career to have bosses and mentors with their own lived experiences of poverty. Willie Jones gave me the afternoon off with no question when Kevin landed at Boston Health Care for the Homeless. When I returned, he brought me into his office and shared his own experiences of being one of the few to make it out and the responsibilities that came with it. Willie truly cared, for his family, for his community. He centered his life around that care and met the responsibilities care calls for, both personally and professionally.

Willie spoiled me. I was unprepared for a different boss years later who bragged to me about getting to know homeless people living on the streets in another part of their city. It was for a report they'd been funded to create. "You have to get out and talk to people, or else you know nothing."

"Yes! I completely agree. That's why I'm here. They're my family, my people, growing up how I did and living where I live." The boss knew my story.

"Yeah, but do you *still* talk to them?" they challenged with a hint of derision in their voice.

"Yes. They're my family." The boss gave me a vacant stare. "They are my neighbors too. My toddler and I say hi and regularly chat with them on our daily walks." I don't know how it was possible, but somehow this boss started looking down their nose at me even more. Did they think I was lying? Were they just innocent of understanding that class status doesn't change so easily? Were they trying to break me down because they believed me too ambitious? I have no clue. I just backed off and smiled politely as my boss continued passive aggressively berating me, refusing to see me for who I was. After that Zoom meeting ended, my wife yelled at me, "Give me their number! They can't talk to you like that." I did not give my spouse my boss's number to go defend me, but, wow, I'm in love.

I was ignorant enough to think (以为) that I could still prove myself and be welcomed by this class of people. I swallowed it and tried to outwork everyone, as I always had. That worked for me as a teenager against the doubts I could ever achieve a top-tier education coming out of Randolph. It worked dealing with social class problems at Swarthmore and MIT, both of which unusually, mercifully, held hard work in the highest regard. It worked early in my career to convince colleagues to stop seeing me as a baby-faced developer, to welcome me to the closing table and to the job site both.

I thought (以为) I could swallow colleagues' classist complaints, superiors' sexist and racist jokes about my marriage, and bosses' bigoted comments and passive-aggressive undermining. I thought (以为) I could code-switch and manage in that world. I thought (以为) I would overcome it all with hard work and achievements. I hope I never need to talk that way again.

Working through the pain didn't work.

In 2016, I was recruited to Seattle to take on a role that called for a mix of real estate development skills and public policy skills, to create both affordable housing and early learning centers.

I hadn't dreamed of leaving Boston. I had a challenging, rewarding job that made a real difference. I had my communities and families. But the offer came at the right time. I realized I needed to go when I started identifying with Beyoncé's *Lemonade* album, subbing Boston for Jay-Z, her love for her husband and my love for Boston both twisting and betraying and giving. Gentrification had gotten out of control. Rents were displacing folks, especially immigrants and artists. Monique Ortiz—whom I would see perform once or twice a week when her residencies were on—got priced out of Cambridge, Massachusetts, and left for a small town outside Austin, Texas.

Even with a decent salary, first-generation professionals like me and many of my friends couldn't get into the homeownership market.

The high prices put down payments out of reach to anyone without access to family wealth, and down payment assistance programs had been designed for low-*income* purchasers and are functionally blind to inherited wealth. Working-class establishments kept closing. Due to a quirk of Massachusetts law originally intended to screw over the Irish in the late nineteenth century, it became far more profitable for business owners in working-class and poor neighborhoods in the twenty-first century to sell their liquor license to a downtown business and close shop than to continue working. I'd begun to lose hope for Boston.

On the positive side, Sung wanted to try somewhere new, to try to build her own communities instead of inheriting mine. My dear mentor, Bev Gallo, told me to go for it, that I could always return, and that the experience would be good for me. Sung and I discussed it back and forth, then made our decision on a perfect summer day bobbing in the Atlantic Ocean at Nantasket Beach. It was hard to imagine much better than that New England beach day, and that was almost reason enough to go searching for new experiences. Everything will change.

I gave notice, transitioned my projects, and Sung and I began our ten-day drive from Boston to Seattle. We threw a second going-away party at a bar in Manhattan, where I lost my voice yelling over loud music chatting with friends. We went to dinner with friends in Pittsburgh, where Sung had to carry the conversation because I'd lost my voice. We stopped in Cincinnati to tour the Avondale Choice Neighborhood, work I'd had a small hand in and felt proud to see. We spent a weekend visiting with friends in Chicago, then drove to Decorah to meet up with my friend—and, I am guessing, future Iowa governor—Rob Sand, who took us on a long bike ride around his rural hometown.

I took a call from my aunt as we drove the most boring stretch of I-90. She told me my mother almost died from alcohol poisoning, again, went to the ER, again, and was going to rehab, again.* Ever since Kevin died, homeless, a husk of his former self, my mother crashed through rock bottom after rock bottom. I grit my teeth because of the shame we associate with weakness. Neither Sean nor Mom took my leaving well. Vacant plains, emptied of their buffalo herds, stretched and stretched and stretched until Sung and I finally reached the Black Hills. We visited Glacier National Park, which was about as empty of glaciers as the Dakotas were of bison. We passed through late-season wildfire smoke in Idaho, and after ten long days, crossed the Cascade Mountains and descended into Seattle.

We vowed a three-year try, but we forgot to agree what happened at the end of three years. I assumed we'd go back to Boston. Sung assumed we might try somewhere else entirely. No matter. By the end of those three years, we had careers, communities, a condo, and our child. Reluctantly, I had to admit Seattle was where we created a home.

Our baby had colic and screamed nearly every waking moment the first three months, then screamed only most of the time for the following three months. That's six times the colic my mother suffered with me, not that it matters, or that I care, really, who's even counting? My daughter slept through the night for the very first time when she was ten months old, stuffed full of mashed potatoes and turkey from her first Thanksgiving.

Sung and I began to make enough money that we could live our modest lives and save for our daughter without worrying too much. I could go to the grocery store and not give a third thought to unit

---

* Relapse is extremely common and should not be a cause of shame. Read Erica Barnett's *Quitter* for more on relapse and alcoholism.

prices. When the pandemic hit, I could even afford to buy all my groceries at Pike Place Market, supporting my community while avoiding the indoors like the responsible liberal I was.

I'd never been still before the pandemic. I'm not sure I'd ever logged even two weeks of sleeping in one place. I hated being still. Waiting tended to infuriate me. Dr. Sharon Lambert, professor of applied psychology at University College Cork, described how waiting can be a trauma trigger.[143] For those of us who experienced the noise of violence as children, who grew to expect it, the silences brought anxiety. They were only silences until something bad would happen again. Our brains learned that waiting equals danger, triggering our fight, flight, or freeze response.

But I didn't have to worry about the price of groceries. I learned to be still. I even began to enjoy doing laundry. I own a stacked Samsung washer and dryer in a small closet. I could do laundry in my own home, and I didn't have to worry about the price of groceries. That's my definition of having made it in life.

Across from my washer and dryer, on the other side of the hall, is an alcove I jokingly call the Belltown Music Hall. I'd always dreamed of having a music room. My Stratocaster I'd played since childhood, my two-string bass that was the four-string I played until I fell in love with Morphine's music and turned to the glass slide my mother used in the '70s, the four-string bass I bought after I reached the professional class, my first trumpet, the tin whistle Mom beat Sean's ass with after he threw it at her, and a child-sized bodhrán drum all hang on a wall decorated to look like a basement club. The floor and shelves are crowded with a keyboard, amplifiers, violin and trumpet cases, effects pedals, a plastic crate filled with percussion toys and baby pianos, and a janggu drum from Seoul. My policy is that when a child in my home asks to use an instrument, I set her up with it.

My friend's little four-year-old, Dalia, blew a perfect note the first time she touched a trumpet. Absurd!

Anyway, after I get my squats in moving wet clothes up to my—my!—dryer, I can close the laundry closet door, lean back, and take in my musical memories. These children discovering the joy of playing instruments. My mother's guitar playing and her generosity. Ending up underneath that bass guitar, staring up at hanging green and black artwork, the Gloucester Art Space's floor bouncing under my back from the mosh pit around me. Irish instruments and Korean instruments. This is decolonial praxis, I tell myself as pretentiously as the liberal arts student I was half a lifetime ago. Best of all, I can walk away from the laundry, and no one will steal my clothes. I have made it. I am home. We created a home.

My mother began to put together longer and longer stints of sobriety after she became a grandmother. She found quality, stable, affordable housing in a LIHTC development near Rhode Island. Tears well in my eyes knowing how close we came to losing her in the same way we'd lost Kevin. She's made a fantastic grandmother.

Ancient Irish people's legal status in their society depended on what their grandparents had created and on what they would leave behind for their own grandchildren.[144] Indigenous peoples of America similarly talk about responsibility across seven generations, which some interpret as the three before you, yours, and the three after you. Recent science demonstrates that trauma changes our telomeres, and thus the expressions of our genetics across generations.[145] Our grandparents' and our parents' traumas live in our bodies. What we do matters for generations.

My daughter and her little toddler friends entered this world as climate change began to run away, as the US threatened to split along its seams, as prospects for an affordable, safe home near jobs became a guarantee only to families already firmly in the ownership class, when a local measles outbreak followed by the global COVID-19 pandemic revealed our inability to cooperate and sacrifice for each other's safety.

No matter what we do, our children and their children are going to live during an incredibly difficult period of history. I continue to work, as hard as I am able anyway, because my daughter deserves better.

They all do.

We did too.

Every one of us.

TWENTY-THREE

Housing: What's Broken?

What fixes homelessness? Homes. What would solve our housing crisis? Housing.

We should not forget that it is, at its core, truly that simple. In 2022's *Homelessness is a Housing Problem*, Colburn and Aldern demonstrated conclusively that the variance in rates of homelessness among cities "cannot be explained by disproportionate levels of drug use, mental illness, poverty . . . weather, local political climate, the mobility of low-income households, or the generosity of local welfare." Their analysis of all available evidence found only two credible measures that explain levels of homelessness: rents and vacancy rates. They state, "The causes of homelessness at the individual or family level is a somewhat complex interaction between individual factors, structural drivers, and misfortune . . . In study after study, the most effective treatment for homelessness is housing."[146] That should be the end of the argument. Precipitating events like divorce, illness, unemployment, addiction, or injury lead to an individual's homelessness, yes, but only in situations where the rent is too damn high and homes are too scarce.

How do we get more homes in the places we need them at prices that people can afford? Local governments must allow the homes to be built, and the public must subsidize the cost of those homes for anyone who cannot afford the construction rent or the operations rent. There are many tactics available towards those ends, but allowing homes to be built and paying for them are absolute, unavoidable necessities for solving our housing crisis.

There's no escaping this fact about our economic system. There will always be people who earn too little for the market to meet their need for a place to live. So long as we keep making more humans, and so long as humans move around during our lives, however much housing currently exists wherever will be insufficient to meet needs over time. We continually need to create homes.

There is no imaginary technology to drive the cost of producing homes to zero. That would require free land, labor, and materials, plus an egregious disregard for the health and well-being of both humans and our environment. And while a humane future cannot be built from such exploitation, historically, these were in fact the USA's housing affordability solutions.

Free or cheap land? Plague and violence depopulated the continent. Settler governments entitled the land by decree, according to their own seventeenth-century English laws and successor systems in the United States. Each individual conquest was unique, but American settlers generally did not compensate Indigenous people or other inhabitants fairly for the title to their lands. That truth felt distant to me growing up in Boston with nearly four centuries between me and colonization. In the Pacific Northwest, it is only a few generations. Living people's great-grandparents took this land with dishonest treaties and with violence. Today, land theft from Black and Indigenous people continues through abuse of legal frameworks. Abuse of heirs' property and allotment is an especial danger to the land of African American descendants of slavery.[147] Speaking of which . . .

Free or cheap labor? Chattel slavery. Indentured servitude. Union busting. Prison labor. Undocumented labor. Offshore labor. Wage theft. America has a long and continuing history of keeping costs low and profits high by exploiting labor. Pundits complain about affordable housing being too expensive to build.[148] Well, everything seems more expensive to build when we adequately pay the people building it.

Free or cheap materials? Colonists and settlers did not take this continent only to live upon it. America and Europe saved on building materials by exploiting taken land, removing its wood, oil, coal, sand, iron, gypsum, copper, gold, rare earth metals, and so on, without proper environmental procedures or compensation to natives nor neighbors. With today's global supply chains, the exploitation continues outside our own borders as well as within.

Poor standards? By the numbers, this is still the United States' preferred solution for housing the poor. In the nineteenth century, this took the form of overcrowded tenements lacking indoor plumbing or electricity. In the Great Depression, Americans built shantytowns, which were at least structures and connected to the postal network and other services. Today, we have tents, cars, and couches. Everybody sleeps somewhere.

We can be better. We can choose not to rely on tents and sidewalks to house our poorest neighbors. We can have standards and still ensure everyone in America has a safe, affordable place to live. We need to correct for housing's inherent market failure below the Construction Rent. And we need to escape government policies that prevent homes from being built in the first place.

The simplest, most efficient way to correct for housing's inherent market failure would be to create a universal housing voucher. We can ensure every person in the US has a safe place to live by funding vouchers that pay the difference between the rent individual households can afford (the only rent that matters) and the operations or construction rent where they live, as appropriate. That would allow the market to build for just about everybody. It would ensure affordable housing developments continue operating in good repair, as infrastructure worthy of a first-world nation.

For a market system to provide housing for all, subsidies are a necessity. But for the subsidies to work—to work for people and to work as a system—strong tenant rights are also a must. Conversely, tenant protection policies are only truly meaningful when people can afford the rent in the first place.

Tenants should have the right to use whatever source of income— salary, seasonal work, social security, housing vouchers, etc.—to pay their rent, and landlords should not have the right to discriminate based on tenants' sources of income. In November 2021, the *Seattle Times* reported that "Seattle got more than 1,300 federal housing vouchers. So far, only 10 people have used them."[149] Two culprits caused 1,290 people to be left on the streets during a pandemic, a record heatwave, civil unrest, and a thick blanket of forest fire smoke. The first culprit was our governments' insistence on separating the worthy from the unworthy rather than fully funding our needs; in this case, HUD's egregiously wrong-minded rulemaking for emergency funds Congress had appropriated. The second culprit was the inability to find private landlords willing to lease an apartment to a voucher-holder due to cost concerns, bureaucratic barriers, and/or discrimination.

Tenants should have the right to stay in their homes unless there is a just cause for eviction. Evictions for physical or monetary damages, sure, those are reasonable for a market system to function and may be a necessary evil. Evictions for convenience or to unreason-

reversed course and routinely let apartments sit vacant until someone is willing to pay the rent assigned by the software, letting the higher rent pay for the vacancy losses.[150] The benefit of this practice to landlord-developers may be even higher because they can show lenders and investors the artificially high rents achieved by this strategy in order to underwrite higher rents in their next development, and so on from there. Articles by *ProPublica* in 2022,[151] reports by whistleblowers from the software firms, lawsuits,[152] and congressional inquiries[153] were actively pursuing the question of whether this practice can be proven to violate antitrust laws. Regardless of the law, the real-world effect has been that this software and the industry's dramatic change in business practices have artificially lowered the supply of available homes and are a driving force behind much of the unprecedented rapidity of rent increases in the twenty-first century.

In his 2023 budget request, President Biden proposed $32.1 billion to renew all existing Housing Choice Vouchers and to expand assistance to an additional 200,000 households.[154] Would that cover it? Does it even come close?

President Biden's own White House reported more than 580,000 Americans were experiencing homelessness, prior to the pandemic even.[155] Meanwhile, its Department of Education estimated 1.35 million homeless students, not counting their parents. The differences are in the definitions, and survey data shows about 5% of Americans experienced homelessness at least once in their life. One in twenty of us. We are a class.

In the affordable housing profession, we celebrated Biden's budget request. The National Low Income Housing Coalition stated, "If enacted, it would be the most significant expansion of housing vouchers in the program's history, and it would put the nation on the path towards universal housing assistance for all eligible households."[156] To be more precise, it would cover fewer than two of every five Americans currently experiencing homelessness. The budget request assumed leaving a Minneapolis-sized population of Americans without homes. Later, the Biden administration declared its "ambitious goal" of reducing homelessness by 25%, which they ironically titled, "All In: The Federal Strategic Plan to Prevent and End Homelessness."

No, that budget request was not a reasonable opening bid. It was not a serious response to a serious problem, and it was not even followed through upon. In the final enacted budget, those 200,000 promised new vouchers had dropped to merely 12,000.[157] Funding for affordable housing capital remained level with the past year, which is a cut after inflation.

I know it's good practice to praise politicians whenever our priorities are included in a budget, but I personally just cannot forgive a Democratic administration whose opening bid proposed to leave hundreds of thousands of Americans homeless and *millions* more people just one bit of bad luck from homelessness.

The Center for Budget and Policy Priorities in October 2021 showed that nearly all housing agencies had at least 1,000 households waiting for vouchers. Most have at least 10,000 households waiting. The San Diego Housing Commission topped the list with 109,088 households waiting for housing help. "Most of these agencies (32) closed their waitlists to new applicants, and many of those with open waitlists have more people on their waitlist than the number of vouchers they have available. Because so many agencies have closed or limited waitlists—some for close to or more than a decade—millions of people experiencing housing instability and homelessness haven't ever had the opportunity to add their names to a waitlist. And the long wait times to receive help may also discourage people from applying, even if waitlists are open."[158]

The same week the administration released that 2023 budget request, Congresswoman Maxine Waters approached a crowd who'd assembled looking for help with housing in her district. In a video of the encounter, the congresswoman clearly looks upset about a false rumor of new Section 8 vouchers that attracted this large crowd. Frustrated, she tells them, "You cannot get Section 8 vouchers here. There's a long line [for the vouchers]. We are fighting in Washington for something called the Build Back Better Act. I put $25 *billion** that we're fighting to give people more Section 8. [159] Now. The money that *is* available is for the absolute homeless under the emergency program. That's what you started signing up for today." She proceeds to tell the crowd that due to their rowdy behavior, the Los Angeles Homeless Services Authority staff who'd arrived to add names to the voucher list had left. "There will be no more applications here today," she said.

A man in the crowd asks calmly, "Are there any more locations, Maxine? Because I'm hearing there is one on Wilson. Another location where they're taking apps?" The crowd begins to chatter as the congresswoman starts to reply, and the man raises his voice to be heard over the din. "Is there any more locations?"

"No, no. Here is what I want you to do. OK. One minute . . . I want everybody to go home."

A beat of silence reigns before someone yells, accurately, "We ain't got no home. That's why we're here." Another yells, "What home we gonna go to?"

The congresswoman reflexively replies, "OK, OK," before the realization of what she said hits her. She turns on her big, bright smile and looks aside before she demands authority again. "Nothing

* An impressive number, I suppose, but not enough to maintain current vouchers let alone expand the program.

is going to happen anymore today. Nothing more is going to happen here today."

Someone else calls out, "Miss Maxine, you need to work with me."

Offended, she replies, "Excuse me! There's nobody in Washington who works for their people any fucking harder than I do. I don't want to hear this. No, no, no."

Congresswoman Waters is a liberal champion. The combined effects of poverty, racism, and misogyny did not stop Maxine Waters from building a storied career, from California Assembly staffer to elected member and caucus chair in the Assembly, to more than three decades in the United States House of Representatives. She achieved divestments in apartheid South Africa. She was one of very few in Congress to get it right on the Iraq War in 2002. She spearheaded legislation to capitalize the National Housing Trust Fund. More than anything, she is well known for unashamedly claiming time and space to speak out for her people and values. I have no doubt the congresswoman cares deeply about these constituents. I'd wager she kicks herself in private over her "Let them eat cake" moment, but her comments before the confrontation caught my attention.

"You cannot get Section 8 vouchers here. There's a long line . . . Now. The money that *is* available is for the absolute homeless under the emergency program. That's what you started signing up for today." The underlying bias—some are worthy of this help, some aren't—already assumes homelessness. This underlying assumption has been a feature of the American approach to housing the poor since English colonizers brought the English Poor Laws to this continent with them. And our system insists against all experience that we all need to play by the rules to beg for what little we can get. I believe that is what the congresswoman was channeling, the accepted rules of our system.

We affordable housing professionals put more time, effort, and creativity into our massive compliance edifice than we do into ending homelessness. Yes, it is important to audit for the legal use of public funds. Yes, unfortunately, it is necessary for us to triage among overwhelming need for starvation budgets. However, we have spent centuries studying, defining, redefining, and monitoring who is the worthy poor and who is not, rather than simply helping people who need help.

In our system, applicants and residents complete paperwork for property managers, owners, developers, funders, public agencies, and third-party specialists to each examine. They each add layers to the paperwork for continual compliance audits to deliver to local, state, and federal bureaucracies. This multibillion-dollar compliance system spans the public, private, and nonprofit sectors. It is both staff-intensive and tech-dependent, so quite expensive. The entire edifice exists so that government agencies can report to elected officials that they funded housing for the people those elected officials said should be housed and that they provided absolutely no resources whatsoever to anybody else who might not fit their definitions of "worthy."

I find it hard to believe that the potential cost of instances of individuals fraudulently living in affordable housing is nearly as high as the cost of the compliance edifice to the public, to the housing system, and by extension, to those people in need of safe, quality, affordable places to call home.

Poor people bear the brunt of our compliance edifice. We sit in waiting rooms, spend hours on the phone, send email after email, fill out redundant reams of paper, track down letters, and call again

ably raise rents? No, those are the sorts of evictions that fueled the greatest humanitarian disaster in Irish history.

Lastly, tenants should have the right to expect only reasonable increases in rent. Many pixels have been spilled in debates over rent control and rent stabilization. As we explored earlier in this book, there is rent, and, well, then there is rent. Reasonable increases in rent to reflect increases in operating expenses are necessary to keep homes in good repair. Large or sudden increases in rent beyond that operations rent are simply wealth transfers. Further, when reasonable lenders and investors underwrite a real estate deal, they do not count on large rent increases to meet their return expectations. The highest annual average rent increase I've been allowed to use in underwriting is 3%. Policies that prohibit egregious rental increases can save people from bad actors without significantly jeopardizing our ability to develop more housing. And were we to have a universal housing voucher, rent stabilization would protect the program from being exploited by egregious rent increases.

Technology may have already surpassed rent stabilization policy's ability to meet that aim, however. Over the last decade, large private landlords almost universally embraced software products to assign rents, removing discretion from their on-site property managers. Because these landlords all use the same products, they are able to achieve the benefits of colluding to raise rents, with the algorithms doing the actual collusion bit.

This technological change accompanied a revolution in how corporate landlords regarded vacancy. Traditionally, landlords had filled vacant apartments with new tenants as quickly as possible. Every day an apartment is vacant, it is losing money. After embracing the business philosophies of Sam Zell and other executives who cut their teeth in 1980s corporate downsizing, these landlords have now

to follow up. And we do it because all this paperwork has life-or-death consequences.

There are two large federal agencies monitoring affordable housing funding, sixty-one state and local housing finance agencies,[160] at least fifty housing departments in state governments, hundreds of city government housing departments, and 2,830 Public Housing Agencies.[161] This is a large, diverse country to be sure. But might we be spending too many resources on targeting our spending too narrowly? Would it not be more efficient to stop worrying whether a few people cheat a system for help they likely needed anyway, and we instead all get to work creating the homes we need? How can we possibly house everyone when our entire system is premised on dividing those we believe are worthy of help from those we believe are not?

We need a universal voucher and tenants' rights in order to correct for the inherent market failures in our housing system. These could make housing affordable, but not on their own. We have much to make up for.

Decades of underbuilding dug us a deep, deep hole, especially in the best job markets. We seem to have stopped building; 76% of homes in the US were built before the year 2000 and more than half before 1980.[162] Most US housing is older than I am, and I am need-to-stretch-before-typing years old. In 2021, analysis by Freddie Mac asserted the US is short some 3.8 million homes.[163] According to research from the National Low Income Housing Coalition, we are short 7.3 million homes affordable to the poorest third of our nation.[164] By the 2023 point-in-time homeless count, 650,000 of us were currently homeless.[165]

Building our way out of our housing crisis will require a large investment in new, affordable housing tailored to the diverse cultures, climates, and landscapes of our nation. But would it cost an unreasonable amount of money? While the national average is about half of this, let's assume it costs $400,000 per home to create housing in job and opportunity rich areas, and assume that the mean rental assistance payment for our 22.2 million currently homeless or housing-insecure people is $1,000/month.[166] That's a one-time investment of $260 billion to build enough permanently affordable homes to cover existing homelessness, plus no more than $266.4 billion annually in a universal housing voucher to address housing insecurity. That's barely one Elon Musk or Jeff Bezos. The voucher funding, mind you, would not be lost to our economy or even stay with the poor. It would flow through to property owners as rent and banks as mortgage payments, and then return in part to the public as tax revenue.

The numbers are large, but certainly achievable if we choose. A few revenue suggestions follow, only so you can't say I suggested spending without suggesting how to pay for it, but there are many other good revenue ideas circulating by people more expert with public finance than I.

An unearned wealth tax would resonate thematically with ensuring everyone in the US has a home. Inevitably, fortunes accumulated in the past—when things were cheaper to accomplish—pass through to current generations, distort the housing market, and then pass on again and again. An unearned wealth tax with a high standard deduction and/or high marginal rates could recycle that excessive unearned wealth into our nation's infrastructure.

An unearned wealth tax would especially fit housing and environmental remediation projects because past abuses certainly contributed to current fortunes, but in ways difficult to precisely assign to individuals. Our current approach is the opposite; we charge tomorrow's people with remediating and redeveloping sites polluted by yesterday's. One of the many reasons housing costs are higher now than in the past is that we are quite literally paying for past mistakes—leaking oil tanks, PCBs, asbestos, lead, volatile organic compounds, and more. Let's pay for the mistakes of the past with the wealth accumulation of the past. Tax unearned wealth.

More resources could come from phasing out the Home Mortgage Interest Deduction (HMID) completely. This would save our federal government $30 billion annually, plus billions more to state governments. Prior to Trump's 2017 tax reform, the HMID cost $70 billion annually. The reduction is due to the fact that now only higher-income households itemize deductions and therefore this benefit. Even at the lower number, we spend 50% as much on subsidizing housing exclusively for the wealthy as we do assisting everyone else.[167] We could choose to change that.

However, no matter how much we invest in subsidizing housing and no matter how we raise those resources, our investments will fail if we do not do one more thing.

We must end zoning as we know it.

Zoning and land use restrictions are the most powerful frontier in using our legal system to segregate people. Exclusionary zoning deserves to go the way of Jim Crow Laws and the racially restricted covenant, to go the way of apartheid and penal laws. In *The Color of Law*, Richard Rothstein argues that "government actions to create a system of de jure segregation were explicit, never hidden; that they were systematic and; not so long ago, well known by anyone who paid attention."[168]

Zoning stops the construction of housing that people need and want, and it uses public resources to defend incumbent wealth and preferences. It drives up the cost of local services by de-densifying, making an exclusive community to enter also an expensive one to continue living in.

Concern trolls protest, but zoning does not improve safety or fairness. The few supposed benefits of zoning—protecting people from hazardous uses, for example—could be better performed by other existing mechanisms. Building codes protect health and safety. Zoning impedes public health. Any consequential damages to neighbors from new development can and should be compensated through mediation and the civil legal system, not through endless zoning battles denying homes to others.

Zoning takes from the young, from people who move, and from impoverished people for the benefit of capital investors and older, wealthier owners through artificially high rents and artificially high sales price appreciation. Without removing this body of harmful and restrictive land use laws, all we can ever do is address a tiny portion of our country's needs. With exclusionary zoning in place, everything else we do is a bandage.

These land use laws are extremely local, and that makes removing them a daunting task. There are tens of thousands of jurisdictions across the US responsible for zoning and land use. The local elected officials who would need to change those laws are disproportion-ately longtime homeowners, disproportionately white and wealthy, and typically elected on off-year ballots with predictably low voter turnout and little to no media scrutiny. There are locally connected and wealthy landlords and developers in each jurisdiction who profit from existing restrictions on housing and the byzantine, expensive processes needed to navigate them. They handicap the competition. Mixing insular decision-making with widespread consequences is a recipe for corruption and abuse of the law. Worse, it is a system nearly impossible to fix from inside itself.

There are any numbers of carrots and sticks the federal or state governments could attach to housing production to hold local governments accountable in the same way they do with antidrug laws, the drinking age, or more recently, mentions of "DEI." Rothstein also suggested that "Congress could amend the tax code to deny the mortgage interest deduction to property owners" in places that fail to allow and construct enough housing.[169] In 1970, Republican Secretary of HUD George Romney proposed that the federal government should deny funds for water and sewer upgrades, green space, sidewalk improvements, and other projects if the local government applying for the funds had not yet revised their land use codes to remove exclusionary zoning and permit construction of subsidized apartments for lower-income and African American households. Nixon quickly fired George. Fifty years later, our housing crisis is larger than he could have imagined.

In 2021, the Biden administration declared "A New Path Forward" by adding provisions to the American Jobs Plan that would begin to question exclusionary zoning. It proposed a $5 billion grant program for jurisdictions that take concrete steps to eliminate needless barriers to produce affordable housing.[170] Massachusetts has operated a similar program to help suburbs plan for growth, Chapter 40R. Time will tell how effectively these carrots work at addressing exclusionary land use policies.

Courts could provide another way through. Zoning codes may unconstitutionally violate the Fourteenth Amendment to the United States Constitution, which reads: "No state shall make or enforce any law which shall abridge the privileges or immunities of citizens of the United States; nor shall any state deprive any person of life, liberty, or property, without due process of law; nor deny to any person within its jurisdiction the equal protection of the laws."

Zoning codes have a disparate impact on housing, health, employment, safety, and property for people of color, families with children, veterans, and the mentally and physically disabled. Zoning codes also have a disparate impact on the lives of the young and people without access to wealth, though the young or poor are not currently recognized as protected classes under US law. Zoning codes also deny equal protection in part by conferring different rights to people who live in differently zoned areas. For example, I pay more taxes but enjoy fewer rights and services as a resident of a commercial zoned area in the City of Seattle than I would if I lived in a single-family 5000 zoned area here. Never mind that thousands of people live on my avenue.

Zoning codes that explicitly mention race could no longer be legally enforced after the Supreme Court's 1917 decision in *Buchanan v. Warley*, which said they violate the Fourteenth Amendment. However, in 1926, the Supreme Court upheld the use of racist deed covenants, a decision that rested on case law from *Plessy v. Ferguson* and the existence of legal Jim Crow segregation laws in neighboring Virginia. That same year, that same Supreme Court upheld zoning in the case of *Village of Euclid v. Ambler Realty Company*. In 1948, a later Supreme Court reversed this one's ruling on racial covenants, ruling them unconstitutional because covenants depend on the collaboration of the judicial system and therefore violate the Fourteenth Amendment. Zoning similarly relies on using public resources to enhance the wealth of some at the expense of the many. Exclusionary zoning has yet to get the second hard look in our justice system that racist covenants received.

The people who created zoning codes in the first place explicitly advocated for zoning as a tool to raise housing prices and to keep Black people out, even if the laws themselves do not mention race.

Is the omission of explicit mentions of race in statute enough to comply with the Fourteenth Amendment? Do euphemisms ensure constitutionality? Or do zoning proponents' own words and zoning's disparate impact evidence violations of our constitutional rights?

Alternatively, Congress could pass legislation to take on exclusionary zoning nationally. Congress could also enforce our rights under the Fourteenth Amendment, which it is directly empowered to do under Section 5 of that amendment. But this paragraph could have ended at "Congress could pass legislation" and been just as much a waste of ink. (Prove me wrong, Congress!)

Imagine what you'd be doing right now if you didn't have to worry about the rent or mortgage. Imagine what the US could be doing if none of us had to worry about our rent or mortgage. Imagine the art, the music, the entrepreneurship, the caregiving, the healing. Just some thoughts for your mind.

Our crisis grew more from mindset than physical reality. The neoliberal belief in controlling access to and profiting from any and every human necessity—water, food, shelter, care, nature—married the Puritan obsession with separating the worthy from the unworthy. They would have you believe the lie that there is not enough to go around, so we must exclude others for our own success. We do not need to accept this ideology as reality. Like Papa taught me, I call bullshit.

Our housing crisis is not an intractable problem. It has a solution: end the practice of exclusionary zoning and appropriate the necessary subsidies. Everything else follows from there.

I estimate that a one-time investment of $260 billion in development capital plus $266.4 billion annually for rental and mortgage assistance could return stability to the 22 million or so Americans who lack safe, quality, affordable housing today and solve homelessness for future generations.

Quibble with these numbers. Open a spreadsheet and do the math yourself. Get far more precise than the estimate here. No matter which way you count it, you will see that the dollar number attached to ending homelessness and housing insecurity in the US is well within the realm of what we spend each year on other priorities.

We need to be honest about what it takes to fix this problem.

We need to be honest about why we choose not to.

Acknowledgments

First, to the women who shaped my life, Grandmy, Mom, Sung, and Niamh. All that I am and could be owes gratitude to you.

To my mentors who have passed, Kevin Rice, Tunney Lee, Willie Jones, and Frank Chopp, may your legacies and wisdom carry us forever. To my departed relatives whose memories fuel my words, Papa Tom Lally, Gar and Barbara Fiske, Kelly Madden, Lance Fiske, T.J. Meehan, Alice Meehan Riley and Frank Riley, Mike Lally, Kyle Fiske, and my Uncle Tommy, who made me a Madden again before he left.

To my toddler pod, we survived the early 2020s by taking care of each other. This book would not exist without you. Finley and Laura; Nyla and Bua; Leela, Rachel, and Neel; Harriet, Arlo, Silas, and Jessica; Ellen, Addy, Mindy, and Aaron; Dalia, Sufi, Sana, and Joey; Lydia, Aria, Emily, and Jeff; Lily, Amanda, and Steven; Deni and Xihuitl; and to honorary aunties Sara, Megan, Constance, and Grace. Liberation is a generational project. We do it for them.

Thank you to my friends and colleagues who read early drafts of this book, including the barely readable block of granite that was my first draft: Laura Gillespie, Patrick Hart, Rachel Ghosh, Jeremy Wilkening, Andrew Bjorn, and Nate Watson. Your insights and encouragement lit the laneway for me. Thanks also to my writer friends who helped guide me into the strange world of publishing with your time, advice, and examples: Qian Julie Wang, Michelle

Kuo, Marcia Chatelain, Andrew Stobo Sniderman, Kenneth Meador, and Hannah DeKeijzer.

Rebekah Borucki, V. Ruiz, Yomari Lobo, Lisa Bond, and the whole Row House community, you make dreams come true. Thank you for believing in this book. Being welcomed into your community was praise of the highest sort, and I am forever grateful.

Nirmala Nataraj, I knew you'd be the perfect editor for this project the first time we met. You showed me what needed doing and encouraged me down those paths, holding my hand when I needed it. I hope I've done you proud. Lore Alexander, your keen and seemingly tireless attention to detail covered over my inconsistent and carpal-tunnel ridden writing, thank you.

Michael Hobbes, thank you for planting the seed in my head that would become this book. May I never end up on your book podcast. Terry Babcock-Lumish, thank you for the initial encouragement that gave me the bravery to take this from a title and concept to the work it became. The Truman Scholarship community helped make all this possible, especially Tara Yglesias, Nate Watson, Claudio Simpkins, Marcia Chatelain, and Monica Bell.

Before writing this book, I walked away from the highest-compensated job that I, my close relatives, or our ancestors had ever had (don't think I got notions; it was still a middle-class salary). Thank you to the bullies and quisling hypocrites who helped push me out the door. You know who you are and what you did.

To the writers and lyricists whose words fueled my work, may your inspiration reverberate: Nick Flynn, John Darnielle, Octavia Estelle Butler, Nasir Jones, Laura Jane Grace, Michelle Zauner, Tupac Shakur, James Murphy, Matt Desmond, Richard Rothstein, Josephine Ensign, Blindboy Boatclub, Katriona O'Sullivan, Chris Thompson, Lulu Miller, Larry Vale, Cathy Park Hong, Greg Colburn, Stefanie Foo, Sasha taqʷšəblu LaPointe, Qian Julie Wang,

Michael Patrick MacDonald, George V. Higgins, Tim Pat Coogan, and James Fucking Joyce.

Thank you to The Community Builders, Inc. Thank you to the fine folks at Preservation of Affordable Housing, Community Roots Housing, Berk Associates, Kitsap Community Resources, City of Seattle Office of Housing, and the Low Income Housing Institute for being wonderful clients who allowed me to pay the bills while writing. Thanks also to the MIT DUSP and Swarthmore College communities, especially Xav Briggs, Mary Jane Daly, Larry Vale, Keith Reeves, and Sa'ed Atshan.

To my family, chosen and biological, I hope I represented us well and do you proud. I exist because of you, for better and worse. Sean, Mom, Grandmy, Jerry, Joe, Amy, Jen, Nancy, Corinne, Julie and the Slarskeys, George, Dwight, Drew, Mariela, Mary, Luis, Connor, Danika, Charlie, Joey, and all the Meehans, the Maddens, and the Irish Fiskes. If I listed you all, there'd be ten Thomases, eleven Johns, eight Josephs, and seven distinct versions of Mary. To my kung fu family, Sean, Kody, Zack, Jason, Andrew, Caryn, Charles, Samantha, Edwin, Tom, Tony, Sethanie, Wayne, Nick, and all the others who've punched me in the nose, you've given my face character.

Randolph, RANDOLPH. You know who the fuck you are and why you're special. No matter how many years or miles between us, you are my hometown.

Niamh, all I've ever wanted to be is a good dad. May you inherit the best of us and be free from our intergenerational bullshit.

About the Author

Jamie Madden (he/sé) is a dad and community development professional with expertise in housing development, public policy, and real estate finance. Jamie earned his Master of City Planning from the Massachusetts Institute of Technology and his BA in Political Science and Chinese from Swarthmore College, but he learned his most important lessons inside Massachusetts's most diverse high school, Randolph Junior/Senior High. Jamie grew up in affordable housing at the Bittersweet Lane Apartments, and he went on to work for the affordable housing industry's leading national nonprofits. His projects have included low-income, middle-income, and market-rate housing; new construction, acquisition, and preservation; rental, homeownership, retail, and early learning centers. He's directly contributed to creating more than one thousand affordable homes. If this housing crisis were fixed, sé would spend his days writing, parenting, playing music, and learning *an cúpla focail as Gaeilge*.

Roles

Professionals from a wide variety of disciplines play crucial roles in affordable housing. Paying for, developing, owning, and managing housing are four distinct roles, which may or may not be performed by the same parties. Maybe you already have the skills to play one of these roles.

Developer – The developer pulls the deal together, pairing financing with design and construction and earning permissions from the relevant authorities for building to occur. A developer can be a public agency, a nonprofit, or a for-profit; a firm or an individual; large or small. Theirs is the only role whose primary interest is that something gets completed. That is doubly true in affordable housing where it is harder to walk away from an infeasible deal and cut losses. Every affordable housing development is infeasible from an economic standpoint anyway, and each tends to have political support. Development is chiefly about compromise. Consensus is mandatory.

Typically, one person has responsibility for the day-to-day work and decisions in the development process, and they answer to managers, executives, and boards for more expensive and consequential decisions. They will be called project manager or project director or vice president, etc.

Most funders of affordable housing require developers to follow specific rules for design, construction, and lease up. The developer, in turn, attempts to hold the architect, general contractor, and property manager accountable for the required outcomes.

Owner – The owner holds title to the property and/or its improvements. They pay the taxes, they receive any remaining cash flow, and their assets would be lost should a lender or taxing agency foreclose on the property. The owner hires and fires the property manager. The owner may have bought the property from a past owner, or it may have been the developer. Both are common. In the private market, there are large firms that specialize in buying, owning, and trading housing, and there are firms that specialize in developing and selling housing. That "merchant builder" specialization is less common in affordable housing with its long affordability restrictions and covenants.

Investor – Investors purchase shares in the ownership of housing. They underwrite the deal and participate in the closing. In the private market, investors put their resources in with the expectation that they will make more money over time through cash flow and eventual sale. In LIHTC affordable housing, investors put their resources in with the expectation that they will profit more through the value of the tax benefits than they could investing that money elsewhere. They do not expect cash flow, nor do they even want it. Income from the property would be counterproductive because the profits were based on reducing tax liability through credits and deductions, not increasing how much tax they owe by increasing income. There are a few investors who underwrite expecting some profit from the eventual sale of the property, and in recent years, some clever traders have been investing in LIHTC housing with the expectation of taking control and/or profiting from sale or use of the housing after the affordability compliance period ends.

Investors theoretically risk losing money, and they price their equity investments accordingly. In practice, the conservative underwriting, partnership agreements, reserve requirements, sponsor guarantees, and insurance policies typical of LIHTC housing mean their risk of default or recapture has proven vanishingly small.

Lender – Bankers are boring. That's why they are crucial. That, and banks are where the money is. Most housing developments include several loans from several lenders. Lenders finance predevelopment with smaller, more expensive loans; construction with larger, slightly more expensive loans; and development/purchase with a larger, less expensive, permanent mortgage loan. Banks should be risk averse because they should never lose their depositors' money, and they size and price their loans according to the perceived risk of the development stage above the cost of money they are paying to whoever's capital they are utilizing. Lenders often have the most stringent underwriting requirements. The banks seek to ensure that the property will always have enough revenue to pay the mortgage.

Design Team – The design team develops concepts, creates drawings and renderings for the community process, specifies materials and products, develops drawings for permitting and to enable a more precise estimate of the development costs, implements *value engineering* when the costs are higher than the budget (which is always), produces detailed construction documents from which the builders will build, and is ultimately liable for design defects. There must be a licensed architect to stamp the final drawings, but there is a much larger team. The developer hires a lead architect—or a partnership between architects, which may help smaller, newer architecture firms get off the ground. A principal or project manager or both from the lead architect meet regularly with the developer to report on progress and inform important decisions. Junior architects produce more detailed drawings. Typically, the lead architect will subcontract specialty design and engineering work to a structural engineer, mechanical/electrical/plumbing/fire protection (MEP/FP) engineer, traffic engineer, and, if not on staff, a code compliance reviewer, LEED-certified sustainable designer, interior designer, construction administrator, or other relevant specialties. The project's landscape architect—who designs the site itself—may work for either the lead architect or the developer. Multifamily design and construction is highly complicated, specialized work. Many mistakes in the process occur from miscommunication between the developer and design team. Collaboration is crucial.

Construction Team – The developer hires a general contractor (GC) to implement the design team's construction documents. The construction contract between the developer and the GC is one of the most important documents to which all relevant parties must agree for a deal to close and housing to be built. It sets out how the work will proceed, what it will cost, how changes and mistakes are to be handled, how disputes are to be settled, and who will be liable in the case of any one of dozens of potential things that could go wrong during construction. There are several common types of construction contracts, including design/build, guaranteed maximum price, and cost plus, which differ around the terms of what to do with budget changes and who bears responsibilities.

The GC might only have a few tradespeople on staff, commonly laborers and carpenters. The GC bids out construction work by trade, coordinating a team of subcontractors for demolition, earthwork, concrete, steel, masonry, carpentry, glazing (windows), plumbing, electrical, heating ventilation and cooling (HVAC), sprinklers, roofing, elevators, fireproofing, insulation, drywall, painting, flooring, casework (cabinets and such), finish carpentry, cleaning, paving, landscaping, and more. The GC details the construction documents with the subcontractors through *shop drawings*, manages the subcontractors' schedules within the overall project schedule, and attempts to direct subcontractors' work.

The GC is ultimately responsible for the construction, and it takes out very large insurance policies to cover losses and pay for construction to be finished should the GC fail in some major way. This is called *bonding*—though a different kind of bond than we went over in the development financing section—and GCs are sized by their *bonding capacity*. Putting $100 million of construction in the hands of a firm that could only cover $10 million, for instance, risks losing up to $90 million in the case of severe construction problems.

The GC ultimately implements the requirements that affordable housing funders attach to developers. It is important for the developer and GC (and design team) to be clearly on the same page about all compliance issues, the tactics to achieve those regulatory goals, accountability for outcomes, and how any problems will be solved.

Property Management – The owner and/or developer typically hires a property management firm, with consent and approvals from the development's funders. The property management firm is responsible for the day-to-day operations of the housing, including marketing, qualifying applicants, leasing, collecting rent, paying bills, maintenance, utilities, repairs, cleaning, emergency management, enforcing rules, mediating resident disputes, carrying out evictions, and coordinating periodic inspections for fire, sprinkler, elevator, HUD REAC, and others. In owner-occupied detached homes, owners are their own property managers. Condominium owners typically share some property management costs through a homeowners' association.

In affordable housing, property management is also responsible for getting applicants and existing residents to satisfactorily complete many documents to certify that they are eligible to move in and eligible to continue living there. At the very least, this will be a look at tax returns, pay stubs, and other records of income to ensure an applicant makes enough to afford the rent but not so much that they are above the lowest income limit prescribed by the housing's funders. It may also be a review of a household's assets, criminal record review, citizenship status, credit score, references from past landlords, evidence of homelessness, and more. If the property manager makes mistakes on the resident certification process, the IRS or other funders could require the owner to repay millions of dollars to the government, and the equity investor(s) and lender(s) of course in turn require the developer to repay them too.

Asset Management – Asset management is the work of owning real estate. The asset management team must monitor the property manager's performance, manage compliance reporting to investors, lenders, and government agencies, and ensure that financial goals are being achieved. Affordable housing owners often perform their own asset management, though may contract it out. Additionally, their LIHTC investors have an asset management team also keeping tabs on the property's performance.

If things are going well, asset management is routine and unevent-ful. When things go wrong, their performance is crucial to moving a property back into financial and physical health.

Resident Services – From small, culturally competent organiza-tions to national firms partnering with government and academia to deliver on theories of change, nearly all mission-driven affordable housing developers invest time, energy, and funding into helping their residents succeed in life.

Resident services often include some mix of programming, affin-ity groups, and individual assistance to help residents as they move into a new home and neighborhood, navigate bureaucracies, pursue education, work on their health, and cover the basics—food, safety, shelter, care.

Staff are often social workers, educators, and/or people with lived experience. They may or may not be from the same firm or report to the same executives as property management. Some firms separate property management and resident services because they want to ensure that residents do not associate the person helping them get a GED and look for college scholarships with the person asking where the rent is and perhaps threatening eviction.

No matter who they report to, resident services and property management staff should be in close communication with each other to best meet their residents' needs, yes, but also to save the property money on evictions, rent loss, and maintenance. It is both more efficient and more moral to invest a little in helping a house-hold avoid eviction than it is to rely on evictions as problem solving.

Accounting – Accountants play an important role in affordable hous-ing, especially developments using LIHTC. IRS rules and reporting requirements for LIHTC and other tax credits are both complex and consequential. The same is typically true with a development's lenders, investors, and public funders as well. Our complex compliance system exists to ensure that 1) no dollar was spent on anyone or anything other than what the source of that dollar specified, 2) that dollars were spent on exactly whom and what the funder intended, and 3) there has been no fraud or legal violations among the financial participants, developer, general contractor, and subcontractors.

Lawyers – Affordable housing in the US today employs many lawyers. During acquisition, attorneys represent the seller(s) and buyer(s) to negotiate and execute an option, a purchase and sales agreement, and other documents. Zoning and land use attorneys review designs against zoning codes and must attest to their conformance. Environmental attorneys detail risks and responsibilities of remediation. Closing attorneys represent each party to the deal—which in affordable housing can be a dozen or so participants—in reviewing, negotiating, and executing that long list of closing documents (see Appendix 2). Attorneys representing the architect, general contractor, and developer review, negotiate, execute, and litigate contracts and liabilities among those parties. The closing attorneys come back at construction loan conversion and permanent closing. Property management and owner firms use attorneys for certain tenant and applicant complaints and also for evictions. I can always tell I am having a bad day at work when I think I should just go and get that JD.

Closing Checklist

1. **Loan applications** – detail the requests of the lenders
2. **Proof of insurance coverage** – no one wants to see their investment literally go up in smoke or under water. Coverage requirements usually include builder's risk, general contractor's liability, general property liability, hazard, fire, flood, earthquake, civil disturbance, commercial general liability, rent loss, and business loss policies
3. **Title insurance** – to compensate investors and lenders in the rare event that a legal claim demonstrates an outside ownership interest, for example, if property ownership was transferred through fraud or if an owner of the property was not party to its development
4. **Beneficial owner certification** – for the bank to show US Treasury compliance with the Patriot Act, paired with other certifications
5. **Guarantees** – in which the development sponsor/owner designates assets to guarantee certain actions, including:

    a. Completion, performance, and loan repayment
    b. Operating deficit coverage

    c.   Repurchase – to agree to buy out an equity investor under certain conditions

    d.   Tax credit guarantee – an agreement to reimburse the investor if the tax credits received differ from projections. Typically includes *adjusters* that will increase or decrease equity payments should the development generate more or fewer tax credits, sooner or later than projected

    e.   Development period taxable income – LIHTC investors want assurances that the developer will be responsible for paying any tax liabilities before the property is stabilized. They are in it to reduce their taxes, remember

6.   **Collateral documentation** – to give the lender legal rights to take compensation in the event of a default

    a.   Signed mortgage or deed of trust lien on borrower's interest in the property

    b.   Assignment of all leases, rents, income, licenses, permits, and contracts relating to each property

    c.   Lien on all personal property owned by borrower

    d.   Lien on all operating reserve and other deposit accounts related to the property

    e.   Assignment of partnership interest, including capital contributions and tax credits

7.   **Assignment of all relevant permits, awards, licenses, contracts, and agreements**

8.   **Copy of executed contract with the general contractor**

9.   **Payment and performance bond** – an insurance policy that would theoretically pay to complete a project if the general contractor fails or refuses to

10.   **Indemnification agreements** – so that the investor/lender accepts less risk, usually includes one for each identified risk

and especially for environmental liabilities and liabilities arising out of misbehavior

11.   **ASTM phase 1 environmental study** and any other necessary environmental studies

12.   **ALTA survey** acceptable to the title insurance company and funders

13.   **Property appraisal**

14.   **Flood hazard determination**

15.   **Geotechnical stud**y

16.   **Seismic study**

17.   **Physical/Capital needs assessment**

18.   **Complete architectural plans and specifications**

19.   **Complete cost estimate**

20.   **Final development pro forma** demonstrating compliance with funders' conditions and terms on budget items such as reserves and contingencies

21.   **Project schedule**

22.   **Sustainability checklists** – LEED checklist, Enterprise Green Communities, Passive House, or other demonstrations of the development's environmental sustainability

23.   **Tenant Selection Plan and Affirmative Fair Housing Marketing Plan** – detailed description of how you will advertise opportunities to rent/purchase the homes to be developed, how you will select among applicants, and a demonstration that it is all compliant with federal, state, and/or local fair housing laws and policies

24.   **Form of tenant lease**

25.   **Market study** – to demonstrate economic demand for leasing or sale of the development

26. **Resident services plan**
27. **Evidence of compliance** with all relevant zoning and land use controls
28. **UCC, litigation, and other searches** on the relevant development entities
29. **Financial reviews** – often a review of the following for each of the relevant entities and their principals:
    a. Audited financial statements for each of the most recent three years
    b. Year-to-date financial statements
    c. Credit reports
    d. Current account balances
    e. Tax returns
30. **General partner management agreement** – the obligations of the two owners of the general partner ownership entity to each other
31. **Proof of funding** – showing each funder that every other funder and allocating agency has made a binding commitment of resources to the development
32. **Subordination agreement(s)** – to clarify in which order lenders have a right to receive repayments and to foreclose
33. **Entity legal formation documents**
34. **Legal opinions** – a lawyer officially stating that the plan as represented is legal in specific ways. Typically includes tax, zoning, and environmental legal opinions but may also require additional opinions
35. **Site control** – evidence of the development's legal right to use of the property, such as a lease, ground lease, deed, purchase and sale agreement, and/or development agreement, plus any easement agreements
36. **Architect's contract**

37. **Representations and warranties** – we mean what we are saying so much that we would agree to it in court. Often includes a focus on environmental issues like lead, oil, hazardous materials, or asbestos

38. **Equity and inclusion agreements - agreements** to target certain percentages of development spending, work hours, and/or operating budgets to people of color, women, small businesses, veterans, locals, the disabled, and/or others

39. **Limited partnership agreement** – this is the detailed, three- to six-inch binder that governs the deal and the obligations of each of its owners

40. **Agreement to when, how, whether, and how much** the limited partner LIHTC investor and the general partner developer entity will pay each other under every conceivable potential circumstance, including adjusters

41. **Allocation of profits, losses, tax credits, depreciation, cash flow, and proceeds** – agreement among the partners for who gets how much of what. In LIHTC developments, the investor LP wants to minimize taxable profits because their return on investment is generated by tax savings

42. **Operating cash flow waterfall** – agreed schedule of the order and amount in which cash flow is spent and distributed

43. **Right of first refusal, option, put agreement, limitations on sale, etc.** – agreements on whether, when, how, to whom, and for how much the property can be sold or refinanced

44. **Developer fee agreement**

45. **Property management agreement, terms, and conditions**

46. **Depreciation schedule**

47. **Review and reporting requirements**

48. **Publicity and/or nondisclosure agreements**
49. **Agreements to the legal rights of each party** under all potential circumstances
50. **Agreements to if, why, how, and when** a partner may exit the agreement
51. **Anything else a funder requests**

The Pro Forma!

The pro forma is the developer's tool, like a graphic designer's creative suite, a court reporter's stenograph, or a Marine's rifle.

> This is my pro forma. There are many like it, but this one is mine.
>
> My pro forma is my best friend. It is my life. I must master it as I must master my life.
>
> Without me, my pro forma is useless. Without my pro forma, I am useless. I must calculate my pro forma true. I must shoot straighter than my investor who is trying to kill me. I must convince him before he convinces me.
>
> Thus, I will learn it as a brother. I will learn its weaknesses, its strength, its parts, its accessories, its printable summaries, and its circular references. (Apologies to the Marines and hoo-rah.)

There are many like it, and because most of your funders and partners use different pro forma models from yours, each project you manage will have many versions to communicate with everyone. And most developers have their own customized pro forma to analyze and manage the development project in the manner that best fits their situations. Developers spend many, many hours with their pro forma, day and night, mastering it and trying to squeeze every last sensible penny to balance the sources and uses for a feasible project. Disagreements and different interpretations of what are sensible ways to balance out a deal lie at the root of many long negotiations during predevelopment. Pro formas each have their own quirks, peculiarities, and priorities, and knowing where to find those consequential quirks is part of the art of development.

The basic sheets of the pro forma are:

1. **Program** – data on how much of everything there is in the development, such as the number of homes, square footage (total and by uses), the amount of parking, etc. The program often starts with a mix of WAGs and SWAGs (sophisticated/wild-ass guesses). The program becomes more detailed and precise as site studies and architectural drawings progress. The program drives cost and source calculations that are based on the number of homes, square footage, etc.

2. **Sources and Uses** – this sheet details the amounts and types of funding (sources) and major development costs (uses). The object of the game is to get the cell that subtracts uses from sources to equal zero. This page charts the expected funding sources, the status of attaining them, and the financing terms of each. Typically, the calculations to estimate the amount of potential mortgage debt and tax credit equity are included on this page. This page interacts with everything else.

   To be financially feasible, a housing development must detail what *sources* the project can generate and show the sources are equal to pay for the *uses*, what it will cost to develop the project. When the costs are higher than the potential sources, the proposal is infeasible. Development firms that are economically driven typically walk away if a deal proves infeasible. Affordable housing development firms may stick with a site and proposal despite infeasible economics if the development is important to the community or municipality, with the expectation that a reasonable amount of public funds will fill the gap and make the development feasible.

Development capital costs—*uses*—typically include:

- Land – purchase price of the site, cost of capitalized ground lease, or cost of seller financing note, plus any option payments and professional fees associated with acquiring the site itself.
- Construction – also known as *hard costs*, construction is the largest part of the budget, and it typically flows almost entirely through the general contractor. These are the costs of labor, materials, and equipment for the building.
- Soft costs – these are fees paid to third-party professionals such as the architect, engineers, lawyers, and accountants, and the various intangible costs of development such as insurance, development period taxes, and government fees.
- Financing Costs – this is the cost the project will pay to get people and institutions to give the developer enough money to complete it, such as loan fees, closing costs, tax credit and investor fees, and capitalized interest.
- Reserves – affordable housing developments typically include capitalized reserves, which are funded at the permanent loan closing or by equity proceeds later in the development process. Reserves exist to assure all parties to the deal that the ownership has emergency funds on

hand should things go wrong. Reserves typically include
an operating expense reserve (usually six months of the
budgeted operating costs), replacement reserve (to pay
for big-ticket items like HVAC equipment or roofing),
and occasionally other reserves that might be required,
like a reserve to fund resident services. It's a similar concept to the tax and insurance escrows that detached house
mortgages may require.

- Developer Fee – in conventional real estate, developers
earn money through rental cash flow, sale, and/or revenue
from related firms like an in-house architect or general
contractor. Those sources of revenue are tiny or absent
from affordable housing. So affordable housing developers reimburse themselves for the costs of development
and try to fund staff to complete the next cycle through
a developer fee. The amount of the fee is a regulated percentage of a project's total development costs, following
a formula set out by the project's public funders. Commonly, a large portion of the developer fee is deferred
to be paid out of cash flow over the first fifteen years of
property operations.

Development capital *sources* in affordable housing typically
include:
- Hard Debt – this is the property's permanent mortgage,
sized based on the amount of income the development
reasonably projects over the loan term. People variously
say hard debt, first mortgage, first position debt, perm(a-
nent) loan, and other permutations.
- Subordinate Debt – also known as soft debt, soft money,
subordinate financing, gap funding, and other combina-

tions—includes the raft of resources made available to affordable housing developments at below-market terms. Most commonly, the federal, state, and local governments make subordinate loans—meaning they only get paid if there's enough remaining cash flow, a sale, or a default for noncompliance—to housing developments. Banks, housing finance agencies, quasi-public organizations, some nonprofits, and philanthropies may also provide subordinate debt. In LIHTC deals, this money should always be structured as debt (i.e., be a loan to the development, not a grant) in order to increase leverage to preserve the project's affordability after the compliance period as well as to increase the project's operating losses and thereby increase the amount of private equity coming into the deal and lessening the burden on other public subsidies. In affordable homeownership or in non-LIHTC deals, these may be structured as either grants or loans. Other structures, like mezzanine debt, might also be utilized. Deferred developer fee, as described above, is also considered a form of subordinate debt, a cash-flow dependent loan from the developer to the project. It is not unusual for an affordable housing development to have a dozen different funding sources, give or take half a dozen.

- Equity
  - * Conventional Equity – in conventional real estate, equity is sized based on the profit the equity investor expects to receive from cash flow and/or the future sale of the property. Real estate investors are essentially purchasing the right to collect cash flow.
  - * Tax Credit Equity – in affordable housing, the rents are too low to provide an acceptable (or any) return

on investment. In developments that include tax credits—typically the Low-Income Housing Tax Credit (LIHTC) but potentially also New Markets Tax Credit, historic, Brownfields, solar, or others—investors earn a return on their investment through tax benefits rather than cash flow. Each dollar of credit decreases the investor's tax burden by one dollar. Investors in affordable housing, especially in 4% LIHTC deals with significant subordinate debt, also benefit from accounting losses the property generates, which are tax-deductible. Each dollar of loss creates a tax savings equal to the investor's marginal tax rate—let's say $0.21 on the dollar. Investors in affordable housing size their investments based on their expected return on investment, the current market price for credits in similar deals, and what the pro forma budget projects in credits and losses. In LIHTC housing, this is typically expressed as the price per dollar of credit. For example, as I write this paragraph, the Seattle LIHTC market settles around $0.93 of equity to a project for each dollar of tax credit the investor is projected to receive. Developments I have personally been involved in have ranged from $0.78 during a recession and housing market collapse to $1.24 in a strong market with many Community Reinvestment Act–motivated investors willing to pay above one dollar for each dollar of credit due to the value of the CRA points to them and the value of additional tax-deductible losses.

3. **Development Budget** – this sheet of the pro forma details the full costs of development. Precision can range from an assumed cost per square foot multiplied by the square footage at the early conceptual phase to a closing version with a detailed budget by line item, contract, and category (acquisition, hard costs, soft costs, financing, reserves, developer fee), and then prorated across distinct portions of the development, such as commercial, affordable residential, unrestricted residential, depreciable, and non-depreciable. This sheet calculates the total development costs, of course, but it also drives the value of tax credit equity by detailing which costs are eligible for the credits.

4. **Rent Schedule** – this sheet charts the homes to be built by bedroom size and rent level. From a basic market standpoint, rent levels vary by the size and assumed desirability of each home but are set—how much do I think I can rent/sell these homes for at the time I intend to rent/sell them? Affordable housing complicates it further because the variety of local requirements and quantity of subsidy sources create a wide number of rent levels to be included. Typically, it includes various percentages of the area median income as set by the funders' policies, expected operating subsidies (usually HUD's published Fair Market Rent), and the assumed unrestricted market rent. The rent schedule drives the potential gross income (PGI), which in turn drives the net operating income (NOI) and the amount of financing the project can expect to generate.

5. **Operating Budget** – the "OpEx" sheet projects the completed property's finances, including expected income by category and the costs of administration, management, utilities, maintenance, staffing, taxes, insurance, reserves, and loan payments. The acronym for the basic unit is the much-loved "PUPY,"

pronounced like a ten-year-old boy wants it to be, per unit per year. The operating budget drives how much funding can be generated based on how much is expected to be left at the end of each year after all obligations have been met, the NOI. Affordable housing models project out at least fifteen years to meet the IRS's minimum compliance period and then as long as the longest loan term, which is often a public funder's subordinate loan at twenty-five to fifty years or so. When properties don't appropriately budget for the future, they cut back on services, maintenance, utilities, and worse as the owner tightens the properties' belt to pay its lenders and stave off foreclosure. Most funders require several margins of error on the NOI estimates' ability to leverage debt.

There are many sheets beyond the basic five, and the composition of the rest of the sheets defines a model. Firms often forbid the distribution of their own pro forma models to protect trade secrets that set the firm's competitive advantages and overall approach. Other sheets a pro forma might utilize include:

- Detailed construction cost information
- Calculations of benefits to investors with more detailed projections into and discounts from the future to arrive at precise bottom-line estimates
- Multiple versions testing possible scenarios and risk profiles
- Models to score the proposal along the guidelines of the relevant funders' competitive processes
- Detailed market information
- Data from comparable projects

- Calculations to check the long-term compliance with all relevant statutes, regulations, and policies. These are especially complex for projects using LIHTC or New Markets Tax Credits
- Past versions of the pro forma, to track a project's evolution
- Accounting of predevelopment spending and/or actual construction spending
- Multiple individual sub-pro formas (pro formae) for distinct uses or phases in a development, such as LIHTC residential, market residential, or retail
- Alternatives to adapt to different project types or to different geographies where funders' rules are different

The numbers in our pro forma represent real people and places. The income numbers are rents and fees our residents need to be able to pay. The uses represent an ability to direct the labor and expertise of hundreds of people, to direct the use of physical materials, and to obtain the right to build. The pro forma is the development's master control panel, through which the project manager coordinates the process of turning numbers on a screen into real homes.

APPENDIX 4

Endnotes

1   Raquel Harati, Dan Emmanuel, Katie Renzi, and Andrew Aurand, *The Gap Report* (The National Low Income Housing Coalition, 2025), https://nlihc.org/sites/default/files/gap/2025/gap-report_2025_english.pdf.

2   Christina Kamis, et al., "Overcrowding and COVID-19 mortality across U.S. counties: Are disparities growing over time?." *SSM - population health* 15:100845 (2021), https://www.ncbi.nlm.nih.gov/pmc/articles/PMC8219888/.

3   Gregg Colburn and Rebecca J. Walter, *Affordable Housing in the United States* (Routledge, 2025), 127.

4   "HUD Archives: Budget Summaries and Congressional Justifications," U.S. Department of Housing and Urban Development, accessed Feb 27, 2025, https://archives.hud.gov/budget/; "Department of the Air Force President's Budget," Air Force Financial Management and Comptroller, accessed Feb 27, 2025, https://www.saffm.hq.af.mil/FM-Resources/Budget/. Compare https://www.hud.gov/cj.

5   Linda J. Blimes, William D. Hartung, and Stephen Semler. *United States Spending on Israel's Military Operations and Related U.S. Operations in the Region*, October 7, 2023-September 30, 2024 (Watson Institute for International & Public Affairs: Brown University, 2024), https://watson.brown.

ENDNOTES

edu/costsofwar/papers/2024/USspendingIsrael. Compare to Housing Choice Voucher cost estimate from 2025 HUD budget above.

6   U.S. Department of Transportation, Federal Highway Administration, *Budget Estimates: Fiscal Year 2025* (2025), https://www.fhwa.dot.gov/cfo/fhwa-fy-2025_budget_508.pdf.

7   Office of the Under Secretary of Defense (Comptroller)/Chief Financial Officer, *Program Acquisition Cost by Weapon System: United States Department of Defense Fiscal Year 2024 Budget Request* (2023), https://comptroller.defense.gov/Portals/45/Documents/defbudget/FY2024/FY2024_Weapons.pdf. $315 billion as compared to estimate from final chapter of this book $244.8 billion.

8

Characteristics	Count Estimate (,000)	%	Source
Total Housing Units	142,153	100%	"2021 National—Housing Unit Characteristics—All Housing Units," United States Census Bureau, https://www2.census.gov/programs-surveys/ahs/2021/2021%20AHS%20Table%20Specifications%20and%20PUF%20Estimates%20for%20User%20Verification.xlsx.
Public Housing	958	0.67%	"Policy Basics: Public Housing," Center on Budget and Policy Priorities, updated September 30, 2024, https://www.cbpp.org/research/public-housing#:~:text=The%20nation's%20958%2C000%20public%20housing,of%20people%20had%20low%20incomes.

Characteristics	Count Estimate (,000)	%	Source
Housing Choice Voucher—PBV	245	0.17%	"Policy Basics: Project-Based Vouchers," Center on Budget and Policy Priorities, https://www.cbpp.org/research/housing/project-based-vouchers.
Housing Choice Voucher— Mobile Households	2,055	1.45%	"Policy Basics: The Housing Choice Voucher Program," Center on Budget and Policy Priorities, updated September 30, 2024, https://www.cbpp.org/research/housing/the-housing-choice-voucher-program.
LIHTC	2,996	2.11%	"Low-Income Housing Tax Credit (LIHTC): Property Level Data," Office of Policy Developnent and Research (PD&R), revised May 8, 2025, https://www.huduser.gov/portal/datasets/lihtc/property.html.
Affordable subtotal	6,254	4.40%	Sum of above

9   Lawrence J. Vale, *From the Puritans to the Projects* (Harvard University Press, 2000), https://doi.org/10.2307/j.ctvjz8123.

10   *Boston Evening Transcript*, Boston, Massachusetts, July 20, 1883, https://www.newspapers.com/image/735325225/.

11   1910 United States Federal Census Suffolk, Boston Ward 17, Massachusetts, District 1522.

12   "1821 Book of Valuations, Boston Ward 12," Boston Public Library, https://archive.org/details/cityofbostontaxr6318bost/page/n850/mode/1up.

13   "Land Owners in Ireland 1876," Failte Romhat, accessed Feb 27, 2025, https://www.failteromhat.com/lo1876.htm. (Barry, Davis, Perry, Blake, Lyons, White, Curtis, Cobb, Gibson, and Ferguson).

14   "Tithe Appointment Books," The National Archives of Ireland,
      accessed February 27, 2025, http://titheapplotmentbooks.
      nationalarchives.ie/search/tab/results.

15   Carmine A. Prioli, "The Ursuline Outrage," *American Heritage*
      33, no. 2 (1996): 101–105, https://www.americanheritage.com/
      ursuline-outrage. This is a history worth learning, with strong
      parallels to Q-Anon conspiracy related violence today.

16   Thomas H. O'Connor, *The Boston Irish: A Political History*
      (Northeastern University Press, 1995).

17   Family lore told to me by my uncle, Tommy Madden, and my
      grandfather, Joseph Robert Madden.

18   Vale, *From the Puritans to the Projects.*

19   Richard Rothstein, *The Color of Law: A Forgotten History of
      How Our Government Segregated America* (W.W. Norton & Co.,
      2017).

20   Vale, *From the Puritans to the Projects,* 255.

21   Yes, government policy provided these housing subsidies specifically
      for white people. See Rothstein.

22   Chapter 707 is now known as the Massachusetts Rental Voucher
      Program (MRVP), and it is a crucial resource that became even
      more so as federal support for the poor plummeted.

23   Colburn and Walter, *Affordable Housing in the United States,* 83.

24   Jeremy Greenwood and Nezih Guner, "Marriage and Divorce since
      World War II: Analyzing the Role of Technological Progress on the
      Formation of Households," *NBER Macroeconomics Annual* 23,
      no. 1 (2008): 231-276, https://www.journals.uchicago.edu/doi/
      epdf/10.1086/593087.

25   *National Household Survey on Drug Abuse, 1985* (United States
      Department of Health and Human Services; National Institutes
      of Health; National Institute on Drug Abuse; Substance Abuse
      & Mental Health Data Archive, 1985), https://www.datafiles.
      samhsa.gov/sites/default/files/field-uploads-protected/studies/
      NHSDA-1985/NHSDA-1985-datasets/NHSDA-1985-DS0001/

NHSDA-1985-DS0001-info/NHSDA-1985-DS0001-info-codebook.pdf.

26 *2021 National Survey on Drug Use and Health,* (United States Department of Health and Human Services; Substance Abuse and Mental Health Services Administration, 2021), https://www.samhsa.gov/data/sites/default/files/2022-12/2021NSDUHFFRH ighlights092722.pdf.

27 Language inspired by John Darnielle, "Woke Up New," song by The Mountain Goats, 2006.

28 Greenwood, "Marriage and Divorce since World War II," 2008.

29 Martha R. Burt, *Over the Edge: The Growth of Homelessness in the 1980s* (Russell Sage Foundation, 1992).

30 Richard B. Freeman and Brian Hall, "Permanent Homelessness in America?," *Population Research and Policy Review* 6, no. 1 (1987): 3–27, https://www.jstor.org/stable/40229999.

31 *Student Homelessness in America: School Years 2019–20 to 2021–22* (National Center for Homeless Education: University of North Carolina at Greensboro, 2023), https://nche.ed.gov/wp-content/uploads/2023/12/SY-21-22-EHCY-Data-Summary_FINAL.pdf.

32 Rebecca L. Hegar and Geoffrey L. Greif, "Abduction of Children by Their Parents: A Survey of the Problem," *Social Work* 36, no. 5 (1991): 421–26, http://www.jstor.org/stable/23715936;

Andrea J. Sedlak, David Finkelhor, Heather Hammer, and Dana J. Schultz, *National Incidence Studies of Missing, Abducted, Runaway and Thrownaway Children,* (U.S. Department of Justice Office of Justice Programs Office of Juvenile Justice and Delinquency Prevention, 2002), https://www.ojp.gov/pdffiles1/ojjdp/196465.pdf.

33 "Data & Trends," United States Interagency Council on Homelessness, accessed March 6, 2025, https://web.archive.org/web/20250305050523/https://www.usich.gov/guidance-reports-data/data-trends.

34 "The Opportunity Atlas," Opportunity Insights; United States Census Bureau, accessed February 27, 2025, https://www.opportunityatlas.org.

35 *2021 Picture of Preservation* (The Public and Affordable Housing and Research Corporation and the National Low Income Housing Coalition, 2021), https://preservationdatabase.org/wp-content/uploads/2021/10/NHPD_2021Report.pdf.

36 Jarrett Murphy, "Tenants Again Sue a Housing Authority Crippled by Federal Cuts," *City Limits*, April 10, 2015, https://citylimits.org/2015/04/10/tenants-again-sue-a-housing-authority-crippled-by-federal-cuts/.

37 Savannah Hawley-Bates, "Rats and Black Mold: Kansas City Tenants Sue Section 8 Apartments for 'Unbearable' Neglect," *KCUR*, April 13, 2023, https://www.kcur.org/housing-development-section/2023-04-13/kansas-city-stonegate-meadows-apartments-class-action-lawsuit-rats-black-mold-housing-vouchers.

38 Emma Whalen, "Tenants Sue Charleston Housing Authority over Egregious Conditions at Gadsden Green," *The Post and Courier*, October 3, 2023, https://www.postandcourier.com/news/tenants-sue-charleston-housing-authority-over-egregious-conditions-at-gadsden-green/article_f3fab112-5e36-11ee-86de-5be71bddda1a.html.

39 Molly Parker, "'Pretty Much a Failure': HUD Inspections Pass Dangerous Apartments Filled With Rats, Roaches and Toxic Mold," *The Southern Illinoisan* and *ProPublica*, November 16, 2018, https://www.propublica.org/article/hud-inspections-pass-dangerous-apartments-with-rats-roaches-toxic-mold.

40 For the record, there were people with Asian heritage all over America by the late nineteenth century, which was why the US' first federal immigration law was the Chinese Exclusion Act and why mobs burned down Chinese neighborhoods from Wyoming to Southern California.

41   State Housing Assistance for Rental Production.

42   "The Problem," National Low Income Housing Coalition, accessed March 10, 2025, https://nlihc.org/explore-issues/why-we-care/problem.

43   Lena V. Groeger, Annie Waldman, and David Eads, "Miseducation: Is There Racial Inequality at Your School?," *ProPublica*, October 16, 2018, navigate to Randolph School District, https://projects.propublica.org/miseducation.

44   Maura Nacey, "Derailed from Success: The Usage of Tracking in American Secondary Education," *The Review*, August 19, 2023, https://virginiapolitics.org/online/derailed-from-success-the-usage-of-tracking-in-american-secondary-education.

45   More on Tunney's legacy in: *Learning from Tunney F. Lee: An Intellectual and Ethical Legacy* (International Laboratory of Architecture and Urban Design, 2023), https://www.ilaud.org/learning-from-tunney-f-lee/.

46   Rock Hushka, Shawn Wong, and Shelley Fisher Fishkin, *Zhi Lin: In Search of the Lost History of Chinese Migrants and the Transcontinental Railroads* (Tacoma Art Museum, 2017).

47   "Beginnings: 1875 – WWI," *The Chinatown Atlas*, accessed February 27, 2025, https://www.chinatownatlas.org/era/bachelor-exclusion-era-1875-wwi/.

48   "Bromley-Heath Development Gets Renamed in Honor of Longtime Tenant Leader," *Boston Housing Authority*, May 18, 2016, https://www.bostonhousing.org/en/News/Bromley-Heath-Development-Gets-Renamed-in-Honor-of.aspx.

49   Vale, *From the Puritans to the Projects*, 3.

50   From 1964 to 1988, the rule prohibited any adult male from living in public housing with a single mother and her children, regardless of their relationship.

51   Chad Freidrichs, *The Pruitt-Igoe Myth* (First Run Features, 2012), http://www.pruitt-igoe.com/about.html.

52   "Policy Basics: Public Housing."

53   "Policy Basics: Public Housing."

54   Families with a person whose immigration status makes them ineligible for public housing can receive prorated assistance based on the number of household members who are eligible, which means these immigrants pay more rent than other households who have the same income.

55   Greg B. Smith, "The Toll of NYCHA's Lead Lies: A Brooklyn Girl Poisoned as Officials Covered Up Danger," *The City*, November 28, 2021, https://www.thecity. nyc/2021/11/28/22806530/nycha-lead-paint-lies-brooklyn-girl-poisoned-public-housing.

56   "Former Low-Income Housing Executive Sentenced to Prison for Embezzling Nearly $7 Million," US Attorney's Office; Western District of Washington, August 27, 2021, https://www.justice. gov/usao-wdwa/pr/former-low-income-housing-executive-sentenced-prison-embezzling-nearly-7-million.

57   Brentin Mock, "The Scourge of Sexual Harassment in Public Housing: Complaints by Women Living in Baltimore Public Housing About Sexual Misconduct from Housing Authority Officials Signal a Larger Problem," *CityLab Justice: Bloomberg*, November 16, 2015, https://www.bloomberg.com/news/ articles/2015-11-16/examining-sexual-abuse-complaints-against-public-housing-authorities-in-baltimore-and-beyond.

58   Shane Phillips, *The Affordable City: Strategies for Putting Housing Within Reach (and Keeping it There)* (Island Press, 2020), 164.

59   "Policy Basics: Public Housing."

60   Michelle Alexandra, *The New Jim Crow: Mass Incarceration in the Age of Colorblindness* (The New Press, 2012), see especially pages 144–148.

61   The BRA used section 221(d)(3) of the Housing Act of 1961 for financing. Congress intended 221(d)(3) to finance nonprofits, cooperatives, public agencies, and limited dividend corporations to redevelop slum areas into moderate-income family housing. It operated through a joint program of mortgage insurance (which enables lenders to provide loans at a lower interest rate because the insurance company bears some of the risk of potential default) and below market rate, long-term loans.

62 Colburn and Walter, *Affordable Housing in the United States*, 117.

63 Will Bredderman, "Will Donald Trump Slash the Kind of Federal Housing Programs That Made His Family Rich?," *Observer*, January 13, 2017, https://observer.com/2017/01/will-donald-trump-slash-the-kind-of-federal-housing-programs-that-made-his-family-rich/.

64 Raymond Struyk and Marc Bendick, "Policy Questions and Experimental Responses," in *Housing Vouchers for the Poor: Lessons from a National Experiment* (Urban Institute Press, 1981).

65 Peter Dreier, "Reagan's Legacy: Homelessness in America," *Shelterforce*, May 1, 2004, https://shelterforce.org/2004/05/01/reagans-legacy-homelessness-in-america/.

66 Colburn and Walter, *Affordable Housing in the United States*.

67 Xavier de Souza Briggs, Susan J. Popkin, and John Goering, *Moving to Opportunity: The Story of an American Experiment to Fight Ghetto Poverty* (Oxford University Press, 2010).

68 Richard Heath, "Washington Park Urban Renewal Program," Right Here in Roxbury Wiki, accessed February 28, 2025, https://roxbury.fandom.com/wiki/Washington_Park_Urban_Renewal_Program-_Part_II-Housing-Academy_Homes,_by_Richard_Heath.

69 "Low-Income Housing Tax Credit." *National Multifamily Housing Council*, July 25, 2025, https://www.nmhc.org/advocacy/issue-fact-sheet/low-income-housing-tax-credit-fact-sheet/.

70 *Affordable Housing Credit Study: A Comprehensive LIHTC Property Performance Report*, (CohnReznick, 2021), file:///C:/

Users/laure/Downloads/TCIS_CRedit-Report_2021_
CohnReznick.pdf.

71 Michael Haas, "CRED iQ's Overall Office Distress Climbs to
19.3%, While the Overall Distress Rate Logs Its First Decrease
in Five Months," *Cred IQ*, March 6, 2025, https://cred-iq.com/
blog/2025/03/06/cred-iqs-overall-office-distress-climbs-to-19-
3-while-the-overall-distress-rate-logs-its-first-decrease-in-five-
months/.

72 By my count, the statutory language of Section 42 is sixty-four
pages. The statutory language of the Tax Code is 2,600 pages. I
didn't measure the other 9,833 sections. Andrew Grossman, "Is
the Tax Code Really 70,000 Pages Long?," *Slate*, April 14, 2014,
https://slate.com/news-and-politics/2014/04/how-long-is-the-
tax-code-it-is-far-shorter-than-70000-pages.html.

73 Elizabeth Kneebone and Carolina K. Reid, "The Complexity
of Financing Low-Income Housing Tax Credit Housing in the
United States," Terner Center for Housing Innovation, April 26,
2021, https://ternercenter.berkeley.edu/blog/lihtc-complexity/.

74 *Low-Income Housing Tax Credit (LIHTC) at Risk* (Freddie
Mac Multifamily, 2022), https://mf.freddiemac.com/research/
duty-to-serve/lihtc-risk.

75 Aaron Gornstein and Ann Verrilli, *Mixed-Income Housing in
the Suburbs: Lessons From Massachusetts* (Citizens Housing and
Planning Association, 2006).

76 "Jackson Sq Redevelopment Initiative," JPNDC, accessed
February 28, 2025, https://jpndc.org/jackson-square-
redevelopment-initiative/.

77 Taryn H. Gress, Mark L. Joseph, Seungjong Cho,
"Confirmations, New Insights, and Future Implications for
HOPE VI Mixed-Income Redevelopment,"*Cityscape: A Journal
of Policy Development and Research* 21, no. 2 (2019) : 185-212,
https://www.huduser.gov/portal/periodicals/cityscpe/vol21num2/
ch11.pdf.

78 Sam Bass Warner, *Streetcar Suburbs: The Process of Growth in*

Boston, 1870-1900 (Harvard University Press, 1978), https://doi.org/10.2307/j.ctvjsf66f.

79   Terence O'Rorke, *The History of Sligo: Town and County* (Dublin: James Duffy & Co., 1900), https://archive.org/details/historyofsligoto00oror.

80   Home Owners Loan Corporation, Area Description p Security Map of Greater Boston, Mass. Area C14, accessed via Mapping Inequality: Redlining in New Deal America,

      https://dsl.richmond.edu/panorama/redlining/map/MA/Boston/area_descriptions/C14#mapview=full&loc=12/42.3138/-71.0811&scan=2/65.3668/-105.2906.

81   Rothstein, *The Color of Law.*

82   Freeman and Hall, "Permanent Homelessness," 3-27.

83   Gornstein and Verrilli, *Mixed-Income Housing in the Suburbs.*

84   Tim Reardon, "New Subsidized Housing Inventory Figures Provide an Estimate of Affordable Housing Available in each Massachusetts Community," *Metropolitan Area Planning Council*, August 4, 2023, https://www.mapc.org/planning101/new-subsidized-housing-inventory-figures/.

85   Lizabeth Cohen, *Saving America's Cities: Ed Logue and the Struggle to Renew Urban America in the Suburban Age* (Farrar, Straus, and Giroux, 2019), 377.

86   Nick Flynn, *Another Bullshit Night in Suck City: A Memoir,* (W.W. Norton & Co, 2004), 54.

87   "Troy Boston Apartments," Equity Apartments, accessed May 7, 2025, https://www.equityapartments.com/boston/south-end/troy-boston-apartments##bedroom-type-section-0.

88   Thomas Morton and Charles Francis Adams, *The New English Canaan of Thomas Morton* (Prince Society, 1883), https://library.si.edu/digital-library/book/newenglishcanaa00mort.

89   Morton and Adams, *The New English Canaan of Thomas Morton*, 126.

90   Morton and Adams, *The New English Canaan of Thomas*

Morton.

91 Morton and Adams, *The New English Canaan of Thomas Morton*, 305 (referenced to Young's Chron. of Mass.).

92 Morton and Adams, *The New English Canaan of Thomas Morton*.

93 William Bradford, *Bradford's History of 'Plimoth Plantation'* (Wright & Potter Printing Co., 1898), https://www.gutenberg.org/files/24950/24950-h/24950-h.htm.

94 Thomas W. Allen, *The Invention of the White Race* (Verso, 2012).

95 James Sullivan, *The History of Land Titles in Massachusetts* (I. Thomas and E.T. Andrews, 1801), https://babel.hathitrust.org/cgi/pt?id=nyp.33433008693487&seq=10.

96 "Chickataubut," The Massachusett Tribe at Ponkapoag, https://massachusetttribe.org/chickataubut; Daniel Huntoon, *History of the Town of Canton* (University Press, 1893).

97 Sullivan, *The History of Land Titles in Massachusetts*. As it is highly unusual to come across a Gaelic Irish surname among the founding fathers, a brief genealogy is of interest here. James served as a king's attorney for York, a member of the Provincial Congress, judge of the Supreme Court, delegate to the Continental Congress, member of the Massachusetts legislature, Governor's Council, judge of Probate Court, attorney general of Massachusetts, presidential elector, governor of Massachusetts, and signatory to the Declaration of Independence. Judge James Sullivan traced his ancestry to English, French, and Irish royalty via the first English (Norman) invaders of Ireland, the De Burghs, the Fitzgeralds, and the O'Sullivans. From about 1200 (the Anglo-Norman invasion) to 1650 (Cromwellian invasion), James's ancestors held royal titles under the English crown, lived in castles, and ruled over areas of Ireland's southwest. After two generations of being on the outs with the British Empire, this branch of O'Sullivans emigrated to Massachusetts in 1723. There, they exclusively married members of the Protestant

Yankee Aristocracy, from families like Bartlett, Wells, Amory, Appleton, Bowdoin, and other names New Englanders are used to seeing on place names. James's brother Major-General John Sullivan was a member of the Continental Congress, president of the Convention to ratify the Federal Constitution, and attorney general of New Hampshire. Their descendants included a lieutenant governor of Massachusetts, a governor of Maine, attorney general and senator for New Hampshire, lieutenant governor of Illinois, and US Consul at Barbados.

Charles Henry Browning, *Americans of Royal Descent: A Collection of Genealogies of American Families Whose Lineage is Traced to the Legimate Issue of Kings* (Porter & Coates, 1891).

98 Sullivan, *The History of Land Titles in Massachusetts*. Also see Morton, *The New English Canaan of Thomas Morton*.

99 "Chronological Listing of Historically Important Events at Ponkapoag Plantation," The Massachusett Tribe at Ponkapoag, accessed February 27, 2025, https://massachusetttribe.org/chronological-listing-of-historically-important-events-at-ponkapoag-plantation.

100 Christina Plerhoples Stacy and Christopher Davis, "Assessing the Impact of Affordable Housing on Nearby Property Values in Alexandria, Virginia," *Urban Institute*, April 19, 2022.

101 Offer not valid in Florida and Texas.

102 Jon Chesto, "Corporate Boston Played a Key Role in Opening New Pine Street Inn Building," *The Boston Globe*, March 17, 2025.

103 An article from 2019 details what the site could have been had the entitlement process not been abused: Lynn Jolicoeur, "Pine Street Inn Plans City's Largest Housing Complex For Those Who've Been Homeless," *wbur*, March 8, 2019, https://www.wbur.org/news/2019/03/08/pine-street-inn-plans-citys-largest-housing-complex-for-those-whove-been-homeless.

104   Tim Logan, "Neighbor Sues to Block Pine Street Inn Project in
       Jamaica Plain," *The Boston Globe*, August 10, 2020, https://
       www.boston.com/news/local-news/2020/08/10/neighbor-sues-
       to-block-pine-street-inn-project-in-jamaica-plain/.

105   "NYHC: Alarming Risk of Rising Insurance Costs for Affordable
       Housing," New York Housing Conference, March 18, 2024,
       https://thenyhc.org/2024/03/18/nyhc-alarming-risk-of-rising-
       insurance-costs-for-affordable-housing/.

106   *Filling Funding Gaps: How State Agencies Are Moving To
       Meet A Growing Threat To Affordable Housing* (Abt Associates,
       2023), https://www.ncsha.org/resource/report-filling-funding-
       gaps-how-state-agencies-are-moving-to-meet-a-growing-threat-
       to-affordable-housing/.

107   Dr. William P. Marchione, "Barry's Corner: The Life and Death
       of a Neighborhood," Brighton-Allston Historical Society, https://
       www.bahistory.org/HistoryBarrysCorner.html.

108   Cohen, *Saving America's Cities*, 238.

109   "History," Charlesview Inc., accessed February 28, 2025, https://
       charlesviewcommunity.org/about-us/history/.

110   Mark P. Keightley, "An Analysis of the Geographic Distribution
       of the Mortgage Interest Deduction: Before and After the
       2017 Tax Revision," Congress.gov, February 18, 2021, https://
       crsreports.congress.gov/product/pdf/R/R46685.

111   "See the Daily Snow Totals from Last Year's Historic Winter,"
       Boston 25 News, January 20, 2016, https://www.boston25news.
       com/news/see-the-daily-snow-totals-from-last-years-historic-
       winter/29565182/.

112   "Kelly Madden Sullivan Obituary," *The Patriot Ledger*, https://
       www.legacy.com/us/obituaries/southofboston-ledger/name/kelly-
       madden-sullivan-obituary?pid=165414363.

113   "The Last Place I Saw You Alive," by John Darnielle, recorded

March 2020, track 7 on *Getting Into Knives*, The Mountain Goats, Merge Records.

114 Phillips, *The Affordable City*, 8.

115 Colburn and Walter, *Affordable Housing in the United States*, 22.

116 Edward P. Cheyney, *Some English Conditions Surrounding the Settlement of Virginia* (1907), https://archive.org/details/someenglishcondi00chey.

117 Gearóid Mac Lochlainn, "Nineteenth Century Landlords of Greater Buncrana," *The Irish Story*, March 27, 2015, https://www.theirishstory.com/2015/03/27/nineteenth-century-landlords-of-greater-buncrana/#.YypIgC-B1pQ.

118 "Inishowen – The Poitín Republic of Urris," *Daily Scribbling*, 2015, https://dailyscribbling.com/the-odd-side-of-donegal/the-poitin-republic-of-urris/.

119 Allen, *The Invention of the White Race*, 78.

120 Parliamentary debate about whether/how the Crown should help English landowners defend or increase rents illuminates the mental gymnastics undertaken by members of Parliament to find any rational justification for colonial rents, which in reality bore no basis to logic other than the absolute maximization of short-term profits. See: HANSARD 1803–2005 → 1880s → 1881 → May 1881 → 27 May 1881 → Lords Sitting VALUATION OF RATEABLE PROPERTY (IRELAND)—GRIFFITH'S VALUATION. HL Deb 27 May 1881 vol 261 cc1429–38.

121 "Story of the Murderhole," The Schools' Collection, Volume 1119: 76, https://www.duchas.ie/en/cbes/4493788/4420868/4536733.

122 "Famine Relieve Letters, Innishowen, Co Donegal," Donegal Genealogy Resources, accessed May 7, 2025, http://donegalgenealogy.com/faminereliefcd.htm.

123 "Interview with Octavia E. Butler," *Locus Magazine*, June 2000,

accessed May 17, 2023, https://www.locusmag.com/2000/
Issues/06/Butler.html.

124 "Harvard and the Legacy of Slavery," Harvard Radcliffe Institute,
accessed May 7, 2025, https://www.radcliffe.harvard.edu/
harvard-and-the-legacy-of-slavery-initiative.

125 Vale, *From the Puritans to the Projects*, 22.

126 Ken Armstrong, "Draft Overturning Roe v. Wade Quotes
Infamous Witch Trial Judge With Long-Discredited Ideas on
Rape," *ProPublica*, May 6, 2022, https://www.propublica.org/
article/abortion-roe-wade-alito-scotus-hale.

127 Matthew Hale, *A Discourse Touching Provision for the Poor*
(Bible in Duke-Lane, 1683), https://historyofeconomicthought.
mcmaster.ca/hale/poor.

128 Vale, *From the Puritans to the Projects*, 77.

129 Josephine Ensign, *Skid Road: On the Frontier of Health and
Homelessness in an American City* (Johns Hopkins University
Press, 2021), 15.

130 Anna Patrick, "Where Are King County's Homeless Residents
From?," *Seattle Times*, July 6, 2023, https://www.seattletimes.
com/seattle-news/homeless/where-are-king-countys-homeless-
residents-from/.

131 Greg Kim, "Does Seattle Bear the Burden of King County's
Homelessness? Kinda," *Seattle Times*, updated March 6, 2023,
https://www.seattletimes.com/seattle-news/homeless/does-seattle-
bear-the-burden-of-king-countys-homelessness-kinda/.

132 Shane Bauer, "5 Ways Prisoners Were Used for Profit Throughout
U.S. History," *PBS New Hour*, February 26, 2020, https://www.
pbs.org/newshour/arts/5-ways-prisoners-were-used-for-profit-
throughout-u-s-history.

133 Bauer, "5 Ways Prisoners Were Used for Profit Throughout U.S.
History."

134   Bauer, "5 Ways Prisoners Were Used for Profit Throughout U.S. History."

135   Mia Gant, "Injustice Hidden Deep in Atlanta's Forest: The Old Atlanta Prison Farm and the South River," Georgia State University, April 12, 2020, https://web.archive.org/web/20230307151806/http://sites.gsu.edu/historyofourstreets/2022/04/12/old-atlanta-prison-farm/?ver=1461682765.

136   Thierry Godard, "The Economics of the American Prison System," *SmartAsset*, updated May 30, 2023, https://smartasset.com/mortgage/the-economics-of-the-american-prison-system.

137   Colburn and Walter, *Affordable Housing in the United States*, 21.

138   Vale, *From the Puritans to the Projects*, 11.

139   Stephanie Foo, *What My Bones Know: A Memoir of Healing from Complex Trauma* (Ballantine Group, 2022). Chapter 13 includes an overview with references to the scientific literature.

140   Gregg Colburn and Clayton Page Aldern, *Homelessness Is a Housing Problem* (University of California Press, 2022), 59.

141   Colburn and Walter, *Affordable Housing in the United States*, 5.

142   J. Wortham and Wesley Morris, hosts, *Still Processing Podcast*, episode 133, "Cathy Park Hong," New York Times Podcasts, April 21, 2021, https://podcasts.apple.com/us/podcast/cathy-park-hong/id1151436460?i=1000519304613.

143   Blindboy Boatclub, host, *Blindboy Podcast*, episode 117, "Speaking to an Expert About Trauma," September 13, 2022, https://open.spotify.com/episode/7A1sQsbB94htbx2WPtrccF. Associated papers available at http://research.ucc.ie/profiles/A011/sharon.lambert%40ucc.ie.

144   Fergus Kelly, *A Guide to Early Irish Law* (Dublin Institute for Advanced Studies, 1988), https://shop.dias.ie/product/a-guide-to-early-irish-law/.

145   Kyle C. Esteves, et al., "Adverse Childhood Experiences:

Implications for Offspring Telomere Length and Psychopathology," AM J Psychiatry 177, no. 1 (2020): 47-57, https://pmc.ncbi.nlm.nih.gov/articles/PMC7273739/.

146   Colburn and Aldern, *Homelessness Is a Housing Problem*, 63.

147   Leah Rothstein, "Keeping Wealth in the Family: The Role of 'Heirs Property' in Eroding Black Families' Wealth," Economic Policy Institute, July 6, 2023, https://www.epi.org/blog/heirs-property/.

148   Judith Crown, "The High Cost of Creating Affordable Housing," *Crain's Chicago Business*, January 16, 2024, https://www.chicagobusiness.com/equity/what-makes-affordable-housing-development-so-expensive.

149   Sydney Brownstone, "Seattle Got More Than 1,300 Federal Housing Vouchers. So Far, Only 10 People Have Used Them," *Seattle Times*, updated November 22, 2021, https://www.seattletimes.com/seattle-news/homeless/seattle-got-more-than-1300-federal-housing-vouchers-so-far-only-10-people-have-used-them/.

150   Robert Evans, host, *Behind the Bastards Podcast*, "Part Two: Sam Zell: the Elon Musk of Real Estate," November 10, 2022, https://www.iheart.com/podcast/105-behind-the-bastards-29236323/episode/part-two-sam-zell-the-elon-104424976/.

151   Heather Vogell, "Rent Going Up? One Company's Algorithm Could Be Why," *ProPublica*, October 15 2022, https://www.propublica.org/article/yieldstar-rent-increase-realpage-rent.

152   Meghan Cherry, Kimen Trochalakis v. Realpage, Inc. et al., Case 2:22-cv-01618 Document 1, (W. D. Wash, 2022), filed November 11, 2022, https://www.documentcloud.org/documents/23304390-2022-11-11-class-action-complaint20719261-final?responsive=1&title=1.

153   Heather Vogell, "Senator Seeks Antitrust Review of Apartment Price-Setting Software," *ProPublica*, November 1, 2022, https://

www.propublica.org/article/yieldstar-rent-increase-senate-antitrust-apartment.

154   "Analysis of President Biden's FY 2023 Budget Request," National Low Income Housing Coalition, March 29, 2022, https://nlihc.org/resource/analysis-president-bidens-fy-2023-budget-request.

155   "House America," HUD.gov, accessed February 28, 2025, https://web.archive.org/web/20250107091022/https://www.hud.gov/house_america/faq.

156   "Analysis of President Biden's FY 2023 Budget Request."

157   Eric Shupin, "President Biden Signs FY2023 Federal Budget," Citizens Housing and Planning Association, December 29, 2022.

158   Sonya Acosta and Brianna Guerrero, "Long Waitlists for Housing Vouchers Show Pressing Unmet Need for Assistance," Center for Budget and Policy Priorities, October 6, 2021, https://www.cbpp.org/research/housing/long-waitlists-for-housing-vouchers-show-pressing-unmet-need-for-assistance.

159   *Y23 Budget Chart for Selected Federal Housing Programs* (National Low Income Housing Coalition, 2022), https://nlihc.org/sites/default/files/NLIHC_HUD-USDA_Budget-Chart_FY23_PresRequest_FINAL.pdf.

160   "State HFA and Associate Member Directory," NCSHA.org, accessed May 7, 2025, https://www.ncsha.org/membership/hfa-members.

161   "Policy Basics: Public Housing."

162   Colburn and Walter, *Affordable Housing in the United States*, 19.

163   Colburn and Walter, *Affordable Housing in the United States*, 20.

164   Colburn and Walter, *Affordable Housing in the United States*, 21.

165   Colburn and Walter, *Affordable Housing in the United States*, 15.

166   The actual average Housing Choice Voucher payment was $950 in 2023 and the mean cost of construction was $165,000/unit. Colburn and Walter, *Affordable Housing in the United States*, 113.

ENDNOTES

167 Coburn and Aldern, *Homelessness Is a Housing Problem.*

168 Rothstein, *The Color of Law*, 243.

169 Rothstein, *The Color of Law*, 204.

170 Cecilia Rouse, Jared Bernstein, Helen Knudsen, and Jeffery Zhang, "Exclusionary Zoning: Its Effect on Racial Discrimination in the Housing Market," The White House, June 17, 2021, https://bidenwhitehouse.archives.gov/cea/written-materials/2021/06/17/exclusionary-zoning-its-effect-on-racial-discrimination-in-the-housing-market/.

Index

INDEX

INDEX

INDEX